Figures in a Western Landscape

CREATING THE
NORTH AMERICAN LANDSCAPE

Gregory Conniff

Bonnie Loyd

Edward K. Muller

David Schuyler

Consulting Editors

Published in cooperation with
the Center for American Places,
Harrisonburg, Virginia

Also by the Author

The Crooked Corridor: A Study of Henry James

Henry Adams: a Biography

A Henry Adams Reader, Editor

Lafcadio Hearn

Babbitts and Bohemians: The American 1920s

Park Maker: A Life of Frederick Law Olmsted

▲▲▲

Figures in a
Western Landscape

MEN AND WOMEN
OF THE NORTHERN ROCKIES

Elizabeth Stevenson

THE JOHNS HOPKINS UNIVERSITY PRESS
BALTIMORE AND LONDON

Chapter 10 was published in a slightly different form in *Montana Magazine*. September 1984.

The Johns Hopkins University Press
2715 North Charles Street
Baltimore, Maryland 21218-4319
The Johns Hopkins Press Ltd., London

Library of Congress Cataloging-in-Publication Data will be found
at the end of this book.

A catalog record for this book is available from the
British Library.

To the memory of five in a tent

CONTENTS

PREFACE

During years of traveling in the region of the Northern Rocky Mountains and its adjacent high plains, visiting this area under the duress of a personal reason, I conceived the idea of writing a book about the people of this distinctive segment of the continent.

I came to see that this was the last American West, and so of poignant interest to Americans of other regions.* Here was the final enactment of our national drama, the mixed good and evil of our acts and ambitions, the result of our belief in who we are and what we are. Westering has always been at the bottom of our freedom and of our excesses.

I was not indifferent to or unaware of the exhilaration of the great, overarching theories that have tried to explain why the American people became different from other people by going to the West. I would keep in the back of my mind these various, successive explanations and their interesting revisions.

My interest was different. I hoped that the rediscovered acts and words of certain inhabitants of this region would give vivid color to general history. My interest is in the single, solitary person and how he or she lived and what he or she thought; my bias is biographical. It is a difficult craft held under the iron rule of fact, yet I was allured by the perception of the art and importance of the choice of materials and emphases.

I began with our most introspective explorer, Meriwether Lewis, and traveled down the generations with a fur trapper, a naturalist, a priest, a trader, some soldiers and native peoples, some early and late settlers and adventurers, both male and female, as well as an outlaw, a journalist, gold and copper diggers, a city builder, and an artist. It is a variegated population in an area much given to individuality as well as, more recently, a stiffening

---

*Apologies to Alaska, which today thinks of itself as a last West; but it is another historical time and place and is an epitaph, not a determinant, of American myth and history.

into two ideologies. It is also a region coming to terms with its own identity.

Biography, the story of individuals, is also always a part of history. I thought that these lives might enlighten us about the human condition of each generation of western change. But there was more that I hoped to show. These people lived in a particular geography. I wanted to see how the landscape of the last West affected the lives and outlooks of these individuals, and also how they, in each generation, affected the landscape within which they played out their dreams.

Figures in a Western Landscape

ONE

The Soliloquies of Meriwether Lewis

In a dark forest of troubles, Meriwether Lewis at the age of thirty-five met an ugly death. He died not only in a maze of what were probably temporary difficulties but also in the depths of a real forest, the narrow, shadowed, and dangerous trail that was the Natchez Trace in the year 1809. Along this way, it was almost customary for travelers to be robbed and murdered as they made their daily miles from one lonely stand to another. Lewis met his end at Grinder's Stand in an isolated stretch of the trail between Chickasaw Bluffs (Memphis) and Nashville. His death has shadowed his life. To regain a sense of who he was and what he was in the discoveries he shared with his friend William Clark, it helps to experience the West with him in his own words. To read the journals, the spontaneous accounts of the days of the journey, is to make an exploration of the inner territory of a mind. These entries belong to literature as well as to history.

The reader soon has the illusion of traveling with Meriwether Lewis. After starting in May 1804 from a point of encampment above Saint Louis, the expedition had fallen into a routine of daily travel by September. One early morning in September in the northeast corner of what is now Nebraska, Lewis had an escape from routine. "Having for many days past confined myself to the boat, I determined to devote this day to amusing myself on shore with my gun, and view the interior of the country lying between the river and the Corvus Creek." He found that "the shortness and verdure of grass gave the plain the appearance, throughout its whole extent, of beautiful bowling green in fine order." Facts entranced him, and he examined very fine wild plum trees much like those at home in Virginia; he noted the "barking squirrels" in this green level plain bordering the river, he estimated the height of bluffs at some distance, and he savored the wild plenty of the free-roaming game animals, "the immense herds of buffalo, deer, elk, and antelopes, which we saw in every direction." He followed from ridge line to ridge line the disappearance and reappearance of a flock of seven antelopes. He watched the male look back at him, then encircle the females on the top of a hill and instigate another flight. "So soon had these antelopes gained the distance at which they had again appeared to my view, I doubted at first that they were the same that I had just surprised; but my doubts vanished when I beheld the rapidity of their flight along the ridge before me. It appeared rather the rapid flight of birds than the motion of quadrupeds." Lewis exhibits in this passage both the sensitivity of his very private reflections and the down-to-earth way he adapted himself to uncertain and haphazard conditions, as when he told of his and the other hunters' stop to eat: "We rested ourselves about half an hour, and regaled ourselves on half a biscuit each, and some jerks of elk, which we had taken the precaution to put in our pouches in the morning before we set out, and drank of the water of a small pool, which had collected on the plains from the rains which had fallen some days before."[1]

The partner, William Clark, whom he had left behind that day tending the boats and boatmen, was Lewis's perfect complement. It was a case of opposites who were also friends. They had served together in the frontier army of the young United States, Lewis under the four-year-older Clark at one time. They had much in common in their background. Both came out of Albemarle County in the foothills of the Blue Ridge of Virginia, from the neighborhood of Thomas Jefferson and his family. Each of them had shared in the westering impulses of many families of this time, Clark's having moved west to Kentucky, Lewis's temporarily to Georgia. It probably seemed inarguable to each of them that it was the destiny of the Americans of the older colonies to wish to move farther west.

His admired kinsman and president had plucked Lewis out of the army to be his aide in Washington, then shared with him heady plans for a western expedition, designating him as his agent for this great adventure. Lewis thought immediately of Clark to be his co-captain. Although Congress would never give the second man equal title, despite the wishes of Lewis, he himself saw to it that, to the men of the expedition, Clark was captain and not lieutenant. After the homecoming, Lewis fought for equal rewards for his friend. In temperament and training each brought some qualities to the expedition the other lacked. In addition they liked and understood each other and managed the sharing of responsibility with good fellowship. Clark is not here the principal interest, but he deserves respectful and admiring attention separately. In order to judge Lewis's journal entries, it is useful to sample those of Clark—those we know he wrote separately. In order that the record would not be lost, each kept a separately written and guarded journal, but each one copied the other's from time to time. Clark's notation of things seen and done are most vividly preserved in his preliminary field notes. He was always vivid, straightforward, blunt, objective, and factual. His writing is not as imaginative or introspective as that of Lewis, but it is sometimes a relief from the latter's occasionally self-conscious literariness. His written notes also reflect behavior sometimes quite different from that of his friend.

Getting the men in shape, Clark was rough and ready, as well as effective. "I order in those men who had fought got Drunk & neglected Duty to go and build a hut for a Woman who promises to wash and Sow." This was early, before leaving the base camp near Saint Louis. He was also immediately attentive to need and practical: "Prior is verry sick. I sent R. Fields to kill a squirel to make him soup." Clark savored the good in everyday life. "A relish of this old bacon this morning was verry agreeable." He was kind to animals: "Saw a Dog this evening appeared to be nearly Starved to death, he must have been left by Some party of Hunters. We gave him some meet, he would not come near."[2] When they came to tribes that ate dogs, particularly fat young puppies, Clark could not stomach this dish, even when, later, it was the only food to keep them from hunger. When they were able to purchase ten puppies to carry along with them Clark could not overcome his disgust. Yet Lewis learned to do just that and to find a plate of dog as good as many other kinds of eating. The contradictions between the two men are interesting. Lewis brought along his own dog Scannon as a companion. He showed the most anger of any occasion when, on the way home, some Indians along the Columbia River stole his dog. He was furious in the hunt to retrieve it, and he hurled threats at the tribesmen who had dared take his dog from him.

Upriver, at the Mandan Fort, which the members of the expedition had built to house themselves for the winter, they were joined by the French-Indian Charbonneau with his captured Shoshone wife (one of two), Sacajawea. Clark was able to see past the differences of customs and manners and to appreciate the human being in the young girl. Clark sometimes called her "Janey," and he helped her in the difficult birth of her son, who became part of their company as they traveled on the following spring. Clark delighted in the antics of the growing child and gave him the nickname "Pomp" for his proud little swaggering manner. Clark, on the return leg of his part of the journey along the Yellowstone, was to name an isolated flat-topped mountain for the little boy, calling it Pompey's Pillar, which some later solemn-minded scholars attributed to classical learning. Clark was usually very plain in his naming of places: "I call this Island Butter Island, as at this place we mad use of the last of our butter." He did not incline to consciously literary description, but he had a natural and forthright enjoyment of pleasant scenery, and he was usually brief and followed a statement of enjoyment with a description of an activity. "We camped on this plain, one of the most butifull Plains I ever saw."[3] He did not explore or contemplate his own reactions. "A delightful day. Put out our clothes to sun." The redheaded man, comfortable in his own skin, was comfortable with others. He could swear and be angry for a short time. But he took each day as it came and lived each hour up to its possibilities and stopped reaching beyond. He was clever in dealing with a variegated lot—Kentuckians, Québec rivermen, Indians of various tribes. He had a keen and friendly eye for human qualities in soldier, slave, woman, child. He was better than Lewis in boat craft, as the latter freely admitted. He was the camp doctor for his own men and for Indians along the way until the Mandans and Nez Perces and others came to think of Clark as a considerable medicine man. He was also good at map making, and it was his map-connections, as he called his map work, that brought geographical knowledge of this unknown land back to the settled areas.

The man Lewis was more puzzling as an individual entity. He had some of the same frontier and leadership qualities as Clark. They had been trained in the same rough school of border soldiering. But he was also introspective, blessed and cursed with the compulsion to look before and after. When the long boring stay with the Mandans was nearing an end, Lewis took the time to write not only about what he and the others were doing—breaking the boats free from the ice, packing supplies, and so forth—but also about what he was thinking as these furious activities went forward. An April 1805 entry is characteristic: "This little fleet, although not quite so respectable as that of Columbus or Captain Cook, was still viewed by us with as much pleasure as those deservedly famed adventurers ever beheld theirs, and, I daresay, with as much anxiety for their safety and preservation."

The sight of the boats, canoes, and only slightly larger pirogues, ready to go, filled him with large expectation. "We were now about to penetrate a country at least two thousand miles in width, on which the foot of civilized man had never trod. The good or evil it had in store for us was for experiment yet to determine, and these little vessels contained every article by which we were to expect to subsist or defend ourselves." Yet he cheered himself, adding ambition to hope (for had not Jefferson shared with him the large and even secret national aims of this enterprise?). "Entertaining as I do the most confident hope of succeeding in a voyage which had formed a daring project of mine for the last ten years [he had volunteered for an earlier abortive Jeffersonian attempt at penetration of the continent] I could but esteem this moment of my departure as among the most happy of my life."[4] Lewis identified himself—in a way, buried his own person—in the life and work of the expedition. This was a kind of self-immolation probably not true for any other member of the group, including his apt and efficient partner and friend, Clark. Lewis's conscious and sometimes unconscious assumptions cushioned him from despairs as he moved along the successful emotional upward curve of the journey and let him down on the downward curve into ordinary life afterward.

Lewis lived in a time that was borderland between eighteenth-century rationalism and early nineteenth-century romanticism. As a man of the Enlightenment, he had confidence in achieving whatever had been carefully thought out and planned. At the same time he belonged to a young generation that had begun to examine its own motives and feelings and to find complications in them, sometimes of sadness and doubt. After Lewis's unfortunate death, Jefferson wrote in a memoir of Lewis that he had observed melancholy in his young assistant in Washington.[5] The months of the expedition were to show in Lewis's writings no sustained melancholy, only a self-indulgent brooding that had a literary flavor and that was dissipated by action. The emotions became excessive only after the expedition had ended and Lewis awoke in a world of new responsibilities over which he had little control.

He and Clark maintained a firm but liberal control over the expedition as it progressed into unknown territory beyond the Mandans. Problems at first seemed solvable, and there was time to gape at wonders. Nothing was more remarkable to Lewis than the "white castles" that they encountered on the upper Missouri River where startling cliffs came down to the water's edge and took on, for the assiduous journal-writer, the appearance of medieval battlements:

> The hills and river cliffs which we passed today exhibit a most romantic appearance. . . . The water, in the course of time, in descending from those hills and plains, on either side of the river, has trickled down the soft sand cliffs and worn it into a thousand grotesque figures which, with the help of a little imagination, and an oblique view, at a distance are made to represent elegant ranges of lofty freestone buildings, having their parapets well stocked with statuary.[6]

Beyond the white cliffs, the juncture of the Missouri with another river coming in strongly from the Northwest presented the first puzzling problem: Which was the true course? Indians and trappers had told them of the great falls ahead on the Missouri, and they assumed that beyond the falls were the mountains and a true passage through them. With a small number of the men, Lewis attempted a brief exploration of the northern branch and returned to the others confident that this was not the Missouri. But it was a clear and pleasant stream (this was spring; at a later period its flow would have been greatly reduced). As some days earlier Clark had satisfied himself with naming another branch of the great river the Judith after the young woman who would be his wife, Lewis pleased himself by naming this puzzling river to be Maria's—after another young woman at home in Virginia. The others continued to disagree, yet went along in a well-disciplined way, content to let Lewis's judgment rule them. (They were to become so individualized and democratized before the expedition was over that, on the Pacific Coast, all, including the Indian woman and York, the black slave, were allowed to vote as to where to place the camp for winter.)

When, within a few days, they came to the falls, Lewis was proven right about the Missouri's leading them to the mountains and on to the Columbia. But the falls—rather, a series of falls and cascades—presented to them the first serious barrier to the way west. The month-long pause at the falls, which was filled with furious work, was an early climax in their journeying. What they accomplished in the seventeen-mile portage was a high point of ingenuity, stretched will, and courage. This time also occasioned some of Lewis's most interesting journal entries.

Scouting ahead, Lewis relished the first sight of the falls. The journal reflects a delight in the solitary enjoyment of a natural phenomenon, a new kind of emotion for his generation. "Fearing that the river bore to the south, and that I might pass the Falls if they existed between this and the snowy mountains, I altered my course nearly to the south and proceeded through the plain. I sent Fields on my right and Druilliard and Gibson on my left, with orders to kill some meat and join me at the river, where I should halt for dinner." He heard the sound of the waterfall before he saw it, then, "advancing a little further, I saw the spray rise above the plain like a column of smoke." As he scrambled toward the edge of the declivity out of which the spray rose, he heard "a roaring too tremendous to be mistaken for any cause short of the Great Falls of the Missouri." This then was the Missouri, and beyond, upriver, were the Snowy Mountains, and a way to be found through them to the rivers of the Pacific. This was a great moment, and Lewis knew it and savored it. "I hurried down the hill, which was about 200 feet high and difficult of access, to gaze on this sublimely grand spectacle."

He either on the spot scribbled his description and reaction or very carefully re-created later in camp his personal wonder at the sight.

I took my position on the top of some rocks about 20 feet high opposite the center of the Falls. . . . Immediately at the cascade, the river is about 300 yards wide. About 90 or 100 yards of this, next the larboard bluff, is a smooth even sheet of water falling over a precipice of at least 80 feet; the remaining part, about 200 yards wide, on my right, forms the grandest sight I ever beheld. The height of the fall is the same as the other, but the irregular and somewhat projecting rocks below receive the water in its passage down, and break into a perfect white foam which assumes a thousand forms in a moment, sometimes flying up in jets of sparkling foam to the height of fifteen or twenty feet, which are scarcely formed before large rolling bodies of the same beaten and foaming water are thrown over and conceal them.

He was wrought up in attempting to find words that would approximate the strokes of a painter or a poet. "I wished for the pencil of Salvator Rosa, a Titian, or the pen of Thomson, that I might be enabled to give to the enlightened world some just idea of this truly magnificent and sublimely grand object which has, from the commencement of time, been concealed from the view of civilized man."[7] (Like the other enlightened men and women of his time, he scarcely credited the peoples already inhabiting this region with any just appreciation of the spectacle.)

The day following the discovery of the falls continued to be filled with wonders, adventures, and narrow escapes for Lewis. On foot and alone, he followed the course of the river upstream, passing one set of falls and cascades after another for several miles, coming at last to smooth water where another large river came in from the west (the Indians' Medicine, today's Sun). He discovered, above this jointure of the two rivers, islands in the Missouri large and secure enough to be the camp at the upper end of the portage necessitating the arduous removal of their goods by improvised carts from below all the waterfalls. This the men would name White Bear Island, for (not as peaceful a place as they had hoped) it was alive with these ferocious and unpredictable beasts. On this second day of reconnoitering, Lewis himself came on a number of interesting animals, one of which was probably a wolverine, which growled at him, another of which was a bison he shot and watched die—"the poor animal discharging blood in streams from his mouth and nostrils." And the last and most dangerous adventure of the day was with one of the white bears that charged him without warning. "He pitched at me, open-mouthed and full speed. I ran about 80 yards, and found he gained on me fast. I then ran into the water." There he turned and outfaced the bear, pointing his espontoon (a combination staff and spear) at him, and found to his relief that at this defiance the bear turned and retreated.

The long day had seemed like a dream, so full it was with wonders, but "the prickly pears which pierced my feet very severely once in a while, particularly after it grew dark, convinced me that I was really awake." The others were very glad about Lewis's return, having grown anxious about his safety. He recorded not only his solitary adventures but also the satisfaction he had in good food at the end of the day. "My fare is really sumptuous this evening: Buffalo's humps, tongues, and marrow-bones, fine trout, parched meal, pepper and salt, and a good appetite."[8] He was a man living his life to the fullest, trying out upon his imagination and senses all kinds of new experiences. He would continue to find this area around the falls a scene of enchantment, a word he used more than once to describe his sensations during this period. When he returned the following year, to stop briefly at the falls, he found the plenitude of bison and wolves remarkable.

Despite the hardships they all endured in manhandling their supplies for seventeen difficult miles, this midsummer pause in 1805 was a time of promise for them. For Lewis, it was probably the happiest month of his life. A little more than a month later, ensnared in puzzling passageways through the never-ending mountains, Lewis measured himself in his journal against his large view of the person he wished himself to be. He was hard on himself:

> This day I completed my thirty-first year, and conceived that I had, in all human probability, now existed about half the period which I am to remain in this sublunary world. [He would live only four more years.] I reflected that I had as yet done little, very little, indeed, to further the happiness of the human race, or to advance the information of the succeeding generations. I viewed with regret the many hours I have spent in indolence, and now sorely feel the want of that information which those hours would have given me had they been judiciously expended. But since they are past and cannot be recalled, I dash from me the gloomy thought, and resolve in future to redouble my exertions and at least endeavor to promote those two primary objects of human existence, by giving them the aid of that portion of talents which Nature and fortune have bestowed on me; or, in future to live *for mankind,* as I have heretofore lived *for myself.*[9]

Lewis, an introspective man, had only chance moments for thought during these days of trying to find passage through the mountains. After a long and dangerous search, they found the Indian tribe whom they hoped would help them. Early parlays with Cameahwait (who was the young chief of this portion of the Shoshones and also, by a fortunate piece of luck, the brother of their own Janey, Sacajawea, who had been stolen from her people a few years before) were difficult, but at last successful. The success was largely through Lewis's patient skill in dealing with the chief, appealing at last to his pride and honor in asking him to give them guidance and transportation. When the Indian was about to deny the expedition absolutely needed help, Lewis wrote that he deliberately took a high tone. He called on the chief to fulfill promises already made and added what was an effective threat, "that if they wished the white man to assist them against their enemies by furnishing them with arms, and keeping their enemies from attacking them, that they must never promise us anything which they did not mean to perform." And it worked. "Cameahwait remained silent for some time. At length, he told me that he knew he had done wrong; but that he had been induced to that measure from seeing all his people hungry, but, as he had promised to give me assistance, he would not in future be worse than his word." Lewis had sounded the right note; he had manipulated the chief's feelings. He cemented arrangements for guides and horses and dissembled his own anxiety. "I directed the fiddle to be played and the party danced very merrily, much to the amusement and gratification of the natives, though I must confess that the state of my own mind at this moment did not well accord with the prevailing mirth."[10]

Lewis and Clark were probably more honest with the Indians than were most of their successors, but they had aims other than those of these strange peoples they met in their way. They knew that the vague promises they extended from an unimaginable white father far off to the east could not all be fulfilled. They also knew that they were carrying out a large political purpose for their own country which would ruthlessly disregard the wishes of the tribes if this should be necessary. They knew that they were making a path first for traders, then trappers and miners, and at last settlers; but they could not know how quickly those generations would follow one upon the other, and how soon the final ones, the people who built houses and towns, would arrive. This process would quickly bring about the ruin of the Indians' way of life on the high plains and in the mountains, the last region where they were relatively untouched. Neither the explorers nor the Indians realized this imminent future, and for the most part the two parties got on well with each other. There was often a social mingling of these intruders into tribal life, and this included an enthusiastic exchange of sexual favors. The Indian women passed back to these men of the expedition venereal diseases that other tribes had carried westward from first contact with whites in the East. The two leaders, out of a kind of aesthetic distaste, have been said for the most part to have abstained. But there were also said to have been a number of redheaded Indians in the next generation of Shoshones and Nez Perces.

In their high and ceremonious tone, as well as in their obvious courage, both Lewis and Clark touched a chord of admiration in the Indians and caused an appreciative response in the chiefs. The two leaders were to be remembered in the oral tradition of various tribes as "real chiefs" and not like those other white people who came after.

As the quotations from his journal show, Lewis kept in mind the large political aims of the expedition, but he also kept a space apart for his private enjoyment of the experience, and the tone of this enjoyment was that of a romantic contemplative. Lewis, whom we know better in his inner thoughts than we do Clark, was thus an interesting, contrary mixture. He was a lover of the land and its creatures, a man who contemplated the scene and soliloquized his enjoyment to himself, quite like the many appreciators of this land in successive generations. He was also a measurer and tabulator of the land and its resources and, eventually, a destroyer and a re-creator, never content to leave the landscape as it had first appealed to him.

The passage through the mountains was grim. The members of the expedition were hungry a number of times, and underfed most of the way. They were increasingly cold, and they lost some of the horses through accidents on the steep trails. It became a problem to find ways to make litters for and to carry sick men; Lewis himself was so transported for the last few days before they burst out of the mountains and into the restorative meadows, where there was game for the men and grass for the thin horses. Afterward, having made their way down the rivers to the Pacific, they found themselves for the winter in a wet and gray land, devoid of the larger game to which they had grown accustomed. They simply endured the cold months, anxious to start home as soon as the snow in the mountains would allow them to do so.

On the Pacific Coast there was a dull time of waiting. The Indians seemed less interesting; these peoples had already been partially corrupted by traders along the shore. Both Lewis and Clark expressed from this time on harsher judgments upon the native peoples they met. Cataloging of discoveries went on conscientiously, but astonishment was dulled. They made a ceremony of Christmas and New Year's Day, but for Lewis this first day of 1806 "consisted principally in the anticipation of the 1st day of January, 1807, when, in the bosom of our friends we hope to participate in the mirth and hilarity of the day, and with the zest given by recollection of the present, we shall completely, both mentally and corporally, enjoy the repast which the hand of civilization has prepared for us."[11] These adventurers were homesick.

The return was delayed several times at the edge of the mountains by the deep snows that held on into June, but they found a way to surmount the drifts by traveling upon their surfaces, guided by some friendly Nez Perces. When they reached a high point, Lewis, taking a moment to look about, expressed determination and will more than enjoyment: "From this place we had an extensive view of these stupendous mountains principally covered with snow like that on which we stood. . . . After having smoked the pipe and contemplating this scene sufficient to have dampened the spirits of any except such hardy travelers as we have become, we continued our march."[12]

The homeward crossing of the terrible mountains was not as difficult in the high snow as they had thought it would be. They were across in three days and rested and were glad at the hot springs on the other side. There they made plans for the remainder of the journey, and they decided on a possibly dangerous course.

In order to see as much of this wide country as possible, they determined to divide the party. Lewis would return to the falls of the Missouri, and beyond, and explore the Marias. Clark would move southeastward to the Yellowstone and follow that river downstream until they would meet where the Missouri and the Yellowstone came together. Dividing the party was a bold plan. Lewis recorded the emotion of separation: "I took leave of my worthy friend and companion, Captain Clark and the party that accompanied him. I could not avoid feeling much concern on this occasion, although I hoped this separation was only momentary."[13]

Clark surely had the better of this division of labor. He saw much new territory, and, aside from losing his horses to Indian marauders, and having to build new boats, he had little difficulty in the descent of the Yellowstone. Lewis had all the trouble. Some way up the Marias, his too small patrol (separated from the rest of his men on the larger river) was attacked in the night by Indians with whom they had had to share an uneasy camp. They awoke to find these suspicious tribesmen grabbing their guns and horses. There was a fight, two Indians were killed, and the whites seized hold of the Indians' horses in exchange for their own, which were gone. Exhausting themselves in a night's forced march, they rejoined the boat crew on the Missouri, but left behind a disastrous tradition among the Blackfeet of the white man as enemy. Later, downriver Lewis had more bad luck, and one of his men shot him in the buttocks on a hunting expedition into brushy territory. He arrived at his rendezvous crippled and lying supine on his boat. Clark doctored his friend, and Lewis rather quickly recovered as they sailed rapidly downstream toward Saint Louis.

Lewis's return journey was too full of anxiety and incident to allow much time for introspective writing. He was also consumed already with the future, the need to consolidate discovery in a permanent record, some kind of publication of the expedition. This was to be his passion during the months and years he had yet to live—such a concern as to blot out some of the self-preserving duties and relationships that might have helped him to a happy postexpedition career.

The immediate shock of a homely element of "civilization"—"some cows on the bank"—was "a joyful sight to the party and caused a shout to be raised for joy."[14] Yearning for streets and crowds and buildings, these men of the expedition looked very wild indeed first to the inhabitants of the little town of Saint Charles, then to those who met them on the Saint Louis docks. In Indian clothes, ragged, threadbare, brown, thin, some of them haggard, they looked as if they belonged to the wild country, whereas inwardly they were shaky with joy at being back in the city.

Expectation must have been very high in the mind of the imaginative Lewis, but he kept his sense of proportion. He saw to it that Clark was rewarded with land and money in the same amounts as he was to receive, although the first gesture of the administration through congressional act was to discriminate and make Clark's reward lesser. In his official report, Lewis recommended his men generously, typically omitting the story of the private who had unfortunately shot his captain. He and his worthy friend parted, Clark to go to Virginia and become engaged to the young woman for whom he had named the Judith River. Lewis was to recommend to President Jefferson that Clark come out to Saint Louis as brigadier general of the great territory they had discovered and as superintendent of Indian affairs. Lewis was shortly named governor, but neglected rather too long to take up his duties, leaving the affairs of the territory in the hands of an acting governor, Secretary of the Territory Frederick Bates, who was already jealous of his own position and unhappy at the approaching accession of a superior. In eastern cities, Lewis was feted with dinners and poems, as well as quantities of public and private praise. This could not have been displeasing to the proud man. One of his chief concerns was in assembling an official history of the expedition and planning a book, which he never lived to see completed. No one at this time could have foretold anything but a smooth and interesting future for the two leaders of the great expedition. This would be so eventually for Clark. It is a great puzzle why it was not to be so for Lewis, why his life, from this time on, should be entangled in embarrassing and increasingly tragic circumstances.

Richard Dillon's biography *Meriwether Lewis* gives a fair assessment of the character of the governorship of the former explorer, admitting his fault in coming late to his new command and his failure to make good reports to Washington, but giving Lewis credit for planning what might have been a better and more peaceful management of the territory if he had lived.

Lewis's unexpected problems with the national administration were caused in part by William Eustis, a new secretary of war who came in under Madison and was suspicious of Lewis politically, thinking him an adherent of Burr (which he was not) and fatally not understanding the expenses Lewis had incurred in trying to get the Mandan Chief Big White back to his home country. This bill—for $500—was refused payment when Lewis turned it in as he thought in a routine manner, along with other expenses he thought legitimate. These damaging refusals to honor his bills set him traveling toward Washington when he was already ill, apparently feverish as well as occasionally delirious, yet riding horseback as much as fifty miles a day through the tangled forests of Tennessee.

Readers of Lewis's *Journals,* who had been present, as if with him, in his adventures and musings in the West, can only speculate as if from the outside upon his thoughts as he moved East to settle his affairs in the capital city. Incensed at what seemed a slur upon his honor, he had sold off most of his assets in Saint Louis to pay his debts. He had made a new will, leaving everything he possessed to his mother. Yet he spoke confidently to friends of his return after this journey to Washington. He then vanished into the dangerous woods of the Natchez Trace.

The story of his death has been the subject of various speculations by a number of writers. Vardis Fisher examined the case closely and objectively in his book bluntly entitled *Suicide or Murder? The Strange Death of Governor Meriwether Lewis*. His treatment of the subject makes for acceptance of the strong probability that Lewis was murdered callously and did not commit suicide, which some of his contemporaries, including his old employer Jefferson, believed. Lewis had appeared suddenly and unexpectedly out of the forest at Grinder's Stand. He was ill and distressed and vulnerable, appearing to have more of the goods of this world than most travelers on the Trace. (His money disappeared and was never found.)

Fisher makes a good argument that the death was a violent, senseless murder for what money he had on him, that it was never punished, but hushed up through fear, the word "murder" having been whispered and passed on orally to the descendants of those in the community who had been afraid of retribution.

The fact of the young explorer's having been cut off in his years of promise makes more poignant the reading of his personal journal. In this record, written daily despite fatigue, and carried through many miles and adventures, Lewis (and Clark in his more down-to-earth portions) preserved the measurements, the distances and directions, as exactly as possible, of the rivers, mountains, plains, and minerals. This had never before been recorded in the English language. Lewis also recorded how all this newness struck into his imagination. He was a man of the advent of a new age, that of the romantic view impinging on the useful, rational view of landscape and life. He brought with him a fresh way of delighting in strangeness and vastness. He found beauty as well as terror in this unknown West.

TWO

Fur Trapper: Osborne Russell

In the spring of 1835, a fur trapper named Osborne Russell found himself faced with his first solitary journey in the wilderness of the Rockies. There were no maps for this region, except in the heads of the mountain men who had been here before (their intrusion into the northern plains and mountains had begun immediately upon the return of Lewis and Clark from their exploration). Russell, still a newcomer, had accepted a dare, or rather a command, from the leader *(bourgeois)* of the band of trappers, a man he did not like, to set off alone and find his way to Fort Hall on the Snake River, somewhere southwestward from a campfire gathering; he was to bring back horses so that he and the other trappers might carry their stiff, stinking beaver skins to trade.

Russell at twenty had come out from the East the year before with Nathaniel Wyeth's party. Wyeth had been determined to be independent of the big fur companies already consolidated with headquarters in Saint Louis or with financial backing in eastern cities. Wyeth had large ambitions to carry his skins to the Pacific, meet ships there, and so start a trade all the way across the continent. After building Fort Hall (young Russell, an innocent in these large plans, had helped raise the timbers), Wyeth had been disappointed on the Pacific Coast; there was no ship to meet him. He left a portion of his group behind to start trapping in the spring. Russell was one of this party.

Russell had seen a fellow member drowned carelessly in too swift a river. He had faced his first charging grizzly and trembled afterward when he killed it by a lucky point-blank shot. He had survived his first Indian fight. He had seen the three Tetons. He had taken a wondering part in a rendezvous of all the boisterous trappers from roundabout and far-off. He had begun to learn to measure the direction and distance traveled each day so that he could go back, or, as he thought, tell someone else how to go again that way. He had tried to learn what names had been given, or had given names himself, to every ridge and river and creek passed along the way. Russell also wrote nightly in a journal that he carefully preserved from the dangers and difficulties of travel.

Russell did not write down the details of trap-setting; it would have been too much like talking to himself about what he and the others all knew. It is from other writers, who came later, that one picks up the technical routine of the work of these men: the weight of the traps (three to five pounds), the laying of five or six along a picked stream each night, the collection of them in the dawn, the clever lethal set of the trap—the body of the trap underneath enough water so that, when the animal was caught and pulled, it could be drowned by the chain pulling on a ring, which then slipped down on a stout stick, set a careful distance in the bank or stream bed, and notched at the bottom to hold the ring and the chain so that the beaver could not escape and get to the surface for air. The animal was tempted by beaver-gland material on a carefully moistened tree limb or twig hanging above water over the trap so that the pathetic creature fell in reaching for the erotic scent.

When the tired men gathered together from their individual trappings, with furs accumulating and supplies deteriorating, "our austocratical director," as Russell wrote in his journal, required that he go back to the fort for supplies.[1] He thought he had to do it or be scorned by the others, although Jim Bridger and his men, who had joined forces with Wyeth's remnant, heartily discouraged him from going. (Bridger was the one of them who knew this land.) But at twenty-one, Russell felt it necessary to prove himself.

He had come West from a small place in Maine and so was drenched in the memory of misty lakes, green fields and forests, and a nearby ocean. He had trapped earlier along the streams of Wisconsin and Minnesota and so considered himself something of a veteran. But this dry and open expanse was to him, as to other easterners, a totally foreign kind of land. This was the first trapping season for the eager apprentice, who did not know that the trade was already diminishing. Although the more experienced men, roughly friendly, told Russell not to go, he felt compelled to make this first solitary journey.

Russell said he would go, out of a kind of yearning fear of the unknown. He set off, following first some of the detailed instructions of his leader, and after two days of leading a horse rapidly going lame, of stumbling over rocky barren ground, and of going ahead without water or food, he woke from sleep to find himself lost. He saw trees and bison at a distance and deduced that water must be there. He decided then and there what had to be the credo of every trapper, to rely on his own judgment henceforth and to learn as he traveled the lay of the land.

As he went ahead, he was to grow out of fear into self-reliance and even a kind of spiritual expansion in enjoying the solitude, the beauty, and the strange and sometimes scary happenings into which he fell as he traveled, slowly righting his direction, falling in with Indians with whom he found he could develop a chancy friendship, talk and even exchange jokes with, for he had diligently tried to learn the Snake language the winter before at the fort.

The Bannocks (kin to the Snakes) with whom he hobnobbed gave him "a good supply of boiled Buffaloe tongues" to take on his way. He stayed with them during a mighty hunt when hundreds of men, as it seemed to him, killed thousands of bison on the great plain before the camp, where the women skinned, cut up, and dried the bountiful supply of food for months ahead. He found his way to another Indian village, this time definitely of the Snakes, not of the dreaded Blackfeet, was welcomed into the chief's lodge, and "passed the time very agreeably for six days among those simple but well fed and good humored Savages" (37–38).

He also wrote that "learning that Bridger was approaching the forks and the party of hunters to which I had belonged had passed down the river and arrived at the Fort I mounted my horse—started down the river and arrived at the Fort next day about noon the distance being about 60 Mls S.S.W. When I arrived the party had given up all hopes of ever seeing me again and had already fancied my lifeless body lying on the plains after having been scalped by the savages" (38).

He had not succeeded in his mission of bringing back horses, and he had been hungry and thirsty and scared and lost, yet he recovered himself, found himself, and survived. Having rejoined his friends at the fort, young Russell had a fine sense of having joined the ranks of seasoned trappers. He had also reached the end of his unsatisfactory contract with Wyeth and his company and determined not to renew that connection. "Now I was independent of the world and no longer to be termed a 'Greenhorn.' At least I determined not to be so green as to bind myself to an arbitrary Rocky Mountain Chieftain to be kicked over hill and dale at his pleasure" (38). He passed the winter with some independents at Mutton Hill, which was forty miles from the fort, and in the spring attached himself to Jim Bridger's party, now, the Rocky Mountain Fur Company having foundered, a part of the more monied American Fur Company. From this time on Russell slipped in and out of arrangements and considered himself an independent. One might choose a good "bushway" chieftain, such as Bridger, in whom one could trust, but circumstances changed from time to time, and Russell was now his own man and recorded his interests, emotions, and meditations in hurried but vivid words in his nightly journal. (The other great chieftains of the trade did not write, so we know them only through others, but this obscure trapper recorded words, so we can know him and, through him, his friends and leaders and occasional enemies.)

Russell was not entirely absorbed in work. He took time out to look about and react to the colors and shapes of the land and to the varieties of "natives" he encountered. There was always the need to look out for danger, especially for solitary trappers; this was true however well one might get along from time to time with the Indians. But Russell liked his situation. One particular valley pleased him. Here he and his mates had discovered a tribe so primitive that they thought it seemed to be living a kind of golden age (an idea Russell seemed to have picked up from a book read). The second time he came to it, he liked the place even better.

> Here we found some of those independent and happy Natives of whom I gave a description [earlier in the journal]. We traded some Beaver and dressed Skins from them and hunted the streams running into the valley for several days. There is something in the wild romantic scenery of this valley which I cannot nor will I, attempt to describe but the impression made upon my mind while gazing from a high eminence on the surrounding landscape one evening as the sun was gently gliding behind the western mountain and casting gigantic shadows across the vale were such as time can never efface from my memory. (46)

The words might be those borrowed from books; the emotion was genuine.

His unselfconscious diary records how little he was all work and no play. After a good stay and sufficient food at one spot, he was accustomed to take a look about: "The next day after eating a light breakfast of roasted venison I shouldered my rifle, and ascended the highest mountain on foot. I reached the snow in about an hour when seating myself upon a huge fragment of Granite and having full view of the country around Me in a few moments was almost lost in contemplation" (63). He continued in an incoherent kind of philosophical wandering among the causes of life itself.

The journal is written white-hot, the words coming out naïve and honest. Russell tells of his being astounded and dazed in the first moments of his first Indian fight—mounted Indians riding to and fro in front of the trapper camp, shooting and yelling. "After Securing my horses I took my gun examined the priming set the breech on the ground and hand on the Muzzle with my arms folded gazing at the novelty of the scene for some minutes quite unconscious of danger until the whistling of balls about my ears gave me to understand that these were something more than mere pictures of imagination" (16).

As he was jerked into a sense of danger during this fight, so he was plunged into the necessity of assessing his leaders. One was better than another; one indeed was terribly poor. He had to learn in short order the tasks that gave him rheumatism very quickly, such as wading in glacier-fed streams. He found there was a necessary loneliness for a single trapper. No one could trap beaver in a crowd; each man had to separate to do this task, and it was then a great relief, in small or large gatherings, to burst forth in jokes and drunkenness.

The surety of a good comrade raised thankfulness to a high pitch. Good talk was welcome. A piece of reading matter exchanged was important. A safe and secure camp, after bad ones, was a pleasure: "Here we had plenty of wood water meat and dry grass to sleep on, and taking everything into consideration we thought ourselves comfortably situated—comfortably I say for mountaineers not for those who never repose on anything but a bed of down" (76).

After a harsh apprenticeship and a taste of the compensations of his new life, young Russell was able to begin to think of himself as a veteran. During this learning time and also in all the years of practice, he was acquiring the skills to survive, and even to enjoy. He did not fall by the wayside or give up or get killed or be seriously damaged. He was a mountain man. He partook of the life that one historian has called the western occupation that needed and gathered around it the greatest assemblage of skills.

Bernard DeVoto wrote of the rough-and-ready fur trapper, ill-clothed, dirty, careless, uncouth, deprived by those who took advantage, often illiterate by other people's standards, as a person of consummate skills:

> It is hardly too much to say that a mountain man's life was skill. He not only worked in the wilderness, he also lived there and did so from sun to sun by the exercise of total skill. It was probably as intricate a skill as any ever developed by any way of working or living anywhere. Certainly it was the most complex of the wilderness crafts practiced on this continent. The mountains, the aridity, the distances, and the climates imposed severities far greater than those laid on forest-runners, rivermen, or any other of our symbolic pioneers.
>
> Treatises could be written on the specific details we lack space even for generalizations. Why do you follow the ridges into or out of unfamiliar country? What do you do for a companion who has collapsed from want of water while crossing a desert? How do you get meat when you find yourself without gunpowder in a country barren of game? What tribe of Indians made this trail?[2]

Not having the ambition to be a leader or an agent for the companies that he saw, at this late stage of the trade, shifting, dissolving, and forming with cynical irregularity, Russell was content to fend for himself and to watch closely the motives and behavior of other men. Traveling partnerships were always shifting, too, but it was a comfort to be occasionally in the company of a friend he trusted and liked. One time there had been four of them together. Two who were Canadians departed, and he was left with the one he considered the best of the lot: "Our Camp then consisted of myself and my old comrade Elbridge, I say old comrade because we had been sometime together but he was a young man, from Beverly Mass and being bred a sailor he was not much of a landsman, woodsman or hunter but a great easy natured fellow standing 5 feet 10—and weighing 200 lbs."[3]

Russell had learned earlier about the dark side of life at very close quarters: about mean-minded camp keepers who cheated the hunters when they came in; about cruelties, those of whites against Indians, of Indians against whites; of the dire chanciness of life itself here where every small expedition was a provocation to the tribes or, rather, to those warriors among the generally friendly tribes who wanted to count coup on this new white tribe intruding into hunting grounds. The trappers at this time did not seem a major threat to the Crows, the Blackfeet, the Bannocks, or the Snakes, simply a chance for horse-stealing, counting coup, or picking up some of the new kinds of equipment—guns, pots and pans, metal knives, and so forth. Often Indians, knowing now the worth of the pelts, joined in the expeditions.

In the midst of the cruelty in which he lived, a lot of it gratuitous to people and animals, Russell indulged a growing consciousness, a habit perhaps fostered by journal-keeping. He had room for both curiosity and compassion. He viewed with pity a poor ewe deer that hunters were shooting at as a target, an animal of too poor condition to be of use as food or hide. He looked with discrimination at the human inhabitants of these mountains; for one, he admired the Flatheads (Salish), "a brave friendly generous and hospitable tribe strictly honest with a mixture of pride which exalts them far above the rude appellation of Savages" (33). He came to share with Flatheads and Nez Perces, as if he were their brother, a fear of the Blackfeet, always on the alert to the cry that the "Savages" over the next hill might be Blackfeet.

One time a group of trappers, feeling the competition that the Indians were giving them in collecting pelts and taking them to the rendezvous to sell, fired on an Indian village that was primarily defenseless. Farther on, thinking to do the same again, they were met instead by unarmed Blackfeet who came out to ask them to come in and smoke. They did so, not making an attack, "for we were ashamed to think of fighting a few poor Indians nearly dwindled to skeletons by the small Pox" (89).

The country was dangerous, but it was also full of diversions. Russell learned in geyser country that a trapper could boil his meat by suspending it in a hot pool. Mention of geyser country in the journal indicates the breadth of Russell's wanderings, from Yellowstone's hot pools in the south to the Missouri or the Marias rivers in the north, from Fort Union in the east to Fort Hall in the west, with mountain ranges and wide plains in between these indefinite and shifting boundaries which mountain men learned to know intimately.

Savoring campfire food, campfire talk in between the lonely journeyings, and in his case reading any book on which he could lay hold, Russell in homely words set down in his journal a philosophy by which to live this dangerous life. He hardly realized that he had come into the trade near the end. Men were now switching from beaver hats to the more fashionable silk ones in London and New York. Life out here, far from the trivial changes in fashion that would eventually affect him, did not get easier.

With a friend named White, Russell endured the most extreme danger, pain, and hardship of his career. The two men were one day unexpectedly surrounded by Blackfeet in heavy woods. White was struck by an arrow first, then Russell. "The Indian who shot me was within 8 ft and made a Spring towards me with his uplifted battle axe: I made a leap and avoided the blow and kept hopping from log to log thro a shower of arrows which flew around us like hail, lodging in the pines and logs" (102). The Indians passed close by through the thickets. The two men, weak and faint from loss of blood, kept quiet and hidden. Resilient, Russell scolded his friend, trying to rally him out of a crying despair. He himself crawled to the water in a lake, water that they were thirsting for although it looked an impossible number of yards away. He brought some back in his hat.

> While I was at this he had kindled a small fire and taking a draught of water from the hat he exclaimed Oh dear we shall die here, we shall never get out of these mountains, Well said I if you persist in thinking so you will die but I can crawl from this place upon hands and one knee and Kill 2 or 3 Elk and make a shelter of the skins dry the meat until we get able to travel. In this manner I persuaded him that we were not in half so bad a situation as we might be. (103)

The two injured trappers slept by the fire. Russell made crutches the next morning, found he could rise, and at last the two of them found an encampment with one Canadian in it. But the camp had been robbed and contained for sustenance only one sack of salt. "We left the place heaping curses on the head of the Blackfoot nation which neither injured them or alleviated our distress." They kept going. Russell treated his wounds with "a salve of Beavers Oil and Castoreum." By the next day "this had eased the pain and drawn out the swelling" (105), and he was on the way to recovery. The three men kept going toward Fort Hall. Near the end of their trek they accomplished a distance of "65 Mls in two days without eating" (108). They made it. Russell was now a seasoned mountain man, liable to be killed, but also liable to scratch, scrabble, and survive in a wonderful way.*

The animal life of the mountains and plains was disappearing. The

---

*Bernard DeVoto used at some length this episode from Russell's journal in his history of the fur trade, *Across the Wide Missouri*. Otherwise he used Russell's narrative only to check the movements of his other principals.

mountain men were killing off their own living. Russell saw this. He wrote in his journal in the fall of 1842, near the end of his time as a trapper:

> In the year 1836 large bands of Buffaloe could be seen in almost every little Valley on the small branches of this Stream at this time the only traces which could be seen of them were the scattered bones of those that had been killed. Their trails which had been made in former years deeply indented in the earth were over grown with grass and weeds. The trappers often remarked to each other as they rode over these lonely plains that it was time for the white man to leave the mountains as Beaver and game had nearly disappeared. (123)

Seeing the realities, Russell determined to leave the mountains, to take himself west to the more civilized Oregon country and find a new way to live. He went on a last hunting trip to provide for his journey. He needed dried elk to pack on his way to the Willamette. A friend who had also decided to leave the fur-trapping pursuit went hunting with him. This other defector from the dying trade was going east to the Green Mountains. The necessities of the hunt did not prevent Russell from climbing a mountain and looking about one more time at the landscape that had twined so deeply into his nerves:

> I ascended to the top of Rosses mountain (on which the snows remain till the latter part of Aug.). Sat under a pine and took a last farewell view of a country over which I had travelled so often under such a variety of circumstances. The recollections of the past connected with the scenery now spread out before me put me somewhat in a Poetical humour and for the first time I attempted to frame my thoughts into rhyme but if Poets will forgive me for this intrusion I shall be cautious about trespassing on their grounds in the future. . . . I killed an Elk and on the following day cured the meat for packing from thence I returned to the fort where I staid till the 22nd Aug. In the meantime there arrived at the Fort a party of Emigrants from the States on their way to the Oregon Territory. . . . I started with them and arrived at the Falls of the Willamette river on the 26 day of Septr., 1842. (125)

He had been in the mountains for almost nine years. He had lived through the whole cycle of apprenticeship, training, and curing as a mountain man. Now, fur trapping having ended, he, like other mountain men, had to find another kind of life. The explorers had come home to find themselves out of place and sometimes disbelieved. The fur trappers also had to settle to other modes of existence, to make a place or never find one in the civilization that was somehow always alien to them.

Jim Bridger, Russell's admired friend and leader, probably the most accomplished of the mountain men, was only thirty-five when the fur trade collapsed. He became a trader at his own fort, Fort Bridger, on Black's Fork of the Green River, a stopping place for immigrants to Oregon. He was also often a guide to various kinds of expeditions, civil and military, into the changing West. Russell became a proper and decent citizen of the new Oregon country, took part in the formation of a provisional government of that territory, helping to pull it away from the British sway of influence. He lost an eye, prosaically but tragically, in an explosion at a mill site. He became Judge Russell in the early government of the territory. He was defeated in a run for the governorship. He moved to California at the time of the gold discoveries there, tried mining, gave it up, ran a boarding house, did merchandising, and shared in financing two trading ships between Sacramento and Portland, but he was bankrupted by a partner who took the returns and absconded.

Russell was in poor financial condition the rest of his life. He lived in bad health in and near Placerville in the California gold country. He had sent to his sister in Maine a corrected copy of his journal, hoping for publication. But the copy disappeared, and he was disturbed that no word came as to what had happened to it. He never knew of its late publication. He died in the Placerville County Hospital on August 26, 1892, long after he had last looked at the mountains that held the beaver streams.[4]

THREE

Naturalist: John Kirk Townsend

Dogs were snarling and yelping. But the young white man confidently approached the village of Indian lodges and only half-threateningly pointed his gun while protecting his game bag. As he expected, women and boys raised yells to quiet the dogs and drag them out of his way, saying: "Iskam Kahmooks, iskam Kahmooks . . . take up your dogs, take up your dogs, the *bird chief* is coming."[1] So John Kirk Townsend wrote in his journal at the end of one day of his kind of hunting late in 1836. He had been in the West for more than two years, and he had found a good temporary place in an Indian village of the Chinooks not far from the Hudson's Bay Company's headquarters at Fort Vancouver on the Columbia River. Here he had a few days of undisturbed hunting in making his discoveries of the new birds of this so far scientifically unexplored and unclassified land.

This was probably as contented a state as Townsend would ever know. After two years of effort and hardship, he seemed to himself to have gathered his resources and to be doing good scientist's work in this wilderness of strangeness, beauty, and terror. Taken in hospitably by a chief of a small band, given the best of bedding and food in the headman's quarters, he was finding what he had come looking for: new species of western birds whose forms and colors delighted him. He went hunting each day with his gun at the ready. He needed an example of each new kind. He carefully skinned the beautiful creatures and pressed the skins into bundles for taking home. He had endured a long journey to reach this place, making his counts, taking his skins along the way. He had gone through some serious difficulties and hardships with his self-respect and pride intact. He, the eastern and inexperienced one of the brigade, had endured with those old veterans of the plains and mountains and come through.

He was looking forward to starting toward home. He was seeing past the grueling days of crossing the wide prairies, fording cold rivers, climbing stony slopes and getting lost, and camping in isolated spots where the threat of attack haunted the campfires. He had the vivid memory of sailing to the Sandwich Islands from the mouth of the Columbia and returning to the hospitality of Fort Vancouver. There, under the thoughtful care of the factor, he had been pressed for a time into service as fort surgeon. The young doctor turned naturalist had another perspective from the care he gave the trappers and the neighborhood Indians. It all went into his journal, which he kept night after night. Now, with the happy accumulation of his new species, he was ready to turn back and carry his packs home—to add to the knowledge being accumulated in eastern scientific societies and, for himself, perhaps to gain some modest fame.

It was all delight when he had set out with his traveling companion, the older, more experienced naturalist Thomas Nuttall, who had made western trips before. The two of them had been given advice in Saint Louis as to the supplies, the clothes, and the horses to buy, and had forwarded this heavy equipment with the main brigade to a meeting point at Independence, where they would all in good order set out across the plains. The two men would make a holiday of this beginning by walking cross-country for the first few days. They were gentlemanly observers, not out to get or to gain anything but knowledge, equable and pleasant in their manners and assumptions, and not above enjoying shooting for sport or excitement. Townsend, at twenty-five, was in the best of moods.

The two men noticed their last church bell. They ate their last lunch at a tavern. Then: "I shouldered my gun. Mr. N. his stick and bundle, and off we trudged again westward ho!" (131). These genial naturalists, civilized and polite to each other and to all they encountered, could not help shuddering at dirty beds in dirty inns, now behind them.

After this easy-going walk over a number of leisurely days, they joined the fur brigade and began their real trip on April 28, 1834, from the outpost of Independence. They became part of the well-ordered discipline of the company of Milton Sublette. He was an old and experienced fur trapper and organized the cavalcade for efficiency and protection. Townsend and his friend pleased themselves by taking their place at the head of the brigade alongside their leader, Sublette, and the New Englander Nathaniel Wyeth, beginning his second westward adventure with an iron aim for promoting both gain and settlement in the far Northwest. (Osborne Russell, whom Townsend apparently did not get to know, was somewhere among the 70 men and the 250 horses that trailed behind the leaders.) The "parade" was something to see as they headed out on the flowered plains when summer had not yet dried the native grasses.

> I frequently sallied out from my station to look at and admire the appearance of the cavalcade, and as we rode out from the encampment, our horses prancing, and neighing and pawing the ground, it was altogether so exciting that I could scarcely contain myself. Every man in the company seemed to feel a portion of the same kind of enthusiasm, uproarious bursts of merriment, and gay and lively songs, were constantly echoing along the line. We were certainly a most merry and happy company. What cared we for the future? (141)

Instead of the earlier, reliable, but difficult Missouri River route, up which one had to push or pull or sail alternately, the way west now lay landward across the prairies. To Townsend, these early days seemed as fresh as the spring itself, and he delighted in the wide and open spaces between the swift running streams, in the innocent troops of animals which more and more frequently crossed their path, and in the flights of bountiful birds. All of these sights called for exclamations in his written account, on several different days: "Large flocks of pigeons passing overhead!" (126), and "We saw today several large white wolves, and two herds of antelopes. The latter is one of the most beautiful animals I ever saw!" (155). And on the Platte, "we saw, also, the sandhill crane, great heron (Ardea heroidas), and the long-billed curlew, stalking through the shallow water" (157), and, at last, a sensation indeed: "Towards evening, on rising a hill, we were suddenly greeted by a sight which seemed to astonish even the oldest amongst us. The whole plain, as far as the eye could discern, was covered by one enormous mass of buffalo" (161).

Beyond the Platte, all was not delight. The land dried out, the green growth browned, the game got harder to shoot and sometimes scarce, and the danger of attack by one tribe or another affected at least the imagination. Townsend and Nuttall learned soon that self-reliance was not only pleasing but also necessary. They learned to make their own camp each night, scrounge for their own food, care for their own horses, and devise ways of conserving their caches of plants and bird and mammal skins. No one else had the time to help them in these private duties. Townsend remembered the loving care that Nuttall used in spreading out his precious plants to dry upon a rock after a wetting in the crossing of a stream. Each one took his place as night guard in rotation with the others and pricked his ears at animal howls or bird calls that might or might not belong to the four-legged or winged kind.

Townsend also learned that he could endure a sudden crisis of danger. They were within the mountains and approaching the longed-for comfort and company of the rendezvous, when this most inexperienced member of the brigade had his nearest escape. Crossing a swift river, he lost control of his horse, then some of his records, as well as his coat, hung carelessly across the horn of the saddle, were swept away. He arrived at the camp cold and in pain. He was stove up with fever and arthritis and condemned to lying for days in a tent while the wild rout of the mountain men's meeting swirled around him and filled his ears. Half out of his head, he endured a rising and falling ebb of songs and obscenities and the drumming of horse hoofs and the sharp cracks of gunfire. "A more unpleasant situation for an invalid could scarcely be conceived" (193). He was in no condition to relish the picturesque coarseness and good humor of the scene, but nevertheless managed to describe it: "These people with their obstreperous mirth, their whooping, and howling, and quarreling, dashing into and through our camp, yelling like fiends, the barking and baying of savage wolf-dogs, and the incessant cracking of rifles and carbines, render our camp a perfect bedlam" (193).

Even in perfect health, Townsend was fastidious to the point of shrinking from this kind of behavior. (Audubon would have shrugged it off, having lived in the midst of it all his frontier days.) Townsend's imagination was rather impatiently scientific. He believed that he was one of a new breed of men, and he wrote hopefully:

> What valuable and highly interesting accessions to science might not be made by a party, composed exclusively of naturalists, on a journey through this rich and unexplored region! The botanist, the geologist, the mammalogist, the ornithologist, and entomologist, would find rich and almost inexhaustible field for their prosecution of their inquiries, and the result of such an expedition would be to add most materially to our knowledge of the wealth and resource of our country. (181)

Political or material gain had been and would be the enthusiastic aim of most western travelers, but this was a new note. A handful of these nonacquisitive travelers would begin to come to the West in the dangerous decades of the 1830s and the 1840s, when the fur trade was not over but was diminishing, and to report what they had seen. This is not to say that there were not sensitive eyes among the earlier discoverers and even the illiterate trappers. They understood and loved the country more intimately than the disinterested scientists, but for the most part they did not write about it or paint it. They were ignored or called tall-tale tellers (and some were). Townsend and his kind were, however, among the first western travelers to go as professionals, of science or art, and to record for the rest of the country the unique nature of the newly opening land.

They came raggedly, individually, each proud of membership in a fraternity of learning or craft. George Catlin, who in 1832 came upriver to Fort Union on the steamboat *Yellowstone,* its first voyage this far, was a painter and also a visionary, who found in the Mandans and the other tribes the confirmation of his belief in the goodness of a primitive man, untouched, or rather unspoiled, by civilization. Karl Bodmer, a Swiss painter, found his chance in being attached as an appendage, almost a servant, to Prince Maximilian of Wied-Neuwied, who came with a kind of ostentatious anonymity as the traveler Baron von Braunsberg. Bodmer's employer was an all-round amateur scientist whose background was the German enlightenment of Goethe and Schiller. He was interested in everything about the life of the Indians, a kind of ethnographer before the profession had become clear-cut.

His painter, Bodmer, who saw and painted many of the same Indians Catlin had, was to create on his canvases—better than Catlin—a stunning and lasting picture of the Indian life of this transient time. His sketches and watercolors of the landscapes through which he and the prince passed on the way upriver were those of a man swallowed up in the immensity of a new and unknown scene, yet capable of rendering the immensity, the strangeness, and the beauty of the landscapes, which allowed only the deer, the elk, the bear, and the mountain sheep a dominion. These two Europeans came the year after Catlin's venture; in 1833 they were passengers beyond Fort Union to the dangerous vicinity of Fort Mckenzie, where the Marias joined the Missouri, and soon had to escape from Indian menaces by traveling as silently as possible downriver at night.

Four years later, in 1837, came William Drummond Stewart, of a noble Scots family, and, with expectations of inheriting a family title and castle, he got along very well with the trappers among whom he traveled and hunted. He brought along another Swiss painter, Alfred Jacob Miller, to record for him (and to decorate his great hall later in Scotland with) the new and strange aspects of fur trapper camps, as well as the lakes and mountains of the Wyoming-Utah border country. Miller, who had traveled and studied in Italy, captured on his small and intimate canvases the only contemporary pictures of trapper life around the campfires of the high mountain country. He made available for the future the look of these men and their pristine wilderness. That these mostly French-Canadians also had a slightly Swiss or Italian air was no accident. The congeniality of the Rockies helped Miller feel at home in these newfound Alps.

Six years after Stewart and Miller, the great and aging John James Audubon, the most zestful and driven painter of them all, made his last great journey into the wilderness by coming upstream into the rich wildlife country surrounding Fort Union, open hospitably to the exotic traveler from the East. He was attempting what he had longed for, a foray at last in the High Plains and Rockies. He never got beyond the fort at the confluence of the Yellowstone and the Missouri, but he was rewarded with the appearances of animals he sought for his last book, *The Viviparous Quadrupeds of North America*. Audubon's powers were failing. But his letters from that spot show how he made the most of this opportunity.

In 1846, following the now familiar land trail, came Francis Parkman. He was a not very well young man from Boston, yet, having a strong will, he endured hardships and sights he did not much care for (for example, the everyday immigrants now sharing the trail), in order to test himself during a western adventure. He admired only those types so far removed from daily life as not to remind him of the common humanity of the citizenry of the American settled states; he found he could like primitive Indians and primitive hunters. They were the kind he was searching for, and he would use them as prototypes of his Indians and whites fighting a lonely war one century earlier in his own eastern woods; they would be the grounding of his knowledge, otherwise gained through scholarly searches, for his history of the French and Indian War.

Through such travelers and recorders—Catlin, Maximilian and Bodmer, Stewart and Miller, Audubon, and Parkman, as well as, in his modest way, Townsend himself, this transient West was to become known to the East. Townsend could not think of history or posterity when confronted in 1834, and in the following years of his sojourn, with the daily problems of survival. The actuality of life among these fellow men of the mountains presented him with sufficient puzzles to resolve. He found that he had to get along with the rough trappers and that, in order to save the birds and animals for the future (and in order to eat), he had to do his share of killing.

One day a fresh young colt, strayed from a nearby tribe, came into the camp, "dancing and curvetting gaily amongst our sober and sedate band." But this day they were hungry, "not having eaten anything of consequence since yesterday morning, I thought the little stranger would make a good breakfast for us." So he shot the colt and they ate well (250).

Antelopes were not very good food, but, after a young female came "running and bleating after us," Townsend lifted his gun and shot her. She was only wounded. Not able to face the animal, he wrote later, scarifying his memory, "I threw my arm around her neck, averted her face, and drove my long knife through her bosom to her heart" (177–78). Early in his experience of hunting bison, he learned to kill the great beast in the particular and difficult way necessary, but only after a waste of life. He had shot a bull and stopped to watch it die as it swayed and bled. Then he found that he had killed the wrong animal; it should have been a fat cow, rather than a haggard bull.

In his professional hunting, with no camera at hand, as decades later would be customary, Townsend had to kill the bright and beautiful birds, or the sleek small animals, of the plains and mountains. This was the only way a collector of his kind had to preserve the knowledge of these creatures. The swift movement and the flashing colors had to be reduced to inert bodies, then skinned and dried, and packed into small compass in order to be wrapped against the weather and prepared for carrying home. This was a paradox: of killing to save. He was not a painter and did not have the transformational art that Audubon, who also shot his specimens, had.

Townsend lost one valuable specimen to daily hunger and was able to smile ruefully at his loss. Once he returned to camp, after a fruitless hunt, to discover Nuttall and the others cooking one of his specimens, a rare owl, which he had shot earlier. He had to grin, take part with the others, and eat his scientific prize once it had been cooked over the campfire. "The bird of wisdom," he wrote that night, "lost the immortality which he might otherwise have acquired" (277).

The increasingly difficult plains and mountain journey brought home to Townsend the nature of life beyond the reach of the settlements. He and the others found the most acute pleasure in the fundamentals of good water, enough food of some adequate kind, a fire at night, and the hard ground to go to sleep on. What would have seemed despicable at home became wonderfully satisfying out here. After deprivation they had "purchased a large bag of Indian meal, of which we made a kettle of mush, and mixed with it a considerable quantity of horse tallow and salt. This was, I think, one of the best meals I ever made" (280).

After being tired from long hours of travel, he could understand the trapper's high spirits and boisterous good humor in finding a good camp. He had recovered from his illness and, farther along beyond another chain of mountains, savored a good stopping place. "Our camp here is a most lovely one in every respect. The pasture is rich and very abundant, and it does our hearts good to witness the satisfaction and comfort of our poor jaded horses. Our tents are pitched in a pretty little valley or indentation of the plain. . . . Near us flows the clear deep water of the Siskadee, and beyond, on every side is a wide and level prairie, interrupted only by some gigantic peaks of mountains" (194).

The comfort of a good campground was always surrounded by uneasiness. The taking of horses was the most immediate danger, but there was always also the chance of sudden death from arrows or bullets. These others, the marauders, whom it was difficult to know, were for Townsend continuing sources of curiosity. He felt alternately fear, compassion, and often disgust. In the near-settlement places he had watched with nausea Indians picking lice out of each other's hair and eating them. He noted that the Indians got "better" and better looking the farther one went from the settlements. Some of the men were handsome, and many of the young women were pretty. Momentarily he approved them.

Townsend found that his white companions' salutary fears—which caused the trappers to take every care to guard themselves and their horses, night after night, and to travel carefully, watching for ambushes—caused an ugly hatred. The Indians also had reason to be fearful. "It must be acknowledged," he wrote, "that this determined hostility does not originate solely in savage malignity or an abstract thirst for the blood of white men, it is fomented and kept alive from year to year by incessant provocation on the part of white hunters, trappers, and traders, who are at best but intruders on the rightful domain of the red man of the wilderness." And he continued. "Many a night have I sat at the camp fire and listened to the recital of bloody and ferocious scenes, in which the narrators were the actors, and the poor Indians the victims, and I have felt my blood tingle with the shame, and boil with indignation, to hear the diabolical acts applauded, by these for whose amusement they were related" (214–15).

He felt a justifiable hate, along with a prickle of fear, stir when they were within reach of the Blackfeet, of whom it was said that the individual warrior "would rather hang the scalp of a 'paleface' to his girdle, than kill a buffalo to prevent his starving" (214). In the face of such an implacable threat, it seemed all right to dislike these particular Indians, and he added his words of condemnation on the subject of this tribe to the words of many others who had felt this fear. An easier contempt seemed all right, too, when one got beyond the scary Blackfeet. On the Columbia the Indian tribes had been fatally touched by the corrupting influence of the whites who had been coming upriver from the Pacific for several decades to trade or, more recently, to preach and settle. Here he found the Indian camps filthy beyond belief, and he shuddered at "the most horrific nastiness of the whole vicinity" (257–58). No longer did these seem noble red men such as Cooper had depicted, but a people to be civilized, by force, if necessary.

When the naturalist neared a settlement of Protestant missionaries in the Oregon country, he looked forward not only to more civilized food and shelter but also to civilized talk. In their last camp, before arriving at this place on the Umatilla River, he and Nuttall had attempted to make themselves more presentable. "Mr. Nuttall's razor was fished out from its hiding place in the bottom of the trunk, and in a few minutes our encumbered chins lost their long-cherished ornaments; we performed our ablutions in the river, arrayed ourselves in clean linen, trimmed our long hair, and then arranged our toilet before a mirror, with great self-complacence and satisfaction." Townsend did not lack a little self-regarding humor. "I admired my own appearance considerably, but I could not refrain from laughing at the strange party-colored appearance of my physiognomy, the lower portion being fair, like a woman's, and the upper, brown and swarthy as an Indian" (277). He could put himself in relation to the missionaries, however different their aims were from his. They at least touched at the peripheries of his own imaginings. He had met the best of their lot (as other writers would testify) in traveling west in the same company with Jason Lee, who had shared work and hardships and had also been a handy and helpful man.

Townsend approved the growing of vegetables in this settlement as a sign of eastern culture. He found vegetables and milk from cattle kept as domestic animals as signs of improvement even more striking at Fort Vancouver, where civilization seemed to be thriving within a small compass in the midst of the surrounding wilderness—all under the careful and liberal governance of Dr. John McLoughlin of the Hudson's Bay Company. He saw the beginnings of American settlement in crude log cabins nearby. (Dr. McLouglin was to get in trouble with his employer, the great Canadian-British company, for being too friendly to the Americans. The conflict over national ownership of this country was building.) But Townsend only reveled, at this time in achievement. He had seen at last "the noble Columbia," and he had some pride in having come through so well all the hardships of the western passage of the plains and mountains. He settled down for a stay, during which he found himself more and more drawn to a consideration of the Indians.

Townsend had no room for tolerance, or even much understanding, within his doctor's rational soul for the mystique or practice of medicine men. He had no patience with them and thought them simply frauds. A few times he intervened to try to help those he thought were victims of their ignorant imposition of superstition. He cleaned and dressed the shocking, suppurating wounds of an eighty-year-old man who had gashed his chest to show his grief for his chief's death. But Townsend doubted that he had helped much in this case. The old man's circulation was poor; he would not heal properly.

As an observer, Townsend became more and more impatient with the Indians' whole way of life, as he came upon examples of poverty, dirt, and needless death from untreated disease. These first missionaries' efforts seemed to him civilized and substantial. "They have, I think, a good prospect of being serviceable to this miserable and degraded people, and . . . the Indians in this section of country may yet be redeemed from the thraldom of vice, superstition, and indolence, to which they have so long submitted, and above which their energies have not enabled them to rise" (319–20).

Thus, in the face of the discomfort that the sight of all this misery put upon him, Townsend fell into an attitude first of pity and then of contempt for these victims of the general white movement west. Comfortable in his beliefs, he found it easy to think that providence might have as much to do with all this: "It seems as if the fiat of the Creator had gone forth, that these poor denizens of the forest and the stream should go home, and be seen of men no more" (333). Manifest destiny met divine predestination there, and his sharper reactions were smoothed into an acceptance of the vanishing of one group of human beings before the advance of another, his own kind.

Townsend was kind and upright. But he did not let personal kindness obscure his professional aims. He learned to put aside any weak scruple that might prohibit the gain of an important piece of scientific knowledge. The great unknown West seemed to him to teem with new pieces of knowledge waiting to be fitted into the grand rational scheme. The new scientist was thus as much an enemy of the way of life of the Indians as the thoughtless and speculative trapper.

Although Townsend's principal business was birds, he was alive to the wonders of animal and human life surrounding him in new shapes. He collected some sample mammals and preserved their skins. The repeated sightings of the antelope, the bison, and the great bear filled him with grateful wonder. Studying the Indians, not only their habits but also their bodily shapes, and the likenesses and differences among the tribes, fascinated him. He thought these matters important to science.

He had taken note again and again of the burial places of the various tribes, platforms in trees or set upon stakes raised off the prairie, or in canoes similarly raised off damp ground; the bodies were carefully wrapped and lifted away from predators. He did not think of himself as a predator, but his scientific aim made him one. He conceived the ambition of taking home not only his bird and animal skins but also sample bodies, or parts of bodies, of these various tribes. The most up-to-date measuring tools of knowledgeable specialists back home could set to work on these bones and skulls and place them in an understood order of the types of humankind. This was before the arrival of the Darwinian theory among scientists, but it was a time of great curiosity and enthusiastic assumptions about the placement of the "races" in relation to one another.

With wondering delight, he found a perfect "specimen." It was the body of a young female in a funeral canoe upraised into a tree. He needed, as he told himself, to "abstract" the skull. He took the body down and carried it off at night and hid it in the storehouse of the fort. But this had been a recent burial. The brother of the dead girl found the grave robbed and came to the fort to claim the body. Under the fear of reprisal, the fort chief, Walker, made Townsend go to the hiding place, remove the Indian mat that had covered the body as if it were a "bale of guns," and deliver up his prized "specimen" to the brother. Townsend recorded the circumstances:

The call was so clearly made out, that Mr. W. could not deny the fact of the body being in the house, and it was accordingly delivered to him with a present of several blankets, to prevent the circumstance from operating upon his mind to the prejudice of white people. The poor Indian took the body of his sister upon his shoulders, and as he walked away, grief got the better of his stoicism, and the sound of weeping was heard long after he had entered the forest. (339)

Townsend had reached a curious overturning of personal morality; he was able to be comfortable with his own action. He was able to think it merely interesting and probably exceptional that this other kind of man cried. He was confident that the incident could be made all right with the trifling bestowal of gifts. These were people with a degree of emotional equipment, but of a kind different from one's own. It probably did not occur to him to question himself as to why he would not take a body from a recent grave in Philadelphia.

After some uneasiness about the plight of the Indians, Townsend had arrived at what was the majority opinion of whites moving west and taking over the lands and game and very existence of these people. He was a good deal more thoughtful and sensitive than most. He was not deterred by this incident, which had not turned out well. He took four more skulls from Indian burial platforms when occasions allowed. He gave himself rather theatrical shivers, as he reported in his journal, at the thought of being found again in such an act.

Now suppose an Indian were to step in here, and see me groping among the bones of his fathers, and laying unhallowed hands upon the mouldering remains of his people, what should I say? I know what the Indian would *do*. He would shoot me, unless [and here the white man shows his clear sense that he is, he thinks, dealing with a different order of humanity and therefore justified] I took the most effectual measures to prevent it; but could I have time allowed me to temporize a little, I could easily disarm his hostility and ensure his silence, by the offer of a shirt or a blanket. (361–62)

This episode happened toward the end of his travels, after the voyage to the Sandwich Islands, a tour of duty as a fort surgeon, and a comfortable stay with an Indian family, in the midst of whose hospitality he had been a pampered guest. He faced now a long return home, with the arduous care of his specimens to make the way more difficult. Rather than to undergo the known privations of recrossing the mountains and plains, he decided to ship passage from the mouth of the great river, circle the two western continents, and return north by an Atlantic passage to his familiar Pennsylvania fields and forests and city streets.

In one last adventure, he visited the ruin of Fort Clatsop, the shelter that the Lewis and Clark men had built for defense during a long, damp, and dreary winter spent on the coast. This moldy structure had been occupied only thirty years before, but change had come so swiftly to this area that it seemed like ancient history. "The logs of which it is composed are still perfect, but the roof of bark has disappeared, and the whole vicinity is overgrown with thorn and wild currant bushes" (362).

The young scientist of a time that he thought much more scientific than that of the explorers wished now only to get on with his career and contribute to the great endeavor of enlightenment. So it was that in December 1836 Townsend sailed for home on a ship bound south from the mouth of the Columbia River. He fell ill on shipboard and was delayed in Valparaiso. He arrived home in Philadelphia only on November 13, 1837, a year after looking back from the deck of his sailing vessel at the dark wooded shores of the coast of the Oregon country.

He described his new birds in the *Journal* of the Academy of Natural Science of Philadelphia (volume 7, part 2, 1837, and volume 8, part 1, 1839). His precious skins were deposited in a forerunner of the Smithsonian Institution in Washington, D.C. Audubon began making queries about buying them and including them in his great *Ornithological Biography*. A large number of Townsend's western birds were at last to be included in Audubon's fifth and final volume. Audubon was to credit Townsend in his descriptions and also to name these birds Townsend's oyster-catcher *(Haematopus townsendi)*, Townsend's finch *(Fringilla townsendi)*, Townsend's cormorant *(Phalacrocorax townsendi)*, Townsend's warbler *(Sylvia townsendi)*, Townsend's bunting *(Emberiza townsendi)*, and so forth. Townsend's mammals were also incorporated in Audubon's last volume, *The Viviparous Quadrupeds of North America*.

Townsend did not finish his own comprehensive project of writing a history of the birds of the United States. Only one part of his *Ornithology of the United States of America* appeared. The completion of Audubon's lifework, *Ornithological Biography*—which was published between 1830 and 1839 and included five hundred birds—was simply too overwhelming. Townsend's work became a contribution to Audubon's volumes and, since his own time, a mostly overlooked one. In his modest career, Townsend was a discoverer, and his findings became a part of general knowledge, but he himself is almost unknown today. He lived only fourteen more years after his youthful journey to the Northern Rockies and beyond, when he was so full of buoyant hope, but those late years did little to add to his reputation. He saw published in 1839 his *Narrative of a Journey across the Rocky Mountains, to the Columbia River, and a Visit to the Sandwich Islands*. But Townsend is usually not mentioned in general books about American ornithology.

During the remainder of his life, from the time of his hopeful return to Philadelphia in 1837, Townsend received modest recognition from his peers, which may have seemed a small reward for his sanguine ambitions. He married, and he fathered a son. He considered adding dentistry to his medical practice, so perhaps he was not a prosperous doctor. He had bad health and believed that a sea voyage might help him, but he never undertook the trip. He died on February 6, 1851.

▲▲▲
FOUR

Trader and Priest: John Owen and Pierre Jean De Smet

Bitterroot Valley runs north-south, walled on the west by high peaks. The Lewis and Clark expedition spent many anxious days in 1805 tracing its course to find a way to the Pacific Ocean. They found their route in the Lolo Pass. On the explorers' return journey the following year, coming down into this valley and to the hot springs at the foot of the pass, was a scene they were grateful to behold; for here, at the foot of the mountains, the way eastward led them home. Seventy years later, the Nez Perce Indians, under the united chiefs, Joseph, Looking Glass, Ollokot, White Bird, Tool-hoolzote, and others, led a whole tribe the same way from west to east, hoping for refuge. The native peoples had never had to discover the pass and the valley. They had known it for generations; it was a passageway for the Indians west of the Continental Divide to come east to the plains to hunt, and for the Plains Indians to move westward to raid. For the newcomers, who came west after the explorers and the fur trappers, this valley was to be the first settled part of what is now the state of Montana.

Before the region became the scene of generous ranches and small towns knotted up and down a long road, it was the place where two very different men, Father Pierre Jean De Smet and "Major" John Owen, struck root. They were the first to make permanent or semipermanent settlements in the valley, and their overlapping lives exerted an influence upon this area between the 1840s and the 1870s. This was a brief time of relative peace in the relationship of whites and Indians. It is a time that can be reconstituted from the words that the two men left behind in letters and diaries. Both the missionary and the merchant loved the valley, established relations with the native peoples already at home here or passing through, and wished that they might die here. Neither did. Fortunately both left relics of their thoughts and feelings in writings, as well as records of what they did.

Reading the letters and reports that De Smet sent back to his superiors in Saint Louis in the 1840s, one can in a sense re-create the character of the man whom the Indians called Black Robe. He was a man who had self-confidence but no vanity, and who had great physical vitality and strength. He was short, stout, sturdy, and energetic. He had no pretense, but had the force of utter sincerity. He came to enjoy riding with the Salish (Flathead) Indians on their bison hunts or sitting down upon the ground with them at campfires, eating his piece of fat bison meat along with the hunters, enjoying their company and exchanging tales with them, the news of two different worlds.

Reading the cryptic notebooks of Major John Owen, one can summon up the warm humanity of the trader, a man of force and humor. He was the first builder of a permanent trading post in the valley, and he hosted, without discrimination, Indians, explorers, miners, surveyors, road and railroad builders, and, at last, settlers, who often stopped overnight or camped alongside his little fortress. Owen gave his visitors shelter, food, and good talk, making an exchange for any goods they might sell him, showing them his fruit trees, grain fields, and small dam. He was an isolated man, lonely for word from the outside world, yet making a small world of his own.

The name of Pierre Jean De Smet has floated in the shallow pool of authentic early northwestern history, but he is little known today except as an object of vague reverence. It is recalled that he was the first Catholic missionary to the Indians of the Northern Plains and Rockies, that he traveled greatly, as an explorer as well as a priest, and that he championed the rights of Indians when no one else did so. There remain a few physical remnants of his career—Saint Mary's Church in the Bitterroot, Saint Peter's west of Great Falls, Saint Ignatius's north of Missoula, and a lake in a national park, Saint Mary's in Glacier, reminiscent of at least admiration of his work. However, his letters contain the whole vibrant life of the man, as well as the look and feel of the new country he explored, the peoples he touched with his words.[1] In the words he wrote to his superiors trying to persuade them to send him off again into the wilderness, and attempting to raise money for his precious missions, he is there alive, triumphant, courageous, persistent, adaptable.

In contrast, the name of John Owen is totally unknown except to curious delvers, yet, like De Smet, he filled an important role in the early history of the Northern Rockies. He was also a writer, in his fashion, or at least he kept a laconic diary of the years he spent as the first permanent trader in the same valley where De Smet a few years earlier had founded the first mission church.[2] Owen also traveled widely in order to obtain trade goods or to take furs and skin to exchange posts such as Fort Hall to the west and northeast to Fort Benton, the last port of call for steamboats on the upper Missouri. Before there were any other settlers in Bitterroot Valley, he adapted his life to the migrations of Indians, trappers, miners, and settlers going farther west to the Oregon country. He was instrumental in causing his surroundings to change from what they had been when De Smet set down his church in Indian country.

An early picture of De Smet's life among the Indians has been drawn from the priest's own writings and paraphrased by his biographer John Upton Terrell. It is an account filled with the fervor and emotion of an enthusiast, revealing De Smet's enjoyment of the daily life of his early missionary effort. He was as at home in Bitterroot Valley as he ever would be anywhere, sitting among his friends of the Salish tribes and telling them stories. When the sounds of building ceased—for nearby the first wilderness church was rising—De Smet told tales. The green floor of the valley stretched around the speaker and his rapt listeners. Beyond was the line of sharp mountains. There were no settlements within hundreds of miles, and all the activities of civilization were far, far away. But De Smet was bringing in as vivid a way as he could a little diluted knowledge of that other world to his Indian charges. He told the gathered audience, in very simple language, stories, as Terrell has written,

> of George Washington, and the founding of the American nation, of Napoleon and Waterloo, of how for eighteen hundred years evil forces had tried to destroy the Church.
>
> One evening visibly moved by the fear that the Pontiff might be injured by the Church's enemies, Chief Victor of the Flatheads arose and told Father De Smet: "If the Great Chief of the Black Robes be in danger, you speak on paper to him in our name and invite him to our mountains. We will raise his lodge in our midst; we will hunt for him and keep his house provided, and we will guard him."[3]

De Smet, with his fine European education and his extensive experience of the American scene (he had come to Saint Louis as a missionary of the

Society of Jesus before being allowed to carry his message into the far Northwest), was able to savor the irony of the offer, yet accept it as well meant and sincere, and to enter into the Indians' own viewpoint. De Smet had a lasting kinship to these supposedly simple souls in the Bitterroot. He genuinely liked and respected them. They returned the regard.

An ingenuous, eager young father, he had destined himself for the western frontier from his earliest days in the new world, and, in fact, from his student days in Belgium. He reached Saint Louis for a novitiate in 1823. He made his first journeys into the edges of Indian country in 1838 and 1839, traveling far enough up the Missouri to see tribes decimated by smallpox and other diseases brought to them by the whites, and to see them degraded by liquor, poverty, and listlessness, yet finding them a people to whom he was irresistibly drawn. He wished to go out and beyond white influence and find tribes untouched by the corruption that white settlement seemed always to bring, and to touch them with the Word. He was himself to be touched by them as deeply.

In 1840 he first encountered the Salish, a peaceful, semi-settled people who had come to meet him near the South Pass, having made efforts for several years to persuade one of the "black robes" of the distant white people to come to them with his God magic. De Smet celebrated mass with several hundred of the Indians on the banks of the Green River, then traveled with them through Jackson Hole, a rendezvous area used by the fur trappers, crossed the Tetons to Pierre's Hole, another rendezvous valley, and continued north, then over the mountains again east with the Indians. He accompanied them on a hunting trip into the dangerous bison grounds of the plains and made temporary camp with them in the vicinity of the three forks of the Missouri.

De Smet wrote long, fluent, and interesting reports to the church fathers about these experiences, trying to persuade his superiors to support what he believed to be an important missionary effort in the Northwest. He had no idea that this country would fill up so quickly with white miners and settlers. He believed that, uncontaminated, these primitive peoples, blessed with an unbelievable kind of moral purity, could make a transition under the good fathers' guidance to a more settled, agricultural, nonwarlike state, and remain so in communities undisturbed by white civilization. It was an idle ambition, but he believed in it for a time. Meanwhile, he enjoyed to the fullest, with youthful zest, his first adventures of traveling and living with these companionable people.

De Smet's first experience of hunting with the Salish was in a camp set up alongside the Madison River, named so for Jefferson's secretary of state by Lewis and Clark. It was ground claimed as a hunting area by the Black-feet, who never hesitated to attack the Salish. But this time all went well, and the young priest relished and recorded his first sight of a great bison hunt:

> In this great and beautiful plain were buffalo in numberless herds. Finding themselves there in the midst of abundance, the Flatheads prepared to lay in their winter meat supply; they raised willow scaffolds about their lodges for drying meat, and everyone made ready his firearm, his bow and arrows.
>
> Four hundred horsemen, old and young, mounted on their best horses, started early in the morning for the great hunt. I chose to accompany them in order to watch this striking spectacle from near at hand. At a given signal, they rode at full gallop among the herds; soon everything appeared confusion and flight all over the plain; the hunters pursued the fattest cows, discharged their guns and let fly their arrows, and in three hours they killed more than 500. Then the women, the old men, and the children came up, and with the aid of horses carried off the hides and the meat, and soon all the scaffolds were full and gave the camp the aspect of a vast butcher shop. [4]

The hunt concluded, De Smet was compelled to start home toward Saint Louis. Members of the tribe escorted him part of the way eastward across what is now Montana toward Fort Union at the juncture of the Yellowstone and the Missouri. During this trek he passed through the future sites of Livingston and Billings and followed the course of the Yellowstone until he reached Fort Union, where he was a guest in the house of James Kipp, the kingly agent for the American Fur Company. Kipp lived in a two-storied house with the luxury of glass windows and a wine cellar. Kipp had already entertained here in some style visitors such as the painters Catlin and Bodmer and was to have the naturalist Audubon as a guest within three years. In this spring of 1840, and in other years to follow, he had the companionship for meals and talk of a sturdy young priest who seemed to have an obsession about establishing missions among the Indians.

The Jesuit order of which the priest was an obedient member never shared the sense of urgency he had in this late missionary activity in the remote Northern Rockies. But De Smet prodded and pushed and wrote letters to important church fathers and published accounts in parochial news-papers that had a winning immediacy. He was able to effect a certain amount of action and, after this first year, busied himself in raising money for his mission-building. He persuaded other young eager fathers to follow him; and he, or his successors, set up one isolated mission after another, first Saint Mary's in Bitterroot Valley, then Saint Ignatius's and Saint Peter's, and others. For seven years he went again and again to the Northwest, and thereafter he made trips up the Missouri or the Platte, as much an advocate of the Indians as a missionary to them. He made friends among them by understanding, sympathizing, and exhorting without patronizing. He impressed them by his mental and physical strength, his honesty, and his courage. He single-handedly accomplished much more than was likely. His expeditions enabled him to visit unknown tribes in parts of present-day Idaho, Washington, Oregon, Alberta, and British Columbia, as well as in trails north and south along both sides of the Rocky Mountain ranges. His travels went beyond the nominal needs of the church and were indeed among the first literate reports of the plants, animals, and people of this territory.

The Indians saw De Smet as a whole man and a holy man, and they added him to their count of medicine men. Unfortunately for De Smet, who would have liked to stay in the wilderness, his success caused his superiors to conceive of him as a useful tool for the propagation of the faith. He was compelled to turn over his mission to the Salish to other priests whom he had recruited. He was allowed to return to Bitterroot Valley only a few more times. He was sent as an emissary of the church on fund-raising trips on both sides of the Atlantic. He continued to yearn for a life with the Indians and, from time to time, managed a trip—with fur trappers, with pioneers, with the army, and, toward the end of his life, by railroad to railhead, then on to where the last dangerous fights of Indians against whites were taking place. He became useful to the U.S. government. In the late bitter years of Indian resistance, he was often the only white man with whom the tribes would talk. De Smet agreed occasionally, sometimes with strong private reservations about his role, to serve as mediator. He tried each time to make the best deal possible for the Indians and to persuade both sides to stop the killing. He saw, from the beginning, the injustices that the Indians would suffer in the unthinking westward movement of gold hunters and settlers.

During his first journey west in 1840, De Smet was said to have discovered gold nuggets and gold sand lying loosely visible along the banks and in the shallow waters of a stream that was probably Alder Gulch, the site of Virginia City, the future gold rush city. He knew that the discovery would turn men mad and bring ruin to his Indians. He kept the secret. Gold in this area was not discovered in an important way until the 1860s.

In 1849–50, seeing the relentless sweep of gold hunters going to California, he wrote:

> Imagine thousands of all countries . . . deserters, sailors, robbers, murderers, the scum of the States . . . with some honest men among them, no doubt . . . all living lawless and unbridled lives. . . . The news of the abundance of gold seems to have shaken the United States to the foundation.
>
> The facts reveal clearly the melancholy future which at no very remote epoch awaits these nations [of Indians], if efficient means are not employed for preventing the woes with which they are threatened.[5]

His missionary effort struggled and succeeded in a small way. The Indians accepted as much of De Smet's ritual and belief as they wished. (Catholic ritual was always more congenial to the Indians than Protestant exhortation.) Respecting the qualities of these peoples, De Smet passionately believed that he could bring them truth. Perhaps he never realized that to them he was another revered medicine man whose message and practice could be added to their own beliefs. But even in his approved churchly mission he suffered disillusionment and defeat. The church, with its comfortable superiors far away from Bitterroot Valley, closed down Saint Mary's in his absence in 1851, never satisfying him with a reason. (The little mission church was reopened in 1866 and remained open until 1891; meantime, some of its lands and properties were sold to John Owen, the first permanent trader to come into the valley and settle.)

In 1859, while the mission was still officially closed, De Smet managed to engineer a long delayed visit to this place that had meant so much to him. The following account is by Terrell: "On the 18th of March, traveling through deep snow, Father De Smet, with tears welling in his eyes, stopped before the door of the church he had built at Saint Mary's. From the surrounding forests came the Flatheads, and many of the old men and women threw their arms about him, weeping in their joy at seeing him again. Black Robe had come back to them. Never had they forgotten him."[6]

After this last trip to the Bitterroot, the sturdy father's health, squandered with magnificent abandon during his early years, began to betray him. The church fathers sent him to Europe to recuperate. On the way he was received by Lincoln at the White House and by the Belgian ambassador to the United States. Terrell quotes what the father had to say about these fine public occasions: "I remain of the opinion that I shall always be more at my ease sitting on the grass and surrounded by savages, each one making his jokes and at the same time eating with good appetite a fair rib or roasting piece of buffalo or fat dog."[7]

After a trip to his native Belgium, De Smet wrote: "I always miss something when I am not among my good Indians . . . I am conscious of a certain void wherever I go, until I come back to my dear Rocky Mountains. Then calm comes back to me; then only am I happy. *Haec requies mea*. . . . After having passed a good share of my life among the Indians, it is among them that I desire to spend a few years that are left me still; it is among them also, if it be the will of God, that I desire to die."[8]

This good end was denied him. He suffered various ills. He died at last, in an almost bare room, at Saint Louis University on May 23, 1872, far from his Rocky Mountains, Bitterroot Valley, and the Salish people. (The Salish were also in the end to be exiled from this area. They were ordered out of the Bitterroot to a reservation north toward the great lake that came to be known as Flathead Lake. Some of the tribe refused to go, and under old Chief Victor stayed behind illegally in the Bitterroot for many years and left wrenchingly, by force, in the end. Victor is a small town in the valley, named for the leader of the Salish who was the friend of both De Smet and Owen.)

John Owen, who had had a career of supplying goods to the army, found an independent place in Bitterroot Valley. His life overlapped that of De Smet. It is doubtful they ever met. But the two men were both deeply attached to the same conjunction of high mountains and deep valley. The trader's career represented a distinct new kind of stability in the valley.

De Smet's original mission had closed down. Owen, a sutler, supplier of goods to the U.S. Army, left off trailing military units and returned from farther west at Fort Hall to this spot that he had determined would be a good place to settle. He had a wagonload of goods, a courtesy title of major (not military at all), and an adaptable nature. The Salish who lived more or less permanently in the valley, and other tribes, who passed through on the way to the bison hunting grounds beyond the divides, were eager for the kinds of hardware, white man's coffee, and tobacco which this man promised to trade for animal skins. The valley was hundreds of miles from the nearest trading posts, Fort Hall to the west and Fort Benton to the northeast. Owen set up his personal fort in the wilderness and contemplated calmly the miles and miles of difficult travel he would have to undertake regularly to supply his post and to sell his hides and furs.

In 1851 he purchased the buildings and grounds of the abandoned Saint Mary's Mission for $250. He laid out nearby a wooden, palisaded fort, built strongly enough to have only sporadic difficulties with wandering Indians. One night they broke in his gate and stole all his horses. But he was to have remarkably peaceful and even friendly relations with the tribes as they moved past his post or settled near him. In 1857, with his trade growing handsomely, Owen rebuilt his fort into a more permanent adobe structure. A rancher's grassy field today holds what remains of the once busy fort: on one side, the outlines only of what were kitchen, mess hall, and trade room; on the other side, repaired rooms that were probably sleeping rooms for the major's people, and his own room with a fireplace, a room that has the aspect of a library, for the isolated trader was a reader.

This enclosure in the wild became an important center for the scattered whites, as well as the Indians. Owen was a genial, hospitable man, and Owen's Fort became a social place for lonely people aching for company. Everyone who passed through the valley stopped a night or two with him. Within a few years a regular U.S. Mail Service brought letters here on a two-weeks' journey from Fort Hall across tumbled mountain ranges. Owen established a comfortable, visiting sort of relationship with the remnant of Catholic fathers who stayed on nearby, although their official mission was for a time closed. The major had an Indian wife who had his respect as well as affection. Unlike most whites who acquired Indian "wives," Owen within a few years made a public declaration of official marriage. He became in time the U.S. government agent to the Salish and to other Indian tribes of the region. His concern and interest went far beyond official duties, and, unlike many of the agents, he did not bilk his "wards," these Indians not yet, of course, considering themselves wards at all.

Owen became an expert on wilderness roads and trails, having traveled in these early difficult years an estimated twenty-three thousand miles north, west, and east from Fort Owen, picking up supplies, delivering furs, or conducting curious explorations. He became a guide and adviser to road and railroad builders in the later decades. He advised John Mullan, who built a famous wagon road west from Fort Benton to the communities of the Pacific territories. He also advised John Stevens when the engineer, hired by the railroad company, was looking for a low passage through the mountains for the route which became that of the Great Northern.

His terse diary shows that Owen was quite satisfied with the life he made for himself in the Bitterroot. In the midst of his people, in his own fortress, he was rather like a Scots laird in his castle, a kind of minor beneficent ruler who showed great care and kindness for his community. His life rotated between peaceful planting and harvesting and somewhat adventurous journeys to exchange furs for trade goods. In this soil new to agriculture, Owen planted grains, set out fruit trees, worried over frost killings, and constructed a gristmill, the first in the area. Above and beyond practical improvements, and the introduction of crops that had never been known here before, the man himself was a liberalizing influence.

Owen enjoyed good food and drink and long hours of talk. He read widely and enjoyed as many books and newspapers as he could lay hold of in his isolated place. Brief notations in his diary show his quiet pleasure in the written word:

Quietly reading all day Myself a Catholic Work with Which I am interested and pleased. [9]

Sunday Called off from labour & Spent the day reading. [10]

I recd some letters & from an old friend a file of N.Y. Heralds from Oct/55 up to April /56 & Some Mormon Works So I have some pleasant & interesting reading matter all of which is News to Me particularly the Siege and fall of Sebasterpol after an Eleven Months Struggle with a heavy cost of blood and treasure. [11]

The geniality of his relationship with the Indians reveals itself in a diary entry about being one day surprised and pleased by an individual gift from a visiting Blackfeet, Keitse Pem Sa, "a fine English double Barrel Gun with some 18 Balls for the Same I took it but had nothing to give him in return but gave him to understand I would Not forget this Mark of his confidence and if I see him next fall while I am over at Fort Benton I shall remember him . . . wrote some letters for Fort Benton & Sent them by the Blackfeet that left today." [12]

On July 4, 1856, he recorded his thoughts about the day:

Friday 4 the glorious fourth passed off as other days in this mountain region I would frequently think about the Merry doings that were goin on in a land far distant the patriotic speeches the analyzing of the Master piece of Jefferson in the Declaration of Independence—Say Nothing about Sherry Cobbler Mint julep & Rum Punches that flowed in abundance until all became Merry & happy all around My old wife off after service berries & it is Now dark & they have not retd Yet. [13]

He had a quiet sense of humor, and from May to August, 1856, followed the fate of his hen Madam Jake:

8 Thursday repairing fence around Wheatfield Set Madam Jake this Morning on thirteen eggs & wish her every Success during her present incubation. [14]

10 Saturday Missed four of my Eggs to day from under Madam Jake how she disposed of them I am unable to Say in all probability she came to the conclusion that 13 was too Many & concluded to relieve herself quietly of some of them. [15]

1 Friday Madam Jake has just taken the field with her brood of four chickens and Seems as proud as a May Day Queen. [16]

18 Monday Madam Jake With three of her brood was Made way with last Night probably a Wolf or Ind Dog. [17]

The Indians did not perceive him as a menace and were individually friendly. Owen's life at his time, as well as De Smet's, represents to us today an early phase in Anglo western life. Owen followed the first explorers and supplemented them by additions to basic knowledge of the region, but he preceded, at least in his early years, the rush and push of settlers. His quiet steady life at the fort was broken only by long and arduous journeys for the sake of trade. Some of the early ones, in which he was a pathfinder, were dangerous.

On September 10, 1856, he set out for Fort Benton. [18] He records that the train consisted of two oxen teams and wagons, as well as fifteen horses to carry supplies back. The human party was composed of "Peter M. Lafontaine, Esq., Delaware Jim, Antoine & Michelle Indians." He reached Fort Benton on September 29 and was disappointed to find "the boats not having arrivd." The rowdy river town had little attraction for him. He endured eighteen days of "tedious delay" before the arrival of his supplies on the riverboat. On October 18 he loaded up his oxen teams and horses, with the addition of a small herd of cattle to drive back home. He camped the first two nights on rivers running out onto the plains from the mountains, and next on a high, dry, and cold tableland, where there was no wood. He had put wood in the wagons, but they were slower in arriving than the advance party on horses.

He noted in his diary (which he seemed to have kept even on his travels): "I went to bed Supperless and cold." He sent back a member of the party to find the others bringing up the lagging wagons. There was a temporary reunion the next day, and the whole party enjoyed a pot of coffee together. Then he and Joe Howard (who seemed to have joined the trading party at the fort) went on ahead with two oxen teams into the menace of a slowly gathering snowstorm. "The storm increased in violence & the Wind Swept over these high bleak prairies over which our track lay a perfect gale which we had to face." They lost sense of any track to follow. The others were somewhere behind but did not catch up.

"The prospect of camping was rather gloomy," but the two men spent the night rolled in their blankets under one of the wagons. Whenever they attempted to look out, the snow sifted in upon them. It was already a foot deep. They had been afraid to leave the cattle tied to the wagons, so they hobbled them and turned them loose. These valuable animals were now lost. The men following behind were inaccessible in the storm. This first day of snow had been Sunday. On Monday it snowed all day worse than ever. They spent sixteen hours again under the wagon, but, when Owen even shifted his position to light a match to see the time, the snow blew in and literally covered them.

They could no longer stay where they were. His companion thought he knew where he could find a coulee that would lead them down to the Sun River, where they might find timber for a fire. They managed to reach the river and lighted bundles of wood during another miserable night. The lost party at last caught up with them simply by chance. These others had killed a horse for food. "We soon forgot our troubles Jim had a pot of Strong Coffee Made which with Nice Venison soon refreshed us all." This was on Wednesday. They awoke up to a clearing of weather on Thursday, but the cattle and the oxen were lost. After a fruitless search, Owen wrote, "I am in rather a tight place." But he comforted himself with an interesting talk with Father Antoine, who was one of his traveling companions. On Friday they found some of the cattle. Howard shot a deer. "The privations of the past were soon forgotten after Supper the pipe and then for long Camp Yarns comparing the hardships of the present trip to trips Made Years ago The Voyageur with a full Stomach & a full pipe is always happy."

They had a miserable enough time the rest of the journey. But they found the oxen. They warped the wagons through the canyons and mud that sucked at them after the snow melted. Having passed the worst of the mountains, they met some Indians who gave them a present of bison tongues. Owen sent Lafontaine ahead to the fort to bring back assistance. On November 16 he reached Hell Gate. On November 18, after a day's ride on horseback of eight and one-half hours, he reached Fort Owen. On November 21 he wrote laconically that "the animal I rode home died."

From this and other hard journeys, Owen came safely back to his valley. He fostered his isolated community. He grew older and stouter and drank a good bit too much. He loved his "old wife," as well as his fruits and grains and spring-damaged vegetables. He was a wise interpreter for the Indians being crowded to desperation. He was a brake upon the pushers, an example of enlightened farming for the new settlers, and a guide to government and railroad surveyors—men bringing new life into his territory.

Like De Smet, in the end Owen was exiled from the Bitterroot. His memory failed, and he was taken to a nursing home in Helena, where he lived several years. He was then sent "home" to Philadelphia in 1877, and, after existing for twelve years, his sense of place and his own identity gone, he died.

FIVE

Settlers: James and Granville Stuart

"We went up to Cottonwood to Pete's grand ball," wrote James Stuart in his diary on Christmas Day, 1861, as if this were the most ordinary kind of entry to be made by a young man spending his days picking gold out of the stream beds and ledges of the remote Deer Lodge Valley.[1] This was in the eastern part of the great Washington territory in what would one day be a part of the Idaho territory, then the Montana territory, and, finally, the State of Montana. Two brothers, among a thin scattering of first settlers, took their enjoyment where they could. They kept informal records of play and work, sharing the writing of the journal, and so left moments behind to be rescued, revised, and republished by the younger brother, Granville, when those early perilous days were long gone.

The ball could not have been very grand, but it was great fun for the lonely pickers and panners from the gulches leading into the wide valley, already with a name, Deer Lodge. James concluded this day's note comfortably happy: "Had a fine supper and then danced all night till sunrise. There were a few students of toxicology occasionally, but they were well behaved and gave the rest of us no trouble. Snowed a little last night." The same neighbors celebrated again a week later. "Everybody went to grand ball given by John Grant at Grantsville and a severe blizzard blew up and raged all night. We danced all night."

The dancers slept wherever they could and awoke to find it forty below outside with a driving snow obliterating all trails home. The Stuart brothers lived eight miles south; others, fifteen or more north. So Johnnie Grant told everyone to stay. They were slightly tired from the night before, so they lay down on bison robes and slept again until early afternoon. Then

Mrs. Grant and the other women fixed a "fine dinner." The guests cleared the floor and began dancing again, "which we kept up with unabashed pleasure until about nine in the evening, when we paused long enough to eat an excellent supper. We then began where we left off and danced until sunrise."

These early Montanans were behaving like folks in the country regions from which they had come, Virginia, Illinois, and Iowa, joining together for help and play. To those back home, the scene indoors—except for the presence of the women—might have seemed almost familiar, but outdoors it would have been strange and frightening. The women were so far all Indian, and the children were half and half. This did not seem odd or out of place to the sparse inhabitants. These others, Snakes and Bannocks, were mostly friendly neighbors, and the settlers put them up on visits, fed them, sent messages by them. The Indians had no great enmity for the scattered settlers, for at this time they seemed to pose no threat.

The mountain tribes reserved their fear and hate for the across-mountain tribes, particularly the Blackfeet, among whom they moved with caution when they went over the passes to hunt bison or take horses. Naturally, the individual horse-hungry Snake or Bannock occasionally took a horse from a white settler. Of course, a settler had to look after his horses and tie them up at the door when threatened by marauders, watch all night with a gun in hand, and set out, helter-skelter, to get them back when they were stolen, occasionally killing the taker.

At this time, the late 1850s into the late 1860s, fur trappers had not completely disappeared from the cold mountain streams, but the profit was gone from the trade. Many of the trappers were dead, and some had returned to the Middle West or to New England to tell tales that no one believed. In the short history of the region, another era was being born, and a sparse but true settlement was beginning. The first explorers had looked about, measured rivers and mountains, and gone home to make reports and influence the federal government's policy. The fur trappers had adapted to the land, become almost another tribe among the Indians, and melted away with the depletion of the beaver. Now there was another lure, gold, but so far it was not very rewarding. A few permanent settlers had stayed where they first set pick to gravel or rock.

James Stuart was born in 1832; Granville, in 1834. At the time of the Cottonwood parties they were twenty-nine and twenty-seven, respectively. They had already tried the California gold fields without any great success, but had learned trail and camp wisdom. In their early youth they had eagerly followed their father to the western edge of the continent. Not prospering, they had in 1857 headed toward home, Iowa, but Granville had fallen ill on the emigrant trail in what is now northern Utah. After a delay of several weeks, a traveler interested them with a story of gold having been found to the north. The trail east being made dangerous by Indian skirmishes and the outbreak of the Mormon "wars," they determined to travel north at least temporarily into the Beaverhead country and see what they could find.

Tired and haggard from hard journeying, for the distance was greater than they had imagined, they crossed the Rockies from what is now Idaho near Monida into what is now Montana:

> As soon as we crossed the divide a wonderful change appeared in the country. Instead of the gray sagebrush covered plains of the Snake river, we saw smooth rounded hills and sloping bench land covered with yellow bunch grass that waved in the wind like a field of grain. A beautiful little clear stream ran northward on its way to join the Missouri River. This is now known as Red Rock creek. The forepart of October gave days of brilliant sunshine, warm and pleasant with no snow anywhere except on the tops of higher mountains and very little even there. (124)

When the Stuart brothers moved into this territory from the southwest, newcomers from the East had done little so far to change things.

The Stuarts would stop first in Beaverhead country, return to the emigrant trail for supplies, move on beyond their first stopping place to what became known as the Deer Lodge Valley, and there set down roots. What had set off a mild gold rush in this region had been a story that a part-Indian, François Findlay, called Benetsee, had found nuggets in Gold Creek in 1852, and it was to this area that the brothers made their way. It was unknown to them that, many years before, Father De Smet had come upon some gold nuggets in one of the streams of the area, quietly pocketed them, and told no one of his find. He did not want the cruel disturbance and unleashed greed that he had observed in the men making their way to California during the rush of the late 1840s. He had feared for the good life of his Indians, the Salish, who were in the path of any such change. So his discovery remained private. At Fort Owen, John Owen also had seen gold in the early 1850s and had noted the fact laconically in his diary.

The Stuart brothers found a small dispersed community in the gulches and soon made friends among these lonely gold hunters. They built small log cabins after living in tents. They got out the tools they had carried from California and joined in the eager digging along first one stream and then another. They found a little gold dust in the gravel and sometimes a nugget. They began to weigh this gold and to estimate its worth. They worked at various methods of panning, digging into the rocky ledges above the streams, or nailing together boxes to make sluices with which to wash the gravel. But they also tried to surround their own place with a farm boy's idea of comfort: a fence against deer, a patch of vegetables. They were grateful always for talk and for play as well as work.

As young men they joined in eagerly in the year's end dances at the cabins of those who, like Johnny Grant, already were firmly established. This life was to be, if not idyllic, at least a small-scale model of a good community for a short period, simply because the gold finds were meager.

An episode in the narrative which Granville later wrote illustrates the life of these so far ingenuous, happy young men. "James and I were both great readers," wrote Granville, "and we had been all winter without so much as an almanac to look at. We were famished for something to read when some Indians coming from the Bitter Root told us that a white man had come up from below, with a trunk full of books, and was camped with all that wealth, in Bitter Root valley."[2]

They saddled their riding horses, loaded a packhorse with blankets and dried meat, and set out with an abandonment of the hard duties of everyday life to find the books 150 miles away. It did not matter that there was no one of their kind, no house at all, and "three dangerous rivers to cross" between them and the trunk full of reading matter. Years later, possibly wiser, Granville wrote proudly of the travail of that journey.

They found fords over the rivers; even so, they were once almost "swept away." When they reached Bitterroot Valley, where very likely they stopped over at John Owen's fort, they found that the elusive books were not in the vicinity. Neil McArthur had left his books in the care of another man, Henry Brooks, who had left Bitterroot Valley to go to Mission Valley. When they found Brooks, they had to argue to buy any books at all. "We told him how long we had been without anything to read, and how we had ridden many days, seeking that trunk, and that we would take all the blame and would make good with McArthur when he returned. At last we won him over, and he agreed to let us have five books, for five dollars each, and if McArthur was not satisfied we were to pay him more." Those were very stiff prices for the time, but they set about joyfully picking their prizes: Shakespeare, Byron, a life of Napoleon, a French Bible, and Adam Smith's *Wealth of Nations*. They never found McArthur, but they held onto the books, at least Granville did; James was to be always more for action, Granville for contemplation.

The diary records a thoughtful and sober life, in between youthful adventures, in the gulches of the Deer Lodge region. The very ordinariness of everyday life seemed protection against the dangers known to threaten each one of them when beyond the reach of comradeship. John Grant was already establishing himself as a cattleman. The Stuarts secured a small herd from across the western mountains and divided their time between digging for gold, growing vegetables, and tending cattle. A day in May 1861 seems typical of their life: "Finished sowing wheat and oats by two o'clock. . . . We went prospecting in the afternoon" (165). They were neither lazy nor fanatically industrious. They took time out to look at the hills, note a new flower, lounge on a creek bank, and read a book.

They had no particular reason to hate Indians in general; they saw them as individuals. Interrupting fence-building, they took action in pitying a wandering and hungry Indian: "Had a visitor. A Blackfoot Indian on his way from the Flathead country. Gave him his dinner and sent him on his way. Doubtless he will stay all night at Johnny Grant's at the mouth of the Little Blackfoot creek, eight miles up the river and try to eat enough to do him to Sun river, for there is no one living this side of there" (166–67).

The writer reflected that they were now living in a somewhat settled condition in places with names: "Our settlement is now known as American Fork. Johnnie Grant's at the mouth of Little Blackfoot is Grantsville and the one above on Cottonwood creek is Cottonwood. We are becoming somewhat civilized as we remain long enough in one spot to give it a name" (167).

Longing for milk, they brought in a few cows from the wandering herd and used them as their own milk cows. In the late spring of 1861, they planted beets, potatoes, and melons. They heard vague news about trouble back in "the States" and wondered what was going on, but any news came to them months late.

It was still a rough-and-ready life. Whiskey traders came, and James wrote: "There are plenty of drunken Indians passing from Grantsville to their camp. I wish those whiskey traders would go on to the Blackfoot country or to Hades" (186). James seems to have had a more restless streak than Granville. He noted in the joint journal that, after an absence of several days, he had come home with $425 in his pocket from playing poker in Grantsville. There were shooting matches, one of which he lost because he did not properly load his new brass cartridges.

In the fall of one planting year Granville and James sold their wheat crop to a settler in Bitterroot Valley for four dollars a bushel. A traveler from that same area came over the mountains and sold a wagonload of vegetables "to the folks at Grantsville and cottonwood, who are all hungry for vegetables" (188–89). An entry for October 14, 1861, records "I have churned five pounds of fine quality butter. Put handles in the picks and sharpened the shovels, and got ready to dig on our mining ditch" (189).

Cardsharps from over the mountains moved into the valley. As a good citizen, and perhaps bored with sharpening shovels, James joined in a pursuit and an arrest. One man surrendered; another, playing cards in a saloon, was shot and was buried with his monte cards still clutched to him. Two others were caught fleeing. One was acquitted after an informal hearing, and the other was hanged by the proceedings organized by the local citizens, after he wrote a letter to his father and made a fine end. James noted that he "walked to his death with a step as firm and a countenance as unchanged as if he had been the nearest spectator instead of the principal actor in the tragedy" (220).

A proper etiquette was developing for these informal trials and executions, although in the communities of Cottonwood, Grantsville, and American Fork/Gold Creek such doings were not, so far, numerous. No law existed in any formal sense, but there were soon tentative efforts made to constitute a community. James wrote on July 14, 1862: "We held an election today. Great excitement, but nobody was hurt except with an overdose of whiskey" (213–14).

Gambling places sprang up. In contrast, the brothers set up a grocery store, and soon it was flourishing. A dentist, apparently a resident, pulled a tooth for Granville. A traveler from Fort Benton with news from the East stayed up all night with the brothers. Despite news about the big fight going on back home, the settlers mostly stayed where they were. The institutions of home were coming into existence here. Churches came into spontaneous being. However, Granville did not go to church. "Am glad I do not have to attend church and sit on a bench two hours listening to some fellow telling us how much better it would be somewhere else, and that we were headed for that particular spot. We may miss some of the good things of life by being out here, but we escape some mighty disagreeable experiences" (151–52). Granville relished the good things of his new place. He was as happy at finding a lake full of trout as he might have been of a gulch full of gold.

"I followed up the creek to a beautiful little lake about a mile and a quarter long and half mile wide. It is surrounded by high mountains in the midst of a lovely forest. There were many trout in it and one lone duck floated on its placid waters. No doubt I was the first human being it had ever seen, for it had no fear of me, and probably thought I was just a new kind of deer, and my horse only an elk" (250).

A period was set to this episode in the lives of the two brothers when James married. How formal or official the marriage was, the diary entry does not tell. But on March 1, 1862, James wrote: "I brought with me the Indian woman ransomed from Narcisses, the Flathead. Powell's wife objected to having her and as we have no cook it seems to fall to my lot to take her over to some of her own people, should she wish to go. I might do worse. She is neat and rather good looking and seems to be of a good disposition. So, I find myself a married man" (198). And he commented in a general way: "Marrying is rapidly becoming an epidemic in our little village."

James was to die young, at forty-one. It is unclear what happened to his Indian wife. But with Granville, it is clear that sometimes the union could be permanent. Only two months after James's marriage, he wrote in the joint journal, "Granville was married today to Aubony, a Snake Indian girl, a sister of Fred Burr's wife. She had been living with Burr's family, is a fairly good cook, of an amiable disposition, and with few relatives" (206).*

The equilibrium precariously established in the wilderness, an agreeably primitive and natural life, to which now some domestic comfort had been added, was doomed not to last. A bigger gold strike than the Stuarts and their friends had ever known in the Deer Lodge Valley occurred not too far away in Bannack, then in Alder Gulch, where the town of Virginia City grew up rapidly and uproariously. The little linked communities in

*A footnote by the editor of the Stuart journal says that "Aubony or Ellen became the mother of nine children of whom three Charlie, Sam, and Mary—Mrs. E. C. Abbott, wife of 'Teddy Blue' of Gilt Edge, Montana—still live. She also adopted two sons of James Stuart" (206).

which the Stuarts had found a home became demoralized. Many of the settlers of Cottonwood, Granville, or Gold Creek picked up and set out for the new gold fields. Granville and James went over to Bannack to try it out for themselves and, although they found that there was "no safety for life or property" there (226), decided to try business in the new town.

They set up a butcher shop in Bannack and dealt in other goods that miners needed. They looked about and did a little exploring and digging themselves, but never struck it rich. They took sober advantage of the needs of the wild, desperate, and exhausted men who were making frantic efforts to take the gravel out of the "crick" and to dig into the hard ledges of rock above the flow. Somehow the two brothers kept their heads and made a considerable amount of money for the time.

After the Bannack discovery, there was an even bigger strike at Alder Gulch, first called Varona City, after Jefferson Davis's wife, then, after objection by the northerners among the mixed mob of miners, Virginia City. Again the Stuarts moved on with the miners, looked about, and found they did best by being blacksmiths and storekeepers.

On October 27, 1863, the diary recorded bad news: "Unusual excitement in town today news has just arrived that the coach that left here for Bannack on the twenty-fifth was held up by highwaymen and the passengers robbed" (258). This seemed outrageous to the former inhabitants of innocently peaceful Gold Creek. Now a kind of anarchism was erupting in the bigger gold-strike towns. From all directions other kinds of people—predators, not settlers—were moving in. It seemed that peaceful settlement could be had only when no immense profit was to be gained. Here in the arc of mountain valleys lying between Bannack to the west and Virginia City to the east, robberies and casual killings became events of everyday life. James's diary entry of September 18, 1862, recorded that Granville and a friend, on a trip from Hell Gate (Missoula), met two "fine looking young men. One of them said his name was Henry Plummer, the other was Charles Reeves" (222–23). Thus, casually, the brothers' journal announced the arrival in the new gold territory of Henry Plummer, whose name would dominate the hectic history of that area for a short time.

Trading, selling, digging a bit on their own, the brothers joined this new society in Alder Gulch, where for a time a frenzy of human activity enlivened what had been bare hills and empty valleys. Despite the deadly froth of criminality that thrived here unabated by any formal kind of law, there was always a substratum of civility in Virginia City, and the brothers took part in it. White women of conscious respectability appeared for the first time in the territory. A lively round of more or less innocent social activities sprang up among the saloons and gambling places; and a school, a newspaper, a singing society, and a historical society came into being as naturally as the less respectable activities.

The brothers made a considerable amount of money out of the opportunities available in the new and complex society of this first real town of the territory. But this less innocent society also cast shadows across the lives and careers of these men, as well as across those of other ordinarily good men of the community. The memoir that Granville was to recast in his honorable and honored old age left out James's taking part in Virginia City in vigilante activities. James was to die young, in 1873; he was known among his contemporaries as a more typical man of his times than the studious Granville. James had gone out on wild-goose chases to find gold in other places than Bannack and Virginia City; he had gambled and occasionally used his gun in ways to incite a careless admiration. If he had lived, he might have made a successful politician of the early days of the state.

Granville enlarged the cattle business he had begun in a small way in the Deer Lodge Valley. He moved to eastern Montana when it opened up after the end of Indian domination. He became one of the dominant ranchers of that region for the brief period when it was the last unfenced range of the whole west. He was bankrupted in the downfall of the cattle kingdom, which had overused the grass and was unprepared for one terrible winter when the freeze did not lift and tens of thousands of cattle died. Meantime, in this newer region he was assumed to be a leader in a vigilantelike project to rid the big ranchers of what they thought of as unnecessary competition from Indians, cattle thieves, or small ranchers setting up in their territory.

Granville lived on into old age, an admired relic of a time past. No longer a rancher, he became president of the Board of Stock Commissioners of Montana. He became a state land agent charged with selecting land for school purposes. In 1894 he was minister to the republics of Uruguay and Paraguay. In 1904 he became librarian of the Butte Public Library. Granville died on October 2, 1918, having lived through cycles of Northern Plains history.[3]

SIX

Editor and Outlaw: Thomas Dimsdale
and Henry Plummer

Two men, relatively young, arrived within months of each other at the scenes of the earliest substantial gold strikes in the territory that was soon— 1864—separated from Idaho and had its own name, Montana. It would not be a state until very late, 1889. Although they never knew each other, the coming of the two men into a kind of conjunction was to make a difference to western legendry and even to western history.

Henry Plummer, who came to Montana from rumored troubles left behind in California and Nevada, reached Bannack in late 1862. Between thirty and thirty-two years old, five feet, eight and a half inches tall, with light hair, a pale complexion (he had quiescent tuberculosis in his lungs), and gray eyes, Plummer was pleasing in appearance, but not imposing by rough frontier standards. But he compelled attention by his cool manner, his social amenability, and his handiness with a gun. He already had a reputation for this accepted regional skill. He was a quick draw who did not hesitate to shoot when threatened, and who, in this new town, after a trial for one such shooting and killing, was both acquitted and forgiven, then elected sheriff of the new county.

Plummer was tried and acquitted in a miners' court before a judge elected by the local population. There was already here a spontaneously erected system of rough law. At first the new sheriff seemed an asset to the system. He was attentive to his duties and was humane to the accused. He made friends with some of the leading citizens.

While the principal needs of the miners were shovels, liquor, and sex, there was also a hunger for a decent kind of life. The quiet man who was the sheriff, who built a jail and attempted to protect life and property, seemed at first a sign of stability. Another newcomer, who was to become the outspoken advocate for citizenship and culture, was the editor of the first newspaper in the territory, the *Montana Post*. It was a lively weekly, written almost entirely by one man, and began publication in the late summer of 1864 in an office on the main street of the growing town of Virginia City. So, for a time, the two most influential men of the territory were Sheriff Henry Plummer of Bannack and Thomas Dimsdale, editor in Virginia City, sixty-five miles of rough trail east of Bannack. The story of Plummer has been told over and over again, but Dimsdale, the writer, who told the version of Plummer's life which has been believed, also deserves attention.

Dimsdale was a thirty-two-year-old Englishman who had been moving restlessly westward for several years. He had come from a family of some pretension in the north of England. He had a prideful but unfinished education, public school and then Oxford for two years, before the family's money gave out. He had tried a new life first in Canada, where he taught school in Milbrook, Ontario. Somehow from Ontario he had made his way to the new gold town of Virginia City.

A surviving photograph shows a formally dressed man with a not unattractive serious face; he has dark hair and mustache, and a straightforward look in his blue eyes. He was to lead an active life in the new town for a few years and, having created a successful newspaper and written a book that was to be read widely, married and shortly thereafter, in September 1866, died in bed of tuberculosis.

Plummer might have done the same—for he also suffered from the century's common disease—if he had not had a more public death, before Dimsdale's. In seeing a kind of historical relationship between them, it is interesting to note that there were other similarities. Both men were noticeably better spoken, better mannered, and better educated than most of their fellow citizens. Each exerted a considerable influence over his contemporaries. Both were admired for their abilities. Dimsdale was taken to the heart of the solid part of the community as editor, teacher, clubman, churchman. Plummer, the popular elected sheriff, the first one of the first county of the territory, was known as a man able to get things done, to get along with and to influence men to do what he wished, and to have an expertness as an assessor of silver mining claims, which was a business that took him away on frequent trips. For Dimsdale, Virginia City was a perfect sphere in which an unknown but handy and gifted man might make a mark as a good citizen. For Plummer, before suspicions arose as to his possible double life, it was a place where he might be a leader.

The connection between the two men was to be that of the word, for Dimsdale was to chronicle Plummer's brief career. [1] When Dimsdale arrived in Virginia City, Sheriff Plummer was only a shadowy but influential figure across the mountains in Bannack. Before being forced to think very much about who and what Plummer was, Dimsdale was happy to be in this new place. Virginia City astounded him.

The life of the place was radically different from that of any place Dimsdale had known in the Old World and also unlike any older American farming community gradually settled and organized. Here the magnet of gold had attracted every sort of comer, men and some women from all corners of the States and from places farther off. Shelters along Alder Creek were at first only hastily erected wickiups, Indian-style brush shelters. But Dimsdale, having come a little later than the very beginning, also saw wood and even stone buildings beginning to rise along the main street, which slanted steeply downhill from east to west with low brown mountains enclosing the scene on both sides. He was delighted, for he felt he was in at the creation of a civilization.

Dimsdale was a visionary. Where there was the reality of a raw simplicity of gouging the earth for what were in its innards, of diverting streams through crude sluices, of piling up ridges of bare earth, of cutting down the green stuff that impeded the work, he saw a clean and peaceful city rising. Instead of a frantic horde of men grappling with nature and with each other for imagined riches, he saw a peaceful community of good men and women working and playing, sending children to school, going to church, voting for enlightened leaders, taking the time to read and to club together for amusement and high-minded ends. He set about, as a one-man civilizer, to institute a number of these developments.

In the winter of 1863–64 he opened the first school in Virginia City. Children were being born. Very young ones were running about the rough roads and among the hard-working and hard-roistering men, playing games in the tailings, and darting in and out of the stores and saloons now going up with great rapidity. In 1929, Annie Moran Durnen, a seventy-four-year-old woman, remembered going to Dimsdale's school. It was "a log building like what almost everybody lived in then, and its furnishing was extremely simple. We sat on benches." She recalled her teacher as "a slim man of medium height and very much a gentleman."[2] It was a private school, and Dimsdale reportedly charged between $1.75 and $2.00 per week. Always ambitious, he was soon offering adults classes at night.

The solitary school in Virginia City seemed to be only a beginning. On June 10, 1865, Sidney Edgerton, the territorial governor, appointed Dimsdale superintendent of public education of a territory that had no other schools. There was no salary, but the title was resonant of an assumed future. Dimsdale's newspaper, the *Montana Post,* persuaded Madison County to levy a school tax, then to open the first public school in February 1866. Having started things, Dimsdale busied himself in a half-dozen public matters. He coruscated with ideas and activities. He helped organize the first Masonic Lodge. He was involved in the founding of a Montana Historical Society. He and his fellow members did not wait long to have a past, a present, and a future. He was a communicant of the congregation of the first Episcopal church of the community and took an active part in the life of the church as a lay reader. He led a singing class. Thus, Dimsdale entered into the social life of the community, a companionable man.

Dimsdale valued his friendship with those he considered outstanding citizens, men such as a former Ohio congressman, Sidney Edgerton, who was territorial governor, and Edgerton's nephew, Wilbur Sanders, a lawyer who later became the state's first senator. Dimsdale was friends with, and highly regarded by, the young merchants Granville and James Stuart. Granville wrote later: "This gentle, kindhearted, Christian man came among us in the summer of 1863. A man of culture and refinement he drew to himself all that was best of society at that time in Virginia City."[3]

As an editor Dimsdale was not only concerned with the good life within his community but also attempted to mold its political opinion, especially in relation to the Civil War. He was a passionate backer of Mr. Lincoln's war. In this place, the stand took considerable courage, for Virginia City and Bannack contained a large number of strayed southerners, soldiers and civilians who had fled trouble at home, but who carried their sympathies with them. Leading citizens such as Edgerton and Sanders, who had come from the upper Middle West, were, of course, Unionist. Many of the miners were prosouthern.

Dimsdale was fearless in writing slanted stories of the war and issuing hotly partisan editorials week after week. He opposed the efforts of the territory's Democratic party to send a delegate to Congress whom he believed was of the wrong persuasion: "This Territory is not southern ground."[4] After the election of 1864, when results had at last reached this far west, his headlines were as slanted as his editorials:

Glorious News

Union Majorities in every State But One!

Hurrah for Lincoln![5]

A November 26, 1864, editorial shows the editor trying to create his own kind of town—at least in words:

> In all parts of our city, every day shows new improvements. Business in all its different branches is prospering. . . .
>
> Considering the very short time we have been congregated here to build up a society we have done well. . . . Substantial, stone buildings have been erected. . . . Water, good, pure, spring water, is being conducted in pipes through our streets. . . . Two fire companies are ready at any moment to combat the destroying and so much to be feared element.
>
> Regular religious service is held by three different churches. . . . A day and night school [is] open for the instruction of the growing generation.
>
> A lyceum, as soon as the stone building is done, will be established.

The editorial also said: "It is almost forgotten that less than twelve months ago, it was not safe to go out at night in our streets, for some of the most desperate villains that ever disgraced a community were prowling about. Thanks to the Vigilance Committee, whoever they may be, nothing is left of those outcasts."[6] So, in his search for the good society, the good editor attempted to smooth over the events that resolved a desperate situation in desperate fashion and made his good town notorious.

The most remembered of the vigilante deeds was the hanging of Sheriff Plummer, who had recently accompanied his respectable wife on a day's journey east, where it was possible he planned to join her later. (Her leaving Bannack caused gossip; it was thought that she had found out about her husband's evil doings). However, Plummer continued to eat his meals at the home of his wife's sister and brother-in-law, Martha and Henry Vail. Taken out of the Vails' house, the lawman was accused and peremptorily hanged. This monstrous climax was a contradiction to Dimsdale's picture of a good community, yet it is from the high-minded editor that we know

what happened in the Montana gold country during the days of the vigilantes' activities. The editor wrote about the vigilantes first in the *Montana
Post,* then made the story into a book, *The Vigilantes of Montana,* the first
book published in the state.

Alongside the efforts of Dimsdale and others to create a quiet, stable,
civilized community, there indubitably existed a high-pitched, roistering
extravagance of life, one unfettered by law or custom. Gold had engendered
violence. In the early months and years of the community, 102 citizens
were killed in Bannack and Virginia City and the miles between—on trails,
roads, and town streets, as well as in alleys, saloons, and dance halls. Many
others had been robbed and beaten. Gold shipments had become the chosen
loot of the outlaws, so it was dangerous to ride the stagecoach leaving Alder
Gulch with gold on board.

There was no official system of law in place. Having received information
that they thought was authentic from the confession of a man about to be
hanged, of the makeup of an organized gang headed by their own sheriff,
the respectable leading men of the community came together and coalesced
in a secret organization patterned after the vigilantes of California a generation earlier. They called themselves by the same name and proceeded with
determination and breathtaking speed to seek out and summarily execute
those suspected of the depredations of the past months. With public hang-
ings they enlisted much support and intimidated any who objected. Dimsdale, who knew but did not reveal who these vigilantes were (it was an
open secret), came to be the justifier of the movement first in the series of
Montana Post articles and later in the book that was made from the articles.
The articles began August 26, 1865, when the most concentrated effort
had already been concluded. Part of his story was directed toward his neighbors to make them feel good about what had taken place. Part of his motive
was to reach the opinion of the States, where criticism of the methods of
the vigilantes had arisen.

Dimsdale's book captured the action and mood of a short moment in
the history of the Rocky Mountain Northwest and has colored opinion about
these events. Only recently has his view been challenged; otherwise, it has
been accepted history. The vividness of the writing has insured readers.
Mark Twain read it with attention and some admiration and called it "that
bloodthirsty little Montana book."[7]

There could be no doubt about the lawlessness of the situation and the need for something to be done. The Stuart brothers' journal validates Dimsdale's diagnosis of the dangers of living at this time in Virginia City:

> Many gamblers and desperate characters drifted in, lured by the prospect of acquiring gold dust without digging for it. It became the custom to go armed all the time. . . . There was no safety for life or property only so far as each individual could, with his trusty rifle, protect his own. The respectable citizens far outnumbered the desperadoes, but having come from all corners of the earth, they were unacquainted and did not know whom to trust.[8]

In this rambunctious setting, where men swaggered down main street wearing guns, it was understood that it was no crime to shoot and even kill if one were directly threatened with a gun. Plummer had earlier been forgiven for doing just that. But robbery and gross, pointless killing were affronts not to be endured.

Earlier, when still accepted by the community, Plummer had gone on business north to Sun River, and there made the acquaintance of Henry Vail, who had been sent to the West recently on a forlorn hope to run what was called an Indian farm, as well as his wife, Martha, and Martha's young sister, Electa Bryan. Plummer became engaged to Electa and married her in Sun River before bringing her home to Bannack. In his absence from the gold town his deputies got into a quarrel, and J. W. Willingham, the best of the rough lot of sheriff's helpers, was killed by the others. It was determined to try the two remaining deputies, Buck Stinson and Haze Lyons, at a miners' court. X. Beidler (he never used a first name) was there and described the outdoors scene graphically. (Beidler became one of the more enthusiastic vigilantes shortly and many years later wrote his memoirs.)

The two men "were sentenced to death by vote of the people. . . . Such trials took place outdoors where crowds gathered to take part as jury. We had built the scaffold and dug the graves. The condemned men were seated in a wagon and surrounded by a guard." Beidler claims that the friends of the men had canvassed the crowd, aroused sympathy, and demanded a new vote. The crowd was to divide itself into two parts, "those in favor of hanging were to go up the hill and those in favor of no hanging were a lazy lot of loafers and naturally went down hill and beat us."[9]

This reversal of conviction by the volatile miners' court was said to have crystallized a demand for a more decisive kind of justice, and the vigilantes secretly organized themselves. Small hunting groups then worked with terrifying efficiency, bivouacking through snowstorms and making harsh and desperate marches across mountain ranges to find the two dozen men they hanged within a few months. One of those located at some distance from the mining towns, Red Yeager, before being hoisted to a tree limb, told the hangman that Plummer was his and the others' leader. None of the two dozen hanged men, including Plummer, had the benefit of any kind of proper defense.

The story of this episode in western history was to be told several times. An anonymous account, *Banditti of the Rocky Mountains* (January 1865), came across Dimsdale's desk before he wrote his own account and may have influenced him. Dimsdale referred scornfully to *Banditti* in an editorial on January 3, 1865, and promised to do better. *Banditti* has a more connected narrative than Dimsdale's, devotes more space to Plummer's career before Montana, and is written in a ludicrously flowery style that detracts from the facts embedded in it.

X. Beidler, who was one of the active vigilantes, dictated and assembled his own narrative, *X. Beidler, Vigilante* (1880). He seems to have been bulldog-like and indefatigable, having as the one purpose in this life the catching and hanging of criminals, without a shred of doubt about what he was doing. He never quit and never got hurt; he was always there. He was laconic and a little humorous, kind to noncriminals, and, not giving himself away, glad to seem harmless when he was not. There is no purple in his prose, which shows a ferocious attention to the poignant detail. When Buck Stinson was being hanged, Beidler recalled that the pull of the rope almost upset the gallows and that the outlaw called out, "Hold on, da———n it, you are choking me."[10]

Nathaniel P. Langford, who wrote *Vigilante Days and Ways* (1890), later did many other notable things—exploring the Yellowstone country and becoming the first superintendent of the park—in addition to having been one of the original vigilantes. He concurred in thinking, along with the anonymous author of *Banditti,* with Beidler, and with Dimsdale, that the vigilantes had done the right thing, but he was more judicious in tone than the others. He frankly condemned the excesses that were part of the movement. He had talked with Plummer during the daily business of life in the gold country and found him personable. In Plummer's early days in Bannack and Virginia City, Langford had thought that this person from across the mountains with a shaded reputation might be reformable. Plummer had married well, was doing a good job for the county, and was sober in manner and deeds. But Langford came to believe in the guilt of the official whom the vigilantes dragged from a peaceful household and hanged without recourse to trial. He became convinced that Plummer's attractive manner was a front for wickedness.

Later public accounts have followed the line of thought initiated by these contemporaries and have succeeded in making a legend of the sheriff who was an outlaw. There have been very few doubters. One of these was Dan Cushman. In his book *Montana: The Gold Frontier* (1973), he allowed as probable truth a doubtful, violent past to the quiet, likable sheriff, yet he found no reason to convict Plummer of the charges that the vigilantes had raised against him. He doubted that there had been an organized gang of which Plummer was the head. "The existence of any *gang* is doubtful, although the rough element knew who their friends were. A bandit organization headed by a single mastermind should have produced an example of organized banditry, but none can be found." He judged Plummer harshly, but said that "the charges set forth would never have stood up in court. Aside from hearsay, inflated in the passage of time, no actual proof exists that Plummer profited by a dollar from road agentry, or planned a robbery."[11]

A thoroughly researched study of the case, *Hanging the Sheriff: A Biography of Henry Plummer* (1987), by R. E. Mather and F. E. Boswell, has raised to a high probability the likelihood that Plummer was innocent.[12] Going to surviving court records in California and Nevada, they have exorcised to a great extent the bad reputation that Plummer brought with him from those areas. In addition, locating information concerning Plummer's relations with his wife and her kinfolk, they have fleshed out the man and made his innocence at least more likely.

Mather and Boswell also show that politics was involved in the eagerness with which the influential men of the area were glad to believe in the guilt of Plummer; they were Republicans, and he was an influential local Democrat and was accumulating power. He was awaiting a federal appointment as marshal at the time of his death. The commission arrived in due course after he had been hanged.

Although the writers of this most extensive study of the Plummer case have raised doubts about his guilt, they have been unable to clinch their case. One very heavy matter that is incapable of resolution is the supposed testimony of Red Yeager, who told his executioners that Plummer was his leader, as well as that of all the others whose names he conveniently gave just before being strung up. Was Yeager's testimony true, or was it manufactured evidence? To Plummer's detriment, it was believed, and the sheriff was hanged. The industrious researchers were able to demolish nearly every clause of the vigilantes' case, but were unable to touch this hearsay evidence. It did not have proof or verification, yet over the decades exerted a malign influence on Plummer's reputation.

Plummer's fate, that of a sheriff who was said to be an outlaw, knowing about the shipment of gold out of Virginia City and Bannack, and directing a gang to the interception of those shipments, was to become one of the West's famous tales, told and retold. The account that carried the farthest was that of the editor of the *Montana Post,* the sheriff's contemporary. Because Plummer's case seemed such a striking instance of duplicity, it has been that part of the story which has remained reverberant. Yet Dimsdale's way of telling the story was to present a pageant of the vigilantes' acts, of which the Plummer execution was only one part. The way in which Dimsdale told his story allows a later reader to see into something dark in both the writer's mind and in the life of that society, which in its naïveté and gusto was then and is now a reflection of an aspect of American life.

The Dimsdale account is instantly vivid and engrossing. Yet the writing is not without obvious faults. The most serious is that the writer did not document his descriptions and conclusions. What he has presented, with some fancy writing surrounding violent episodes, is an account of one hanging and then another, these street scenes strung together as a chronicle but without much concern for ultimate cause and effect. He simply states or accepts the guilt of each successive hanged man and goes on with enthusiasm to make the reader see the sudden and violent death.

Dimsdale was also ignorant of the life Plummer had led in California and Nevada and simply retailed garbled stories current in the gold towns. It is probable that Dimsdale never had a firsthand encounter with Plummer, although he may have seen him. The young English editor's other faults are of an endearing kind. He paraded his learning, with quotes from Shakespeare, Milton, and Oliver Wendell Holmes. These authors are employed to furnish monitory tags at the head of episodes. The chapter "Trials of the Road" is headed:

I'll read you matter deep and dangerous
As full of peril and adventurous spirit,
As to o'erwalk a current, roaring loud,
On the unsteadfast footing of a spear.

—Shakespeare

High learning was furnished for the inhabitants of the cricks and coulees of Madison County.

Despite his faults, Dimsdale had a born writer's virtue, the ability to carry his readers headlong through his story. He strung together violent scenes as if by an observer who was there and who heard every word, groan or curse, uttered, and exalted with and shuddered with the spectators. When he reported or made up an action, Dimsdale had a stiletto pen. He was probably a witness to some of the events he described. He also probably coaxed out information from those who had viewed such scenes, but that he had missed.

When Plummer shot his former friend Jack Cleveland (a man some said might tell things about his past), Dimsdale wrote that the latter said: "Plummer, you won't shoot me when I'm down" [having fallen from the first nonfatal shot], to which Plummer replied, "No, you d—d son of a b—h, get up."[13] The shooting having ended successfully for Plummer with Cleveland dead, Dimsdale commented as a good storyteller: "Singular enough it must appear to the inhabitants of settled communities that a man was being shaved in the saloon at the time, and neither he nor the operator left off business." Under an elected judge, Hoyt from Saint Paul, and an elected jury, Plummer, who was thought to have been provoked by threats, was acquitted by eleven to one. Dimsdale's verdict upon the verdict was that "government by the people *en masse* is the acme of absurdity" (39). Dimsdale's intent in telling his story of the series of vigilante executions was to prove that a secret verdict by responsible leading citizens was preferable. The verdict was always arrived at secretly before the public sentence and execution.

When the vigilantes hanged five outlaws at one time, the gallows being the roof beam of an unfinished main street building, Dimsdale reported, as if from the words of eyewitnesses, the chaffing exchange of one of the men to be hanged, Jack Gallagher, to a friend in the crowd: "Say, I'm going to heaven! I'll be there in time to open the gate for you, old fellow" (166).

When the next man of the five, Boone Helm, was to be hanged, it was as if the writer were there. Helm, gazing at his friend dangling from the rope's end, said: " 'Kick away, old fellow: I'll be in Hell with you in a minute'. . . . He then shouted, 'Every man for his principles—hurrah for Jeff Davis! Let her rip!' The sound of his words was echoed by the twang of the rope" (167).

The one hanging that Dimsdale was most anxious to justify in his narrative was that of the sheriff. For the sake of his story it was too bad that this execution took place rather early in the career of the vigilantes. The momentum of his account rather slowed after this point. But all through the story of the vigilantes as he told it, he made the point over and over that Plummer had been evil in the disguise of affability. The very success of the narrative for its generations of readers has been this twist, the story of the bad man wrapped in the disguise of a good one.

Even Dimsdale had had to admit that "Plummer was a man of most insinuating address and gentlemanly manners under ordinary circumstances, and had the art of ingratiating himself with men and even with ladies and women of all conditions." But he added severely: "It was only when excited by passion that his savage instincts got the better of him and that he appeared—in his true colors—a very demon" (257). This was an assumption on Dimsdale's part; it is doubtful he had ever seen Plummer in his "demon" guise.

What happened in January 1864, according to the more thorough researches of Mather and Boswell, was as follows. On January 10, armed men came to the door of James and Martha Vail and asked to see the sheriff. Plummer was lying down, not having felt well for some time. He assumed at first that the men, who let him think so, had come to ask his aid in looking for a suspect. He went with them to Wilbur Sanders' house and found there that he was the object of the group. From there he was taken under Sanders' leadership to the gallows that he had himself erected for the hanging of a criminal. His deputies, Buck Stinson and Ned Ray, also had been rounded up, and the three men saw that they faced imminent hanging with no opportunity for defense. In the midst of the crowd, Ned Swift, a young man who had admired Plummer since first knowing him at Sun River, was extravagant in his grief. Plummer pulled off his scarf and told the men to give it to Swift. He asked for time to attend to his business affairs and to see his wife, and he asked for his sister-in-law, Martha Vail, with whom he boarded, to be sent for. (Martha Vail had first opposed her sister's marrying Plummer, but had since become his friend.) Meantime Mrs. Vail was being lied to at her house and calmed down and kept away until the whole thing would be over, the managers of the scene knowing how notoriously weak the crowd was in the face of female tears.

Plummer asked for time to pray, but was hustled toward the noose. There was no stand to put him on, and Plummer was unceremoniously seized bodily by several men and pulled up, hand over hand, strangling, then dropped (93). Stinson and Ray were hanged expeditiously, too. The three were left hanging until their bodies froze. Then there was a two-month orgy of hanging every man suspected of ill doings.

Other witnesses reported Plummer's manifest anxiety when he found out what was happening to him, and his casting about for help, as well as his quiet self-control at the end, his giving a remembrance to the sobbing friend in the excited crowd, who, if any among them thought the deed bad, were being held back by the pointed guns of the Vigilance Committee. But Dimsdale, writing later in the fervor of wanting to convince, made the scene better from his point of view than it had been.

> Plummer exhausted every argument and plea that his imagination could suggest, in order to induce his captors to spare his life. He begged to be chained down in the meanest cabin; offered to leave the country forever; wanted a jury trial; implored time to settle his affairs; asked to see his sister-in-law; and, falling on his knees, with tears and sighs declared to God that he was too wicked to die. He confessed his numerous murders and crimes, and seemed almost frantic at the prospect of death. (148)

Dimsdale did not reveal that the respectable men of the community who plotted Plummer's death had, only a few weeks before the event, accepted an invitation for their families to dine at Thanksgiving at the Vail house. On this occasion, Plummer, the Vails' boarder, sent to Salt Lake City for a $40 turkey and for wines to decorate the table. (Plummer lived in a hotel but spent time at the Vails and ate his meals with them.) It was as if, on this occasion, he acted as the host. The Sidney Edgertons and the Wilbur Sanderses, already talking of a way to rid themselves of a political enemy and a man who might be a brigand, sat down to eat with him at a meal he had provided.

Dimsdale's book tells how after Plummer's death the other suspected criminals were then apprehended and hanged. Usually Dimsdale could allege the crimes for which these men were so expeditiously executed. But his narrative shows that a fair court procedure was never instituted, although there was a solemn pretense of accusation, corroboration, then swift execution, usually in front of the population of either Bannack or Virginia City, a crowd at which the guns of the vigilantes were pointed. Dimsdale relates more than one patently unfair execution and does not criticize the act. It is as if he cannot see or comprehend the gross exaggeration of a claim for justice.

One particular case arouses what can only be called posthumous pity. John Dolan was captured in Salt Lake City by the duly instituted lawman John McGrath on suspicion of robbery of $700. The lawman promised Dolan he would not be turned over to the vigilantes, but he was. Dolan confessed the deed and promised restitution of $400 owed to the victim of the robbery, $300 having been already recovered. However, he was marched to the scene of execution, a guard surrounding him from rescue by the crowd outside the rim of armed vigilantes. Dolan confessed his crime and said he would make repayment, that he had been drunk when he did it, that he had never been accused before of such a deed, and that he was well-known and not considered a criminal. "He then bade them all good-bye, and requested that some of his friends would bury his body. The rope was placed round his neck; the plank was struck from beneath his feet, and the corpse swayed to and fro in the night breeze. He never made a perceptible struggle" (222).

The crowd became disorderly, the vigilantes' guard threatened them with their guns, and the crowd knocked over a wagon in panic. Dimsdale makes no mitigating remarks but adds, in the reported words of a principal vigilante, a moralizing warning: "He reminded them that nothing but severe and summary punishment would be of any avail to prevent crime, in a place where life and gold were so much exposed" (223).

Whereas Dolan's execution seems excessive, that of another victim, in Dimsdale's reporting, seems inexcusable. The excitement of permitted violence had loosed other emotions in the community, often among those not of the organization of the vigilantes. A number of helpless Indians who lived near the camps were pointlessly murdered, or their tents shot into in a happy-go-lucky way. The case of the Mexican (the Greaser, as the miners called him) Pizanthia displays both the colloquial power of Dimsdale's narrative and the community's prejudice.

Suspecting Pizanthia of crimes, the vigilante mob attacked the cabin in which he had barricaded himself. He fired at the attackers. The mob replied with an excess of weaponry. They found an old abandoned howitzer and shelled the cabin. They dragged the wounded man out, shot him as he lay helpless at their feet, then hanged the dead body.

> Over one hundred shots were discharged at the swaying corpse.
>
> A friend—one of the four "Bannack originals"—touched the leader's arms and said, "Come and see my bonfire." Walking down to the cabin, he found that it had been razed to the ground by the maddened people, and was then in a bright glow of flame. A proposition to burn the Mexican was received with a shout of exultation. The body was hauled down and thrown upon the pile, upon which it was burned to ashes when the fire burned out. [14]

At the end of this description of a particularly violent killing, Dimsdale states flatly: "The truth is, that the Vigilance Committee simply punished with death men unfit to live in any community, and that death was usually, almost instantaneous, and only momentarily painful." Thus the crusading editor let himself be swept beyond justifiable reasoning.

Dimsdale's fault was that he loved a new civilization to the point of blindness. He wanted passionately for his new town and countryside to be safe and to thrive. So he loaded all his partiality on the side of the better citizens—as it seemed to him—who organized a law when there was no adequate one in place. He blindly believed that all they did was commendable and excused them when they were not really excusable.

There was more in his attitude that is interesting. Dimsdale exemplified a double attitude. Something in outlawry and violence attracted him. It is the split view of the westerner, a view distilled clearer in this isolation, but also true, if less clearly seen, in all Americans behind the surge westward. He was passionately for the good, the pure, and the uplifting; yet he had a morbid fascination about the fate of those outside the pale of everyday goodness. This has been part of the attraction of his flawed book through the decades. Mark Twain's description is not off the mark: it is a "bloodthirsty" book.

What happened after this heady indulgence in violence? There was a pause, perhaps some shame. But there was also a diminution of casual murders and robberies. The acts of the vigilantes seem to have been shamefacedly justified and enjoyed by later generations. The violence of good men was latent, ready to burst forth again. There was a case later in eastern Montana when Granville Stuart and a group of prosperous ranchers banded together and again took the law into their own hands to hang poachers and rustlers, whites and Indians, those suspect to, and competitive with, the good men of the new cattle range. Dimsdale, who encapsulated this attitude in a book, is an interesting case, a man who loved civility and culture, yet was fascinated by evil and excused violence.

So how did they all turn out? Having watched with satisfaction a calming of outlaw activity in his beloved new land, Dimsdale married in May 1866 and died in September of that year, of the disease that might also have carried off the sheriff, if he had not died otherwise. Before returning to his native Ohio, Sidney Edgerton had been territorial governor. His nephew Wilbur Sanders stayed on and became the first senator from the constituted State of Montana. Electa Plummer faded into a background of teaching and, after ten years, of marriage in South Dakota, living again near her kinfolk, the Vails, who had moved there. She had six children. Henry Plummer became a notorious memory, an object of bemused interest, half reprobation, half fascination.

SEVEN

Soldiers: George Crook
and John Gregory Bourke

I tried to make myself believe it was a grand thing to have my garments saturated with water, my feet cold and wet my miserable straw hat torn by the breezes, no tent, no blanket, no supper to speak of. This, I said to myself, is heroism and I am a first-class hero; but it wouldn't work. Like Banquo's ghost, the thought would not down that a good hot stove, with plenty of champagne and oysters would be good enough for the likes of me and it was then I made up my mind, if I ever married an heiress, to live for the remainder of my days in a brown stone front and retired from the hero business forever.[1]

The writer of these words, painfully put down in a diary carried on horseback through expeditions against Indian tribes, was a twenty-nine-year-old lieutenant in 1875, an aide to one of the three principal generals who in January of the following year were ordered to put an end to Indian raids and depredations on the Northern Plains and compel these free-roving peoples, mostly Cheyennes and Sioux, to come into reservations and become all at once sedentary farmers, wards of a far-off government. John Bourke was a small actor on the scene, but he had a good place on the stage, a large scene that would make legends of other individuals. His observations, recorded nightly, read today, restore a sense of the way it was in those days, the reactions of a good observer of the happenings of an eventful year.

John Bourke's vantage point for the event of the climax of the Indian wars on the Northern Plains was as aide-de-camp to General George Crook. Crook was the most commonsensical of the western generals detailed after the Civil War to fighting the Indian tribes in this last region of their stubborn recalcitrance.

Crook was always as plain as he could be, and also competent, forceful, and not much bothered by undue sensitivity. In contrast, his aide lived in his nerves and emotions. Both were professional army men, thinking that they were doing right in this strange war. Both carried with them in these early days some of the prejudices of their own civilization. Yet both were open to impressions and ideas that enlarged and in some ways overcame or changed some of these preconceived ideas.

The Indians, variously grouped in the different cultures of their tribes, who faced these soldiers, outrunners and protectors of railroad builders, miners, settlers of new towns, and diggers in the unplowed land, lived in an entirely different world of reference and emotion from the whites who were gradually shoving them aside. These native wandering peoples, who had moved into this land of high rolling prairies from the east and north, were loosely associated societies, with many different languages and beliefs. Yet they shared an all-pervasive sense of religion, a worship of the holiness of every object of daily life, and of the visible aspects of land, sky, weather, plants, animals. They practiced elaborate and daily rituals, including their activities of warfare, which they carried on stripped of everyday clothes and decorated with sacred signs in amulets, headdresses, and painted body and facial symbols.

The white world they faced was becoming, in this decade of the late nineteenth century, compartmentalized, so its religion was separated from the rest of life. That life had become a powerful driving force, very like the fierce railed movement of the trains that were pushing west. Although this civilization had sent missionaries earlier into the West, it was for the most part by this time a secular culture, in love with things and with an egalitarian hunger for a better individual living, which it seemed this open West could give. The troops of these western outposts were usually the poor of the eastern cities. They drank too much and often deserted when hardships and dangers grew to be too much, yet in skirmishes and battles fought desperately hard against an enemy whom they feared or despised and did not understand at all. Behind them was a resistless push of a whole people moving on into this area of Northern Plains and mountains, the last part of the great American space to be filled.

The year 1876 was one of decision. It was to bring to climax much of what had gone before since the Civil War years. In the 1860s the internal

American struggle and its aftermath had diverted federal resources from the West. Scattered settlers had suffered from sporadic and individual tribal attacks wherever the line of settlement was thin. Yet this movement of people went on inexorably. Three forts—Kearny, Reno, and Smith— established along the Bozeman Trail (from what was to be Wyoming into what was to be Montana), and designed to protect the gold trail to the little settlements of Bannock and Virginia City, were not guarded very well, and Indians inflicted heavy losses on these small army outposts.

In 1868 the U.S. government, with great ceremony, summoned the tribes of the Northwest, principally the Sioux, to a gathering to make a final settlement. A Peace Commission, authorized the year before by Congress and President Andrew Johnson, met Sioux and Arapahoe at Fort Laramie. The Americans thought they were gaining a peaceful right-of-way for their railroads to pass through Indian territories; at least some of the Indians thought they were gaining their own land for their own use ("half of the present South Dakota that lies to the west of the Missouri River . . . and as a permanent and exclusive hunting ground the wilderness country beyond the North Platte and Republican rivers 'so long as the buffalo range there in numbers' ").[2] The white men were confident that the bison would soon be gone and that the Indians would then have to go on reservations. The army evacuated the three threatened forts, and the Bozeman Trail was closed.

The agreement did not hold, however. The railheads kept moving west; settlers kept drifting in, either for land or gold. When a large gold discovery was made in the part of western South Dakota supposed to have been given to the Indians, the brief integrity of the treaty was broken. A young colonel noted for his reckless gallantry, George Armstrong Custer (by courtesy general, an honorary brevet rank conferred in the late war), was ordered on an expedition into the Black Hills in 1874 to ascertain if the gold strike was true. Miners were already pouring in; the government made only a futile and consciously hypocritical effort to keep them from having authentic claims. Fighting was expected and planned for.

What people behind the frontier never realized was that most of the battles in the 1860s and early 1870s had not been and would not be formal military engagements, but a series of U.S. Army attacks upon unarmed, usually sleeping, Indian settlements in which women and children, as well as whatever men happened to be in the village, were killed. Frontier whites were frightened and horrified by small-scale but deadly attacks upon farmhouses and settlements, where rape, mutilation, and death followed. Americans in the settled East had understood nothing and wished to know nothing about the Indians' own sense of outrage at being pushed back again and again. The reaction of white people was as savage as that of the various pressured tribes.

On November 29, 1864, Colonel John M. Chivington of the Third Colorado Cavalry, its service due to expire in twenty-four hours, attacked the peaceful Cheyenne and Arapaho encampment of Chief Black Kettle at Sand Creek, Colorado. Under a misguided leadership, these troops carried out a senseless massacre of Indians who thought they were under the protection of white men. Before the fighting began, the colonel is reported to have said: "I want you to kill and scalp all, big and little, nits make lice."[3] An eyewitness (an interpreter) reported: "They were scalped, their brains knocked out; the men used their knives, ripped open women, clubbed little children, knocked them in the head with their guns, beat their brains out, mutilated their bodies in every sense of the word." In their history of the Indian wars, Robert M. Utley and Wilcomb E. Washburn stated that "two hundred Cheyennes, two thirds of them women and children, perished."[4] Black Kettle escaped, only to die not much later in another similar massacre. The soldiers paraded in Denver, showing off their scalps.

On January 23, 1870, searching for the Blackfeet village said to be holding a murderer wanted for an attack upon a ranch, Colonel Eugene M. Baker attacked the wrong village—a sick village, suffering from smallpox, and with its able-bodied men away, hunting meat for the winter. The soldiers attacked in a cold dawn and without warning. The chief, Heavy Runner, ran out of the village toward the soldiers and held up a paper of which he was proud, telling that he was a valued friend of the whites. He was shot down among the first. The teepees were fired into, and mostly women and children and infirm old men were killed. The shelters with all the village supplies were then burned, and the survivors were turned out into below-zero weather with no protection.

Such was the "war" that had been carried on. The commanding generals of these scattered outpost regiments, General William Tecumseh Sherman in Washington, D.C., and General Philip Henry Sheridan, the field commander in the West, had learned a certain kind of warfare, the first in marching through Georgia, the second in marching up and down the Shenandoah Valley. There they had learned well the effectiveness of subduing civilians. Utley, a historian of the Indian wars, wrote: "Both Sherman and

Sheridan believed in the effectiveness of total war against the entire enemy population" and were carrying out this policy in the West.[5] Although the ostensible American orders, issued to the various tribes by a newly formed Indian agency, were simply for them to gather on designated reservations, the spirit of enforcement was not civil or peaceful. Many of the Indians never heard of, or believed in if they did, the moral or legal weight of these commands. These orders had no legal force; the Indian Agency had no authority above or counter to the solemn treaties previously signed.

In 1876 John Bourke's general was to be the first of the commanders in the field to move against the Sioux and Cheyennes. The other two (General Alfred Terry in Fort Lincoln on the Missouri River to the east in Dakota, and Colonel John Gibbon with troops in two western Montana forts, Fort Ellis and Fort Shaw) were not yet ready to move. Crook was as usual prepared. He was ordered to make a preliminary move north from Fort Fetterman in central Wyoming. Therefore, on a cold first of March 1876, Bourke, with eyes and mind wide open to a new experience, was in a good position to see how things would work out in this strange northern territory. Crook's rather generalized orders were to search out and attack any likely, unready Indian campsite or village found in his path and give it a salutary lesson. This was to be a signal to the other scattered Sioux and Cheyenne encampments to heed the commands of the white men and move themselves forthwith into designated reservations. There was arrogance in the planning, as well as a lack of knowledge of the Indians' state of mind and newly gathered strength. What Crook accomplished in this first movement of the season was to stimulate the tribes to a unity and fierceness of purpose they had not had before.

Before he was ordered to move his operations north from Arizona, Crook had for the time being calmed the scene there and put the Indians to work rather peremptorily and dictatorially on the reservation, but at the same time he had sought out means for them to run their own show and to develop a way to make their own new kind of living (he had brought in sheep from California for a herd). He respected the Apaches and intended that they should remain on their own land. He hoped to keep out the corrupt Indian agents, or at least diminish their role.

Crook now moved north along the abandoned Bozeman Trail at the head of nine hundred men, ten companies of cavalry, two of infantry, as well as a wagontrain and a packtrain of mules, along with ambulances and white and Indian scouts. Crook thought mules were better than horses in difficult terrain and rode a fine mule. His packtrain men were highly professional. Crook took pride in them. He thought that his own devisement of carefully burnished supplementary supply aids and his strong reliance on scouts, mostly Indians, was superior to the customary way of carrying on war in the West. The tall, athletic general rode at the head of his troops with his gun across his pommel. However, the first days of the march sorely tried these finely tuned troops. The weather was bad. Bourke wrote in his diary about the situation when Crook's men had reached the Powder River. Snow was six inches deep and the wind was blowing.

> As we were without tents, we had nothing to do but grin and bear it. Some officers stretched blankets to the branches of trees. Others found a questionable shelter under the bluffs. One or two constructed nondescript habitations of twigs and grass, while General Crook and Colonel Stanton seized upon the abandoned den of a family of beavers which a sudden change in the bed of a stream had deprived of their home. To obtain water, holes of suitable dimensions were cut in the ice here found to be 18 inches thick. . . . Our men shared with their animals their own scanty allowances of blankets as the bad weather and poor rations have made our animals look gaunt and travel worn. Mustaches and beards were coated with long pendant icicles several inches long.[6]

When the scouts, who had gone ahead as secretly as they could, returned to say that a village did indeed lie ahead on the Powder River, the general magnanimously designated Colonel Joseph J. Reynolds to take a small body ahead to make the attack. Crook and the main army remained camped behind, while still farther back was the wagontrain. Bourke chose to go with Reynolds. Bourke candidly laid out the rationale of this kind of attack: "If a single one of these large villages could be surprised and destroyed in the depth of winter, the resulting loss of property would be so great that the enemy would suffer for years; their exposure to the bitter cold of the blizzards would break down any spirit, no matter how brave; their ponies would be so weak that they could not escape from an energetic pursuit, and the advantages would seem to be on the side of the troops."[7]

Writing of this attack years later, using his notes of the time, Bourke was honest about the emotions of the past. Initially the attack was a complete surprise, with an ordered line of horse soldiers running into and through the village, at a slow, measured pace at first, then faster and faster into a

wild gallop. "The fun had begun" (274). The riders skimmed right through
the encampment, shooting into tents and into people, and being in turn
shot at by the warriors, who had very quickly seized their weapons and
fought back desperately, aiming at horses and bringing down the riders in
a tangle. Despite the momentary exhilaration, the battle did not go as
planned. The Indian fighters gathered together most of the women and
children and retreated to a bluff above the village and began pouring down
arrows and gunfire on the troops milling about in the camp below.

Reynolds had divided his troops, and they did not all arrive at the same
time. Those on the scene, sending out patrols to combat the fire from the
bluff above, began to destroy everything that the Indians had left behind.
The grand purpose was destruction. They piled up supplies for great bonfires. They ravaged the tents of their poles and piled on the fires food and
furs and religious relics. Wrongly assuming that this was Crazy Horse's
village, Bourke wrote:

> Crazy Horse's village was bountifully provided with all that a savage could
> desire, and much besides that a white man would not disdain to class among
> the comforts of life. . . . There were many loose robes of buffalo, elk, bear,
> and beaver; many of these skins were of extra fine quality. Some of the buffalo
> robes were wondrously embroidered with porcupine quills and elaborately
> decorated with painted symbolism. . . . Every squaw and every buck was
> provided with a good-sized valise of tanned buffalo deer, elk, or pony hide,
> gaudily painted, and filled with fine clothes, those of the squaws being
> heavily embroidered with bead-work. Each family had similar trunks for
> carrying kitchen utensils and the various kinds of herbs that the plains'
> tribes prized so highly. There were war-bonnets, strikingly beautiful in
> appearance, formed of a head-band of red cloth which reached to the ground
> when the wearer was mounted. . . . Of the weight of dried and fresh buffalo
> meat and venison no adequate idea can be given; in three or four lodges I
> estimated that there were not less than one thousand pounds. As for ammu-
> nition, there was enough for a regiment. . . . One hundred and fifty saddles
> were given to the flames. (277–78)[8]

The lodges and their poles were added to the fires, and exploding poles
came down dangerously among the soldiers. The gunfire from the bluff
continued and became more dangerous. The Indians threatened to cut off
those who had gained the village. "At this moment private Schneider was

killed" (275). Already three men had been wounded, "one in the lower part of the lungs, one in the elbow-joint, and one in the collar-bone or upper part of the chest" (274).

After the destruction was completed, Reynolds gave a hasty order for pulling back, disgracing himself with his men, for he left his dead and wounded behind. They moved away as if in retreat and did not stop until they reached Lodgepole Creek, where they awaited the arrival of the general and his troops. Meantime, they were cold and hungry and without supplies and could only think of the meat and furs they had destroyed. The Indians harassed them continually and stole back from them the seven hundred ponies that they had captured. Bourke wrote: "No guard was set over the herd, and no attempt was made to protect it, and in consequence of this great neglect the Indians, who followed us during the night, had not the slightest trouble in recovering nearly all that originally belonged to them" (279). They were seen driving the ponies off, and no effort was made to follow them.

Crook was tight-lipped about what had happened. To give the Indians less excuse to hang on, he ordered killed the hundred ponies left. Fifty had their throats cut; fifty were shot.

> The throat-cutting was determined upon when the enemy began firing in upon the camp, and was the only means of killing the ponies without danger to our own people. It was pathetic to hear the dismal trumpeting (I can find no other word to express my meaning) of the dying creatures, as the breath of life rushed through severed windpipes. The Indians in the bluffs recognized the cry, and were aware of what we were doing, because with one yell of defiance and a parting volley, they left us alone for the rest of the night. . . . Steaks were cut from the slaughtered ponies and broiled in the ashes by the scouts; many of the officers and men imitated their example. (281)

Crook could do nothing but pull back all his troops, and, when they were settled, he brought court-martial charges against Reynolds and Noyes, another officer of the command. The Indians had escaped, the ponies had been lost, and his dead and wounded had been left behind, probably to be mutilated. What might not be remembered (and to history it has been largely forgotten), a small raid on a harmless village, should be recalled as the beginning of the summer's troubles. The Indians had fought better than had been expected, they had carried off their own dead and wounded, and they had saved most of their horses. The survivors of this small Cheyenne encampment struggled on to Crazy Horse's camp, then to Sitting Bull's, leaving dead women and babies in the snow. Their story gave added fire to the later actions of the chiefs who would direct what would become in the months to come the largest concerted action of Indians against American troops.

The larger consequences of this action could not be known at this time. Crook's men rested thankfully. They ate heartily again; they warmed their chilled bodies; they suffered amputations of frozen toes. But this rest was only preparation for the large action promised by the generals in the East. The signal came in early June, and three armies began to move toward what they thought would be an end to the impudence of these scattered savages: Crook from the South, Gibbon from the West, and Terry and Custer from the East. Bourke's part in this was once again as aide to Crook, and this time, in full spring weather, the movement north seemed very different from what they had undergone three months before. Now wild roses were blooming in all the creases of the prairies, and the heavy-headed grasses brushed their horses' flanks with pollen.

Somewhere in these large spaces between the armies were a number of loosely allied Sioux and Cheyennes, with a new sense of purpose as yet undetected by the army planners. The generals had constantly underrated the High Plains Indians and had considered them to be simply a large nuisance to the constructive opening of gold fields, the building of railroads, and the possible settling of white communities. These two peoples were very ignorant of each other. Many of the Indians who were soon to be part of the Custer fight had never seen a white person before and did not know what the green paper stuffed in the pockets of the dead cavalrymen was. (These men had recently been paid and had had no time to spend their money.)

To these wanderers on the wide plains, these Cheyennes and Sioux, there seemed still to be enough space for them, enough game to stock their camps, and a chance for the old life to go on. Sitting Bull consistently scorned calls to come into a reservation. Sitting Bull, of the Hunkpapa Sioux, and Crazy Horse, of the Oglalla Sioux, now allied, scorned submission or reconciliation. They did not believe in any of the series of promises the white men made. They had no notion of placing their land and lives into the hands of newcomers ignorant of a proper way of life between the sky and the earth and between the four sacred points of direction.

Two kinds of warriors and two kinds of life were to clash in this dry hot summer, meeting in a dire series of battles such as had not been known on the plains before. Crook and his aide took part in the first of these, the Battle of Rosebud; Custer and his men, in advance before Terry's army, were to take part in the second, the Battle of Little Bighorn. Because there was not good communication between Crook's command and Terry's command, between the parts of what should have been a concerted effort, there was no coordination of the divided army efforts. The Indian fighters were roughly a unified command under Sitting Bull and Crazy Horse. Therefore Custer, in advance of Terry, was to know nothing of the Battle of Rosebud fight and advanced overconfidently against unsuspected strength. After escaping from near disaster at Rosebud, Crook was to know nothing of the Battle of Little Bighorn until long after it was over, although it took place less than fifty miles from where he and his men rested after their battle.

A fateful history might not be recognized by those taking part in it. Advancing in pleasant weather on June 16, Bourke had the individual's view of a big confused event, and his writings convey something of that scene and time to the reader, making one see and understand what it was like at the moment. Crook's command had come upon the main body of the Sioux and Cheyennes on the bend of the Rosebud River and plunged straight ahead into what was to be the largest pitched battle between federal troops and Indian warriors so far. The tribes had been reinforced by Sitting Bull's calls for a gathering and by Crazy Horse's anger at what had recently happened to the encampment on the Powder River.

This was to be an all-day battle between well-matched and well-trained fighters on both sides. It was to be a close fight for the white men. Crook had to pull back without gaining any objective after the Indians, tired of fighting, pulled back first. It was claimed as a victory, but Crook was sensitive about this day for the rest of his life. In the mixed and confused seesaw of fighting, various units of cavalry were led almost into disaster several times in near ambushes. Once Crook's main force had a narrow escape from entrapment in a canyon, the Indians cleverly leading it into it by deceit about their concealed strength. Only Crook's Shoshone allies scented the danger and warned the commander in time. For at least part of the day, Bourke fought along with three or four other whites among the

Shoshones and came to appreciate their courage and resourcefulness as allies.

> I went in with this charge. . . . There was a headlong rush for about two hundred yards, which drove the enemy back in confusion; then was a sudden halt, and very many of the Shoshones jumped down from their ponies and began firing from the ground; the others who remained mounted threw themselves alongside of their horses' necks, so that there would be few good marks presented to the aim of the enemy. Then, in response to some signal or cry which, of course, I did not understand, we were off again, this time for good, and right into the midst of the hostiles, who had been halted by a steep hill directly in their front. Why we did not kill more of them than we did was because they were dressed so like our own Crows that even our Shoshones were afraid of mistakes, and in the confusion many of the Sioux and Cheyennes made their way down the face of bluffs unharmed. (312–13)

After the rigors of the Battle of Rosebud and the sense of having with little margin escaped from a disaster there, Bourke and the others of Crook's men must have welcomed rest at the base camp that the general designated. It seemed a peaceful spot blessed with good grass and a well-filled trout stream, with the highest peak of the Big Horn Mountains rising above them. Close to the general, Burke was doubtless aware of the worry in his commander's mind but, like a good soldier, left it to the general. He remembered this episode as a time when the isolated troops experienced a great relaxation of nerves and an enjoyment of the possible comfort of a good camp in a beautiful, mostly undisturbed setting. Small groups of Indians harassed them, and there was at first a tightening up of discipline and a rehearsal of maneuvers; overall, however, everyone began to enjoy himself. It was as if he had time to look about and appreciate this country of the Indians.

Contests were held daily to see who could catch the most fish from a stream where the trout seemed almost to give themselves up willingly to homemade hooks and grubbed-up and unlikely flies and worms. Wrote Bourke: "My notebooks about this time seem to be almost the chronicle of a sporting club" (321). The general did not fare very well at fishing one day, but he was forgiven, for he "saw bear tracks and followed them, bringing in a good-sized cinnamon, so it was agreed not to refer to his small number of trout" (322). Cavalry and foot soldiers exercised in moderation. Parties went out for elk and bison to roast on the campfires.

But there was plenty of leisure. Foursomes sat in front of tents and played whist.

On July 1, Crook sent out a search party of twenty men with Frank Gruard, a scout, to see if they could locate either Indians or troops. Instead the Indians found Crook's scouts and almost destroyed them. The little party returned to the base camp after two days of hiding, scrambling in fear. They were tired, hungry, and tattered, and two men were out of their heads. Their condition would seem to say that at this point the Indians masked the advance north. But when they returned, Crook was not in camp, but off on a pleasurable expedition with a small, choice party to try to climb the summit of the nearby Big Horns.

Ostensibly Crook's purpose was to look for movement on the plains, but the atmosphere was that of a party. The group included six officers and four newspaper correspondents on detachment with these troops, a mule-pack to carry supplies under the care of one of the skilled mule skinners. It was to be a strenuous and enjoyable four days in the mountain air, with fine views, snowbanks to play in, a mountain lake to bathe in, and companionable campfires and good roast game each night.

Reaching the top of Cloud Peak was exhilarating for Bourke: "I sat upon a snowbank, and with one hand wrote my notes and with the other plucked forget-me-nots or fought off the mosquitoes" (327). It may be imagined that in this escape Bourke might have had time to look before and after. He found himself in an alien but interesting world, and one worth trying to understand. He had got here by a roundabout route. Like the general, Bourke had had active service in the Civil War, but in quite different circumstances.

Eighteen years older than Bourke, George Crook, a West Point graduate, had already had army service before the war in the far West, in California and Oregon when those areas were very primitive. He had fought Indians and also come to like them, and he learned very early some of their survival ways. He disapproved with a kind of puritan conscience of the immoral treatment of the leftover tribes in these regions by the white men, whom he came to know there and on the whole despised. After wartime service, he rose to army prominence in the Southwest and became a brigadier general in 1873. His former enemies in Arizona, the Apache tribes, called him Gray Fox or Three Stars and on the whole liked him, or at least had respect for his word.

Crook's aide was also a West Point graduate, but under very different circumstances. In June 1876, taking his ease on a snowbank in the Big Horn Mountains, John Bourke was thirty years old, a young man with old experience already. He was the child of Irish Catholic immigrants in Pennsylvania. He had volunteered for service in the Union Army in the Fifteenth Pennsylvania Volunteer Cavalry in 1862, lying about his age, which was sixteen. He served as a private throughout the war, at places such as Stones River, where he won a Medal of Honor and never told how he earned it, Chickamaugua, Chattanooga, and Atlanta. It was only after the war was over that Bourke secured an appointment to West Point. He was commissioned a second lieutenant in 1869 in the Third Cavalry, and he arrived in the Southwest to begin fighting Indians (the Apaches) in 1870.

In June 1871, the then Lieutenant Colonel Crook arrived in this region to take command. He chose the handsome, intelligent Bourke as his aide. In his memoirs Bourke recorded all the ups and downs of Crook's generally successful career fighting, then governing, the Apaches (also fighting off what he thought was the baleful influence of the new Indian Agency). Bourke had one particularly terrible memory of those days when soldiers, having trapped in a cave an unyielding band, poured merciless gunfire into the opening, killing men, women, and children. "It was exactly like fighting with wild animals in a trap; the Apaches had made up their minds to die if relief did not reach them" (196).

So Bourke had known horrors in the Southwest before he came to the high Northern Plains. But he had served a general who did not scorn reconciliation and who had some sense of the worth of his Indian adversaries. Crook hoped for some kind of civilian and Americanized life for the tribes. Some of his ideas would prove premature or unrealistic, and his effort at reconciliation in the Southwest had already been countermanded by other officers who had succeeded him in Arizona.

In the summer of 1876, after having had some at least temporary success with the southwestern Indians (they would break out again after he left the Arizona command), Crook was up against unreconciled and unconquered Indians, a loose confederation led by gifted men, Sitting Bull as strategic planner, and Crazy Horse as field commander. They had brought together two of the branches of the Sioux, the Hunkpapa and the Oglalla, and they had the illusion that they might fend off this hated invasion into their unmarked and unplowed lands.

The little mountain-climbing expedition that Crook had engineered was the last happy event of the summer for him and his men. The remainder of the summer was grim indeed. Crook found out on July 10 that on June 25, even before he went off to Cloud Peak, the eastern portion of the "Grand pincers movement" under Lieutenant Colonel (by courtesy, General) Custer had met the same Sioux as those of the Battle of Rosebud. His portion of a badly divided force was destroyed, but the two other arms of his regiment—that is, the men under Reno and Benteen—sent off from him as part of a plan had survived, though badly mauled. The Sioux and Cheyennes had simply walked away after killing off the men whom Custer had led downhill and across stream into the much larger assembled gathering of Indians.

The bad news kept beating upon Bourke's general, day after day, beginning on July 10. On that day a message reached Crook's camp in a roundabout route from his commander, General Sheridan, telling this commander of the southern part of the pincers movement that Custer and his men had died. On July 12, three army men, tattered and exhausted, came into camp with General Terry's dispatches, giving Crook the same news. Within days some Crows, also telling the same story, arrived. Crook—no doubt alive to missed opportunities, but characteristically expressing outwardly no inner agony—had to wait and wait to move, under Sheridan's orders, for the arrival of a reinforcement of more troops from the south. So for the moment Crook and Terry and the third commander, Gibbon, missed whatever chance they might have had to round up scattering tribes who were moving away from troops and into the hills and prairies west and north of where the troops were. Neither Custer's rashness nor Crook's methodological efficiency prevailed against the Indians that summer. Yet it did not greatly matter in the long run. The outcome would be the same. The Indians had won the battles of 1876. They would lose the war.

Not knowing about the Indians' difficulties—small groups beaten in skirmishes, scattered tribes finding fewer and fewer bison, little groups always on the move—Crook's men waited into August before receiving the order to join General Terry. A joint sweep of the two forces netted very little. Then they separated again, Crook and his troops moving eastward toward the mining settlement of Deadwood, South Dakota, hoping to entrap Indian encampments on the way.

Good grass for the horses and mules was scarce. Then the rains turned the ground into mud. Troopers suffered from an accumulation of untreated ills: "neuralgia, rheumatism, malaria, and diarrhea," as Bourke was to remember. "Lieutenant Huntington was scarcely able to sit his horse, and

Lieutenant Bache had to be hauled in a 'travois' " (322ff.). They had not gathered enough food to carry on the march, and they chased down jack rabbits, tried to use alkaline water for coffee, and dug up patches of wild onions to make horse meat more tasty. For they were reduced to eating their own horses. However fond a trooper might be of his personal mount, he had to ride his horse until it dropped, then shoot it, and, if he had the appetite, eat it. At Slim Buttes they captured a village, then marched on toward Deadwood. At last nearing that white encampment, they saw coming out to them wagons full of food, and at last they ate, ending the "horse meat march."

Looking back at the summer, Bourke found he admired the allied Shoshones, with whom he had fought better than this ragtag population of white miners and hangers-on. In November Bourke was detailed to go on a raid with Colonel Ronald Mackenzie, an officer with a reputation somewhat similar to Custer's. This was once again an attack on a peaceful village and the destruction of it. This was a village that had peaceful inclinations, but the attack was merciless. Once again everything belonging to the Indians was burned in weather that was thirty degrees below zero. Bourke ascertained that fourteen babies froze to death in their mothers' arms in the retreat. Eventually this remnant of the Cheyennes (Dull Knife's village) came into a reservation.

This was the gradual, painful beginning of the end of the Indians' resistance. For a time Crazy Horse and Sitting Bull led their tribal followings beyond the reach of troops, Sitting Bull at last across the border into Canada, then, forced by hunger and the pressures put upon him by both nations, back again after years at last to a reservation. Never conquered, Crazy Horse was persuaded in 1877 at last to come in as he thought freely and proudly, and he was entrapped. Finding himself about to be put in a guardhouse instead of in a voluntary conference with the authorities, he resisted and was stabbed to death by a soldier's bayonet in the struggle. Sitting Bull lasted longer, even for one year away from the reservation taking part in the white man's world as a performer in Buffalo Bill's show. He was later killed by Indian guards on the reservation, surprised sleeping in his own cabin with his wife and, fighting back, shot down in the struggle and buried unceremoniously in a quicklimed box.

The year after the Battle of Little Bighorn also saw the great and poignant march of Joseph and Looking Glass and the other Nez Perces, riled beyond endurance by the invasion of their own ground, the Wallowa Valley. They also won all the skirmishes and battles, but lost in the end at the foot of the Bearpaw Mountains, not far from at least a temporary refuge in Canada. Shortly after Sitting Bull's death, American troops and Indians fought their last battle in the Northwest at Wounded Knee on December 29, 1890, again many of the Indian dead being women and children.

The world would be different for the general and his aide after this year of conflict on the Northern Plains. Crook would continue to climb the ladder of authority, finally attaining command of all the forces in the western fields. Yet he had been betrayed by the army more than once in what he regarded as most sacred, his word. He had called in Crazy Horse (and was not present when that chief was killed) with the promise of an eventual settlement in his own land. Crook thought this best for the Cheyennes. But the higher command overruled him, and it was only by a heroic effort that some of the Northern Cheyennes later were to escape from a hated reservation in an unhealthy part of Oklahoma and return to a portion of their own land in southeastern Montana. Crook was to be betrayed several years later even more flagrantly in a promise he had made to the Chiracahua Apaches after he had returned to active service in the Southwest. A people whom he respected and whom he thought could now live peacefully on their own land were gathered up and shipped on boxcars to Florida, then to Alabama, and at last to Oklahoma. Crook did not live to see a small remnant of them at last returned to their own region, but spent years fighting a battle for them.

After more active duty in the Southwest, in which his aide Bourke shared, when he succeeded in bringing Geronimo back peacefully from Mexico (and had this arrangement betrayed by others' contrary management), Crook settled comfortably into headquarters first in Omaha, then in Chicago. He astounded newspapermen by his open-door policy for questioners and by his informality. He dressed and spoke plainly, went to the theater occasionally, played poker with friends, and every year got away to the West for fishing or hunting trips.

What is most surprising is that this man, who had lived the regimented army life all his adult existence, became a public speaker for Indian rights. This behavior was not only unpopular but also considered eccentric and unpatriotic. Crook made little of the courage that this kind of action required but, in his stoic and somewhat limited tendency toward introspection, probably took no account of it at all. Martin F. Schmitt, who edited Crook's abbreviated autobiography, includes a quotation from the pamphlet

Letter from General Crook on Giving the Ballot to Indians. The general thought little of the arguments used against Indian enfranchisement: "I wish to say most emphatically that the American Indian is the intellectual peer of most, if not all, the various nationalities we have assimilated to our laws, customs, and language. He is fully able to protect himself, if the ballot be given, and the courts of law not closed to him."[9]

Crook accepted an invitation to come to speak in Boston on behalf of the Boston Indian Citizenship Committee in February 1887. He spoke several times in different locations in the city, among them the old South Church. An excerpt as reported in the Boston *Post* on February 28, 1887, gives the tone:

> The Indian is a human being. One question today on whose settlement depends the honor of the United States is, "How can we preserve him?" My answer is, "First, take the government of the Indians out of politics; second, let the laws of the Indians be the same as those of the whites; third, give the Indian the ballot." But we must not try to drive the Indians too fast in effecting these changes. We must not try to force him to take civilization immediately in its complete form, but under just laws, guaranteeing to Indians equal civil laws, the Indian question, a source of such dishonor to our country and of shame to true patriots, will soon be a thing of the past. [10]

Entertained by Edward Everett Hale and others of the Boston progressive elite, the general, feeling himself old (although he was only fifty-nine) and not quite well, recuperated by going fishing in Wisconsin: "In one day he caught 135 bass. 'I could have caught more but got ashamed.' "[11] Crook died of an overstrained heart three years later on March 21, 1890. The fighting years had been hard on him. He had carried on a particularly vigorous and unsuccessful fight to have his particular tribe of wronged Indians, the Chiracahua Apaches, returned to their western homeland. He, as well as Bourke, had visited them in their unhealthy southern detention and been greeted by them with tears and embraces. Crook had never quite achieved objectivity in viewing the Indians as a separate culture. He continued to think of his own culture as "civilization" and as a norm to which the Indians must aspire; yet he had liked them and admired them, as a direct result of the fighting years.

Bourke continued his army career, disappointed of promotion beyond the rank of captain, as an aide to Crook both in headquarters duty and again in the field in the Southwest in the campaign against Geronimo in the early 1880s. In the Omaha headquarters Bourke exercised his considerable social charm in the lively pioneer life of that city. He happily married Mary Horbach and had an emotional headquarters of his own to which he could return from duties elsewhere.

Yet, after the end of most of the Indian fighting, Bourke found that an easeful life did not suit him in the new world. He was wistful about the pleasures and luxuries he missed when he had been cold and hungry on the banks of the Powder River. He never settled down into slothful self-content. Nor did he like the kinds of energies that seemed to hum and crackle in the civilian world, which had taken on new activities while he was away. It was a world that he had not made and in which he did not feel at home. He thought the country had been brought to "a sad state," and he disliked those he thought were riding high—"bum politicians, shyster lawyers, pudding-headed presidents, vacuous-minded Cabinet Officers, Shylock stockbrokers, watered Rail Road deventures, Anglo-maniacs and professional agitators who go around among working men inciting them to unnecessary strikes." [12]

Bourke's interest in Indian ways, habits, and artifacts, as well as the companionship he had felt for such riding companions as the Shoshone scouts, transformed him into a person with a new purpose. He who had seen and enumerated the beautiful things that his fellow soldiers in the Reynolds fight had piled up and burned—decorated robes and hides, quilled and beaded clothes, headdresses, pipes, and weapons—now sought to save and to understand such objects. With the tolerance of his old commander, Crook, and with permission gained from General Sheridan, Bourke attained for a number of years a detached command and the freedom to seek out the customs and the works of Indian culture. He was allowed helpers and modest transport and the backing of the Smithsonian Institution in Washington, D.C., and began traveling all over the Northwest, then mainly the Southwest, searching for relics of this other life which had touched his own.

A full account of this remarkable transformation of the Indian fighter into one of the new breed of early ethnologists in the United States is told in *Paper Medicine Man* by his biographer Joseph C. Porter. Here, one might make a romance of contrasts. The West had used up the intense young life of Bourke, and he found that that particular West was dead. He was not dead, however, and he made another short and intense life out of latent interests that had teased him during his years of Indian fighting.

Bourke found he needed to tell the story of his army years and did so with zest, using diary entries of the times of the harsh campaigns. His book, *On the Border with Crook,* embodies the emotions of the time. It was published in 1891, the year after Crook's death. Before and more generally after his belated active engagements as an aide to Crook, he busied himself in studying the people he had fought. The same year as the publication of this book, he also published a writing that had grown out of a new and growing interest, a purer kind of study, an impulse of scholarship and science. This was his monograph, *Scatalogic Rites of All Nations.* This study would have a curious and interesting influence later. In 1913, seventeen years after Bourke's death in 1896, Sigmund Freud in Vienna would publish with his own introduction a new edition of this work. Freud spoke of Bourke's pioneer study admiringly: "It is not merely a courageous undertaking, but one of great service, to make this work available to German readers."[13] Finding nothing human alien to himself, Freud found help in this objective study of the Indians' frank and obsessive expression of the excremental and obscene elements in their own human nature.

During these crowded years when Bourke became a regular contributor to scholarly journals, most of his researches would be with various southwestern Indians, but some of his earliest ventures were in 1881 in the Northwest. He went to Fort Hall, which was already a relic of American history, and saw those walls that only forty-seven years before young Osborne Russell had helped construct. The Bannock and Shoshones remembered Bourke and treated him as a friend. He was allowed close scrutiny of their way of life and added his opinion to an argument about Indian clan life.

Bourke agreed with Hubert Howe Bancoft that Lewis Henry Morgan was wrong in attributing to these northwestern Indians the same kind of tight tribal organization as he had seen among the eastern Iroquois. A little later he observed an Oglalla Sioux sun dance with the disinterested passion of a scientist. He entered even more intimately years later into Apache ceremonies. Stripped to his underpants, he danced bemusedly alongside half-naked fighting men, experiencing the ritual from the inside, in a purification rite in a sweat lodge. He was characteristically both fascinated and amused by his experience. "I sang: that is I joined in the chorus and wasn't put out, as a more critical or less kind-hearted audience would have insisted upon doing."[14] He vividly described the heat and the sweat and the tangle of arms and legs inside the lodge and the relief of rushing out into the air and dipping one's body in the nearby stream. He was combining the two sides of ethnological research, that of fieldwork and that of library work and talk and correspondence with colleagues, all this crammed into an event-filled time.

When detached from Crook's occasional commands, Bourke had a comfortable headquarters in Washington, all the resources of the growing Smithsonian Institution, and the sponsorship of heavyweight patrons such as John Wesley Powell and Francis Parkman. Bourke read all the current masters of anthropology, a new science in the making, and took on a belief in a stage-by-stage growth of every culture from primitivism to civilization, eschewing any racial or cultural prejudice, but in the end opting for a belief in the desirability of the growth of any primitive culture in the direction his own white northern European or North American kind of civilization. Yet his immediate reactions and sympathies toward the Indians contradicted these beliefs. Bourke also seconded his general's public speaking out for Indian rights. He was still hoping for a raise in rank and so was somewhat fearful of expressing himself too publicly.

After Crook's death, Bourke no longer had a protector in the army. There was jealousy of him and his supposedly easy duty. He was pulled out of his detached service abruptly and sent to Texas to command a border post. There, performing a kind of duty for which he was not suited, he was both inept and unhappy. Bourke died young, at forty-nine, on June 8, 1896, as Porter reports, "of an abdominal aorta which had eroded and destroyed three vertebrae."[15] Porter pronounced an end in tune with Bourke's nature: "In keeping with his own request, he was buried without services or ceremony at Arlington National Cemetery."

EIGHT

Survivors: Pretty-Shield
and Nannie Alderson

An elderly Indian woman living on the Crow Reservation in southeastern Montana, bent and wasted by time, yet constitutionally cheerful, told her story to a sympathetic white listener, Frank B. Linderman, in the 1930s. A spare, hard-used, but undiminished and mannerly white woman told the story of her life to a sympathetic writer, Helena Huntington Smith, in the 1940s on a ranch near Sheridan, Wyoming. The tellers of these life stories did not know each other; it would have been impossible. Yet their lives slipped past each other under the same sky, upon the same ground. To a later viewer, taking the longer and the larger look, it might seem that these two lives—upon both of whom life pressed down hard—marked a transition, the passing of one era, the beginning of another. The two writers, transcribers of these lives, suppressed biases and sometimes preserved the words, and at least the honest attitudes, of the two different existences, an Indian woman who remembered the tribal life, a white woman who was part of the beginning of ranching life. Linderman, himself a part of an ever-changing West, had written about or transcribed other Indian lives, most notably that of Plenty-Coups, the Crow chief. Smith had, before this, acted as the transcriber and shaper of E. C. ("Teddy Blue") Abbott's story of the last open range, *We Pointed Them North*.

Linderman introduces Pretty-Shield as a revered medicine woman of her people, the Crows or Absarokas of southeastern Montana, occupying a shack and caring for numerous grandchildren, her two daughters having died, and her husband, who had been a Crow warrior, long dead. The writer had had great difficulty before in finding a Native American woman who would talk about herself. Pretty-Shield was unusual, not only willing, but eager, to talk. She immediately conveyed to him her willingness through an interpreter friend, another elderly Indian woman who spoke English. Linderman saw at once in her a remarkable youthfulness and resiliency despite the harsh circumstances of her everyday life. She was full of the past and sharp about the present and very quickly established an easy relationship with this white man, whom she soon called Sign-talker because he understood and spoke the sign language that gave shadings and subtleties to their communication.

The rancher's widow whose life might be juxtaposed to Pretty-Shield's had reached a kind of safe haven as an older woman, living with a capable daughter who with her husband ran a dude ranch for visitors to the West, already a tourist attraction. Nannie Alderson keenly remembered the short-lived joys and long-lived hardships of her early life in the West where she came as a bride.

A few years apart, in their younger years the women had visited the scene of the death of Custer and his men. Pretty-Shield had been taken by her husband, Goes-Ahead, to see a battle site that had acute memories for him. He had been one of Custer's Crow scouts. He retold to her how he and the other scouts had warned the determined soldier chief that there were too many Sioux and Cheyennes massed below along the small river and that he would fail. Their campfires had seemed endless to the scouts who had reconnoitered the scene before the white soldiers had arrived at the top of the bluff opposite. The Indian scouts had been ignored or, rather, scorned, and Goes-Ahead had stayed in the advance long enough to see Custer fall in the first charge across the river. When he and the other scouts saw the futility of it all, he had got away with some difficulty, to live and tell the tale.

Pretty-Shield's vivid memories of her husband's story, filtered through time and the Indian opinion of the event, contained, Linderman thought, much truth left out of the myth-making version that for many years white people had believed. As an older woman, she was eager, curious, interested still, and understood clearly the importance of her memories.

With a strong sense of fate, these scouts had felt frustration at Custer's stubborn stand: "But Son-of-the-Morning-Star was going to his death, and did not know it. He was like a feather blown by the wind, and *had* to go."[1] Yet Pretty-Shield, of a tribe that had been allied with white men, would not say everything condemning of the dead man. "He would not listen. . . . And he was brave, yes, he was a brave man." The event had reverberated through the years in her mind. It was an event as momentous to the Crows and the other Indians as Troy had been to the Greeks and Trojans, and it would take on similar epic proportions in the re-telling.

Custer's story was something quite different for the young wife of a rancher, Walter Alderson, in this country cleared of Indian dangers by the battles and skirmishes that had followed Custer's defeat and death. On a pleasant afternoon excursion out of Crow headquarters, where Nannie and her family were staying as guests of the superintendent, the young doctor of the reservation took Nannie to see what was left of the famous nearby battle scene. They were simply visitors, tourists in the later designation, coming to see a place where something important had once taken place. The companionable doctor

> enjoyed the country and would take the ladies driving almost every after-
> noon. It was late summer and the days were beautiful. No matter where
> we went on our drives, we would always wind up at the scene of Custer's
> last stand, above the Little Big Horn. There was a wonderful view up there,
> with the Big Horn mountains to the southwest and a long, low ridge to
> the west; and as we looked over the valley where the Sioux camp had been,
> we could almost see Custer's blue-coated troopers marching over the hills,
> on that terrible June morning.[2]

Nannie said that the dead men had been hastily buried in shallow graves and were later to be properly interred. "But at the time I visited the scene, thirteen years after the battle, the bones had not been removed. The rains had washed them and the coyotes disturbed them, and in many places they were lying on the top of the ground, all scattered about. I picked up a little bone from a hand one day." Two of the men from Pretty-Shield's village had not returned from this battle, and the "people mourned, crying for their dead, and for Son-of-the-Morning-Star, and his blue soldiers, who had so foolishly died."[3]

For Pretty-Shield, this looking back at the past of her people had seemed to signal a closing down of any way toward freedom, spontaneity, opportunity, purpose. For Nannie Alderson, it was invigorating to contrast her and Walter's present life with that momentary defeat in the past; life was an opening up—of opportunity and freedom—despite everyday hardships and difficulties of ranch life in this harsh land. In the two stories, set down side by side, later readers may see that Custer's fall was a painful hinge between one way of life and another.

It is not possible to make an exact correspondence or contrast between them, yet there is a poignancy in the differences in their younger years. Pretty-Shield's childhood was a well-nurtured happiness; Nannie's was a painful sequestration from natural well-being from which she flung herself away in going to the West when she married.

Born in Union, West Virginia, on September 14, 1860, Nannie was the child of a lawyer, Hugh Tiffany, who died at twenty-seven, a captain in the Confederate Army, killed in the stunning southern victory at First Manassas. In June 1864, Nannie's mother remarried: "I remember my colored nurse taking me down into the kitchen where old Uncle Caesar was getting the wedding breakfast ready."[4] The war ended in a long drawn-out aftermath of hard times, regret, and emotional intransigence. Yet Nannie's circumstances were not those of physical or financial hardship. Perhaps the appurtenances were merely leftovers, but she was "bred up to silver and old mohogany, pretty clothes, servants and leisure,"[5] as her recorder wrote. Yet hers was not a happy childhood. She was handed over to her grandmother for most of the year and was allowed to visit her mother's household only in summers. She thought, whether true or not, that her mother, finding her not pretty, was disappointed in her. She went to a school for girls who "were taught a smattering of music and French and other polite subjects, but not much of any of them."[6] But there was fun in roaming the woods with other children, "gathering berries or chestnuts—my stepsister Betty and I, and several pickaninnies."

Something of importance happened to Nannie when she was sixteen. She was sent to Kansas for the summer to stay with the sister of her father, Elizabeth Tiffany Symms, who, with her husband, had "pioneered" on this western border in the 1850s. Nannie remained with her aunt from September until June and was readily "infatuated" with the West.

> What an experience that was! Kansas then was the west. I felt that the very air there was easier to breathe. In Union you had to have your pedigree with you to be accepted anywhere, but in Atchison it didn't matter a bit who your ancestors were or what you did for a living; if you were nice

you were nice. . . . What impressed me most was the fact that a girl could
work in an office or a store, yet that wouldn't keep her from being invited
to the nicest homes or marrying one of the nicest boys. This freedom to
work seemed to me a wonderful thing.[7]

Nannie came again to Atchison the next year and remained for four years,
which changed her life.

In Atchison, Nannie became acquainted with a Baptist minister's family,
the Aldersons, the father having come to Kansas as an abolitionist. She
heard the story of one of their sons, Walter, who had revolted against a
strict upbringing and at thirteen had run away to Texas. At twenty-two he
surprised his family by turning up. He told cheerful tales of dish-washing,
stagecoaching, horse racing, and cow-punching. Once Nannie and Walter
found themselves sitting up together at night over his father's sickbed.
Walter shared with Nannie Tiffany his resolve to go in with a partner, Joe
Zook, and take up land in Montana for cattle raising. He asked Nannie
if she would go with him, and she replied, apparently with no hesita-
tion, that she would. They returned to West Virginia for the wedding on
April 4, 1883. Then, traveling by the new railroad line to Miles City, they
set out across the plains toward Walter's ranch site. Recently slaughtered
bison littered the way toward the juncture of Lame Deer and Rosebud, only
a few years after General Crook's hard-fought battle with the Sioux near
this spot. Their four-room log house, a proud one for the time and place,
was going up. Nannie brought few domestic accomplishments to it. A
friend in West Virginia had given her lessons in making plain underclothes.
She had had another lesson in the esoteric art of making hot rolls, but not
much else about cooking. Yet she faced this lonely life with youthful high
spirits.

In the same sweep of the broad horizon another very different life was
being lived out. Born in 1858, or a year or two earlier, Pretty-Shield had
grown up in the all-encompassing arms of the tribe. It had been an almost
unconscious growing into who and what one was. She looked back on her
childhood as a time of a great deal of playfulness. She had not seen a white
man until she was six years old, and these were three unthreatening, wandering fur trappers. It was these early days that Pretty-Shield wished to talk
about with her white questioner. He discerned early that it was going to
be very difficult for her to talk about the days and years after the tribe's

confinement to a reservation. The records of the agency said she was seventy-four years old, but she was eager and forward in her talk and manner. She said right out what she thought and felt. "We were a happy people when I came onto this world, Sign-talker. There was plenty to eat, and we could laugh. Now all this is changed."[8]

Fending off a begging grandson by digging out of her pocket a silver dollar and giving it to him, she said: "I wonder how my grandchildren will turn out. . . . They have only me, an old woman to guide them, and plenty of others to lead them into bad ways." She told her questioner: "One of my grand-daughters ran off to a dance with a bad young man . . . I went after her." "I felt ashamed of striking my grandchild. I am trying to live a life that I do not understand." But she added later: "I have never let myself hate the white man. . . . But he changed everything for us" (239).

What she remembered best of her childhood was the fun she had had in growing up in what seemed a secure community. Perhaps she colored the past generously out of a pinched and bleak old age, but her recollective emotions seemed true. After a day's talk with her interlocutor (they met and talked many days), she went home from the schoolroom, where the interviews took place, to "a bare shack where she and nine grandchildren slept upon the floor" (39). It was the freedom she remembered, a child's world unfettered even in the middle of an ordered society that had ceremonies and customs for every occasion. Warming to Linderman's easy manners, and the ease with which her friend Goes-together interpreted, and with the white man's use of sign language, she told him more and more of her close-held memories.

Pretty-Shield and her childhood friends, mostly little girls of her own age, played at games that were imitations of grownups' serious occupations. They made little teepees in imitation of the real ones. They constructed tiny travois on which to haul play goods. They conducted play sun dances without any sense of sacrilege. They also in small ways helped in all the women's tasks, including gathering berries and digging roots, when needed. Yet they also wandered off from set tasks to make up games to play, slide down banks, swim, and pretend all sorts of things. She retold sayings, songs, and beliefs of this childhood, making come alive for Linderman a world in touch with all the animal creatures of the plains and a spirit world that was close at hand and deeply believed in. Often a "person," as she said, would appear to someone to lead him or her either the wrong way or the right way. And these "persons" were as real to her as her playmates, as the older people of the village, and as the animals who lived in her world with great intimacy.

"The antelope are a strange people" (114), Pretty-Shield confided as with intimate knowledge, then told a tale of antelope who were not really antelope leading some young Crow girls astray. She spoke intimately of the chickadee as a remarkable little bird that tells by its song when winter is coming: "Ahhh, Ahh! The chickadee is big medicine, Sign-talker. . . . Do you know him well?" (152). Linderman had to admit to himself that he did not know the chickadee as this woman did with such faith. She told him that the ant people were her particular guides and friends. They had given her the names for her children and grandchildren, "and even now the ants help me. I listen to them always. They are my medicine, these busy, powerful little people, the ants" (166).

Pretty-Shield was given away by her mother (as perhaps Nannie Tiffany was by hers), but she remembered no ill effects, so closely sheltered had she been by ties of kinship in the community. The Lakota (Sioux) had killed the husband and two little girls of Pretty-Shield's maternal aunt. So, Pretty-Shield's mother, a Mountain Crow, generously gave the three-year-old child to this sister, Strikes-with-an-Axe, a River Crow. "This separation from my mother and my sisters was in fact not a very real one, because all the Crows came together often" (21). She thought she was probably happier in her aunt's lodge than she might have been in her mother's, although she was at first too young to help her. She recalled a reunion of the two clans. "It was springtime. A crier, on a beautiful bay horse, rode through the big village telling the people to get ready to move to the mountains. . . . How I loved to move, especially when the clans were going to meet at some selected place, always a beautiful one" (21).

In the midst of their play, she and some of her companions had a mishap. That was the time they lost the baby! So Pretty-Shield found a story to tell Sign-talker, and she filled the telling with the childish terror that she had felt that day. The village was moving in berry time. Pretty-Shield and several of her friends were lingering behind the end of the general movement of the tribe and playing carelessly along the way. They went swimming in a creek and while there spoke to a woman trying to catch up. She had stopped to water her two horses, her own riding horse and a packhorse on which she had placed her two-year-old baby girl, very tempting to the band of half-grown, thoughtless girls who liked to play mother, better with a

live baby than with a doll. Pretty-Shield offered for them to take care of
the baby so that the mother could go on ahead and catch up quickly as
she seemed to want to do, promising elaborate care of their charge. They
fussed over the baby at first, taking turns with it, then somehow in one
of their races they forgot her. Pretty-Shield had tied the packhorse to her
own and had been dragging it along helter-skelter in the game. "When I
suddenly remembered, and looked back at the pack, the baby wasn't there!
. . . Sign-talker, I cannot make you know how quickly my heart fell to
the ground, and how loudly I cried out, 'Stop! Stop! We have lost the
baby!' "[9] Worse, it was getting dark, and, not too far off, a broad band of
bison was moving across their path, between them and the camp ahead.

The girls hunted in panic along the ground the way they had come,
fear filling them not only for the lost baby but also for themselves, as the
herd moved slowly closer and closer. Then, providentially, a small group
of young hunters, out to secure bison calves for the evening meal, came
dashing over a rise. They laughed at the girls and teased them about the
enormity of their deed, but scattered to look for the baby. At last they
could be seen gathered on a hilltop, sitting their horses in a circle, looking
at something on the ground. The cruel young men made a joke of it and
let the girls running toward them think something terrible had happened.
Arrived at the hilltop, Pretty-Shield saw a peacefully sleeping baby on the
ground, unhurt and now safe. Pretty-Shield picked up the baby and, evad-
ing the bison, attained the camp after dark, to face recriminations from
the outside and feelings of guilt from the inside.

Recalled to the present from that past, Pretty-Shield said that the baby,
grown up, had died, but that her own grandchildren were "still with us."
She added: "I hope that I can save my grandchildren. But times have
changed so fast that they have left me behind. I do not understand these
times. I am walking in the dark" (70).

When Linderman asked Pretty-Shield about the way a Crow woman
matured, she answered out of a comfortableness with the customs of the
tribe. No, one did not love before marriage; love came after marriage, and
she affirmed that in her case it had. He asked her about child-bearing, and
Pretty-Shield was matter-of-fact. "Crow women do not lie down when their
babies are born" (146). She went on to describe with graphic simplicity
the process of birth and the aftercare of mother and child.

Pretty-Shield would not, or could not, talk about the daily lives of her
people after they were penned in reservations. She was even-handed and

did not altogether blame the whites. She told how in the old days they could stand the cold and quickly recover. "Now my people wear gloves, and too many clothes. We are soft as mud" (84). She implied that the softness was moral as well as physical. She fiercely asserted her own identity. "I do not hate *anybody,* not even the white man. I have never let myself hate the white man, because I knew that this would only make things worse for me. But he changed everything for us, did many bad deeds before we got used to him" (249–50). She spoke briefly about wanton killings by the white man, of hunger coming, of her people beginning to drink the white man's whiskey. (Crows had earlier refused to do this, unlike many other tribes.) "Our wise ones became fools, and drank the white man's whisky. But what else was there for us to do?" (251).

Everything bad seemed to find its meaning for Pretty-Shield in what she had seen of the death of the bison: "Ahh, my heart fell down when I began to see dead buffalo scattered all over our beautiful country, killed and skinned, and left to rot by white men, many, many hundreds of buffalo. The first I saw of this was in the Judith basin. The whole country there smelled of rotting meat. Even the flowers could not put down the bad smell. Our hearts were like stone" (250).

It was going to be hard also for the white newcomers. On the two-day trip across the rough plains south of Miles City, making their way toward the promised land of their new ranch, Walter and Nannie had seen and smelled dead bison, but these sensations aroused perhaps some pity but more curiosity—a sight as of some happening of nature. During the night stop halfway home, they stayed in a "road ranch," where in the next room were fifteen men, all of them vibrant, as the young newly married couple were, with hope for the future. She recalled: "They were all young, nearly all seemed to be Easterners, and they were all going into the cattle business. . . . Everyone, it seemed, was making fabulous sums of money or was about to make them; no one thought of losses; and for the next year my husband and I were to breathe that air of optimism and share all those rose-colored expectations."[10]

Even the prospect of their rough-hewn log house did not daunt Nannie when she arrived at it. It was larger than most log houses of that place and time, and it looked to be susceptible to improvements. She told Smith that "we didn't mind the hard things because we didn't expect them to last. Montana in the early eighties was booming . . . a feverish optimism possessed all of us. . . . It all looked so easy; the cows would have calves; and two years from now their calves would have calves, and we could figure it all out with a pencil and paper how in no time at all we'd all be cattle kings" (54–55).

Nannie took into the house the young cowpunchers who worked for her husband and his partner, Joe Zook, and she found them unbelievably polite and kind and trustworthy. Gamely, she went horseback riding, although her clothes were all wrong and dragged against her legs. She even tried to join in an early roundup. "In 1883 we were all very young. . . . If we were empire builders we didn't feel like it or act the part. We made a game of everything" (52). She breathed the air of this new land gratefully. "Hardships, during these months, were far from being first in my thoughts. There was so much that wasn't hard. The ranch at Lame Deer was in a wide valley watered by a lovely little creek, between pine-studded hills. Our front door looked out upon a particularly symmetrical hill with one pine tree on it" (45).

Nannie soon found, however, that the West was easier on men, harsh as their lives were, than on unprepared women. She remembered that she made many ludicrous mistakes. She tried to wash clothes in alkali water. She attempted to cook with little understanding of the proper ingredients for biscuits. She shored up her pride in the midst of domestic failures by caressing the old silver and china she had brought with her from West Virginia. She found she had to invent new ways of doing things with no store near at hand. Her daily work was drudgery, but she looked out her door at the pine on the hill and often walked down to the newly built corral to watch the men breaking the wild broncos that they needed for their daily work. "I would leave the dishes standing in the kitchen and run down and watch, sometimes for hours. My husband always rode the ones that bucked the hardest" (55).

The house from whose door Nannie watched the goings-on in the corral was a source of quiet pride to her. There was no such house in all that wide area of scattered ranches. It had four rooms, real floorboards, and bookshelves for her father's books. "On the walls, which were lined inside with muslin and papered with a flowered paper, hung two lovely etchings and old-fashioned portraits of Mr. Alderson's parents. My dear grandmother's silver candlesticks stood on the stone mantel" (72).

Things happened as if by a deliberate cruelty of fate, as well as to prove to the newcomers that the land was stronger than they were. Nannie had gone to Miles City to have her first baby, Mabel, and stayed for a time in cramped quarters with an uncongenial couple. At the time of the birth, Walter had come from the ranch to be with her, and he received a telegram saying: "Indians have burned your house. Come immediately with sheriff and posse" (99). So Nannie brought her first child home to ruin.

Filled with a stupid mischief, a white ranch hand had shot at an Indian camped nearby and grazed his head. The Cheyennes revenged themselves in an orgy of fury by burning down the house, carting away all movables, pulling up and burning even the fence posts, and shooting their dog. Their careless hand, Hal, had left the country as a fugitive. Silver and china and pictures were gone, so now they had no tangible traces of the past. The Aldersons moved to another location, then to another, and another, but never had a house as good as their first one. They had other accidents with Indians. One time a cowboy shot an Indian through the arm, but in this case Walter tended to the man's wound and befriended him. An older dispossessed Indian adopted the Aldersons as his family and helped Nannie look after the children, who tended to wander freely into the prairies and coulees, already more at home here than their parents were.

Nannie had three more children, two more girls and a boy. Her second child was born back home in West Virginia, but the two last ones were born in spare and even dangerously deprived circumstances on the ranch, with only the chancy help of a nearby neighbor as midwife. Nannie also had a miscarriage when alone except for the ranch hands who tiptoed around her in embarrassed carefulness. Life did not, after all, get easier. It got harder.

As the years went by, the benign aspect of the new life was shadowed. Nannie was not always exempt from fear when strangers came by. Alone in the house one day, Nannie fed a morose stranger with some trepidation and had a gun strapped to her waist under her apron. Homelier evils afflicted the hospitable Aldersons. Sometimes casual visitors—cowboys who asked for a bed for the night, Indians when they arrived at the door hungry and cold in winter—left behind unwelcome nuisances. Nannie struggled then to rid the house of lice and bedbugs. In the beautiful isolation of their ranches, she neglected her teeth and suffered from toothaches. She knew she did not have the proper clothes for her children and made makeshift garments out of sacks.

Nature itself seemed to be unfair to them after years of endurance and hard work. Walter shared with the other cattlemen of the region a great disaster in the terrible winter of 1886–87, when drought, then merciless storms and long-enduring below-zero freezes, paralyzed this new business upon the overgrazed plains. (This was the year the cowhand Russell drew a postcard picture of a starving calf.) Cattle died by the tens of thousands, and in spring their stinking carcasses were in windrows against the new fences. Walter had been prudent in his management and had weaned his calves and fed them by hand the fall before, and more of his survived than those on neighboring ranches.

When the hard times of the early 1890s of the nation spread to the West, even prudence and good management could not save the Aldersons' ranch. However, Nannie was to recall this time of growing difficulties as a fortunate one for her children. They were to remember a "happy childhood," as their mother recalled almost wonderingly. "They had more freedom than many modern children whose mothers know more of psychology than I did. And children thrive on freedom. Most of the time they were outdoors and away from me, living and learning for themselves. For hours they roamed at will out of the range of 'don'ts' " (170). The land itself gave these children something of the same sense of kinship as Pretty-Shield and her friends had had before.

It would be difficult for Walter Alderson and his generation of ambitious and hard-working cattlemen to realize that this was the beginning of the end of their great cattle kingdom in eastern Montana. This occupation would have to be transferred elsewhere to less hard-used range land, and the next episode of western use of this land would be wheat-growing.

While her children were becoming native to the place, Nannie had never quite resolved her feelings about the Indians who lived here. She came to like individual Crows or Cheyennes who showed personal attachments to her husband or children, but she stiffened, as others of the pioneer generation did, into a not very generous or imaginative view. She saw these strangers coming to her door hungry or cold, and she fed or sheltered them, but she also had a lingering fear of them, or sometimes a contempt of what seemed their weaknesses. Her first thought was: "How . . . could anyone fear such poor, miserable creatures?" (47). Chief Two Moons, who, as Nannie thought to herself, had, only a few years before, taken part "in chopping Custer's Command to pieces," became a regular visitor. "Now he was just an old beggar who came around to our house asking for coffee. He was absurd and squalid-looking, with his dirty cotton shirt turned wrong side out, and his white man's pants with the seat cut out, which he wore like a pair of leggings over a breech clout." But Two Moons had his own thoughts, as well as humor. He asked Walter how many horses he would take for his wife. It was a kind of mutually appreciated joke between the two men. Nannie also disapproved of white men who took Indian wives. "They would come and live off you if they could, and any white man, who fell a victim to the charms of a black-eyed Indian girl, was sure to have a huge tribe to support forever after" (185).

Yet Nannie could have moments of admiration, in which she did justice to individuals. She saw in the character of the Cheyenne chief Little Wolf some greatness, although his wife "did our washing." "He was a pathetic figure of a deposed king, but there was a dignity about him, despite his poverty, that was touching. I was always convinced that despite his reputation as a chief who had bitterly fought the government, he had in him to be a good American if only the 'Great Father' could have been made aware of his great heart and his capacity to serve" (186). Little Wolf and Walter were friends and had eloquent and complicated conversations in sign language.

Enduring for a time, Walter, like many others, had at last to give up cattle ranching. Bad weather, as well as the drying up not only of grass but also of funds from banks, failing here in the West as they were all over the country, persuaded him to make a necessary if bitter change. He thought he might raise horses in a small way; he had always had a talent with them. He and Joe Zook amicably broke their business ties as ranchers and decided to try for opportunities in Miles City. Walter Alderson became deputy county assessor under Zook as county assessor. In some ways the move was a relief to Nannie, who knew that her children needed better schooling than she had been able to give them. Mabel, the oldest child, was now ten.

Schooling could be had, and new and stimulating life for the children, but a full-time job for the dispossessed rancher was not so easy. Miles City turned out to be "a scene of grave disappointments" for Walter (255). He invested in a small local coal mine, but had bad luck with those who went in with him. Nothing was gained. However, Zook had appointed him as his deputy, and things looked up. Walter bought a horse on which to go about this travels as deputy tax assessor. It was ironic that this horseman, who got along so well with horses, should be killed by his new horse, Seven Dollars (the amount he had been lucky enough to pay for a serviceable mount). Alone in the stable, caught between two horses savagely fighting each other, Walter was kicked in his head, which fractured. He was found face down and unconscious on the floor of the stable, and his wife was called. He lived six days, never getting better, and died on March 18, 1895, twelve years after his marriage in West Virginia to the twenty-three-year-old Nannie Tiffany. Now at thirty-five, with four children, and no income, Nannie set about supporting herself and her children in the West still new and, at this time, the mid-1890s, suffering from the effects of a national as well as regional bout of hard times.

Nannie set about doing what she could. She kept a boarding house in Miles City. She catered food. She moved back to the southeastern part of the state, which seemed like home to her, and became postmistress in the little town of Birney. She became a kind of institution there, her house a center for gatherings of the informal, western kind. She was able to buy and keep a piano in her log house, and it became the center of friendship of the Birney area.

When her West Virginia mother learned of the rough informality of some of these gatherings, she was scandalized. But Nannie now belonged to this culture and understood it. Her son, Walter, who had herded cattle and broken wild horses since he was twelve, grew up a rancher. Here Nannie came to settle in her spare, firm older years. It was here that her interviewer found her and got from her the story of a life that was not so unusual in this first generation of settlers on the high plains.

Nannie Alderson was a survivor, an endurer, as another contemporary woman was, a woman she would never know. It is only a later viewer who can see the similarities between them and the differences in their circumstances, the one belonging to the future, the other to the past. Although Pretty-Shield had perhaps more humor and liveliness, she kept her eyes on the past, whereas Nannie saw possibilities in a future, at least for her children and grandchildren. Pretty-Shield could not be so sure.

NINE

Coppertown People

In the sixth decade after Lewis and Clark's small expedition had crossed from east to west the great northern territory that would become Montana, a few miners discouraged at the pickings in Bannack and Virginia City put down their shovels in the arid soil that would become Butte. There was enough gold and silver in this forlorn cup in the top of the Continental Divide to hold the newcomers. It was hot in summer, cold in winter, naked to all weathers. But the alluring metals attracted other disaffected or hopeful men from many places. Butte grew slowly at first, but was never again without men digging for elusive metal in a straggling settlement.

There was to be no real burgeoning of Butte until Marcus Daly, a rough-and-ready and very intelligent miner, came to the conclusion that copper, which underlay the gold and the silver of the hill, was a marketable product. Less immediately attractive than gold or silver, copper was becoming useful and even necessary to the growing industrialization of Europe and the United States. Daly had arrived in 1876 and secured a silver mine, the Alice, which fulfilled its promise. Yet in 1880, he purchased, foolishly it seemed, a mine called the Anaconda, for $30,000. This was to begin the fantastic growth that would make Butte notorious all over the world. The 1880s, 1890s, and early 1900s would be the glory days. Exploration and rivalry created the first complex city of Montana and one that, for this period, was eccentric and unique. From its hill would come, for the period, more copper to fill the needs of industry than from anywhere else in the world. It is from this time of the cruel, funny, and remarkable life of Butte that the memories of a few of the inhabitants convey vivid, partial views of what the town was like then.

Outsiders always found the place remarkable, both physically and humanly. Sometimes those who lived there did also. Berton Braley, who later achieved a transient fame as a facile reporter and verse writer, learned his craft on two of the town's newspapers. He wrote in his autobiography, *Pegasus Pulls a Hack,* how Butte struck him when he arrived, innocent of all presumptions. It was "bleak, gaunt and ugly to the unaffectionate eye; a camp on a scarred and barren hill." But he found, as many others did, that "you ceased to be aware of its ugliness, and instead found a certain strange loveliness in its raw colors and rough contours."[1] Mary MacLane, one of the natives who was to achieve a notorious reputation outside Butte, wrote of her town, where often the air near the mines was bad: "The brightness of the day and the blue of the sky and the incomparable high air have entered into my veins and flowed with my red blood."[2]

Another native, the novelist Myron Brinig, who was to be a competent writer of well-made and popular novels, some of them set in his hometown, remembered his growing up as a sheltered member of a Jewish family from Rumania who were storekeepers, and becoming part and parcel of the life of the town. He also was aware of the surprise that Butte was; it should not have been there at all. But if one came down out of the mountain road, "it is as if a giant had been sitting on the top of the Rockies playing with many colored dice that he had rattled in his palm and then thrown into the valley below." And at night, he said, "fires burned holes through the dark blue tent of the sky."[3]

In remembrance of his childhood, Brinig took gleeful joy in the color of the individuals who had lived here and in the variety of national types: "blue-eyed lads from Ireland with rich brogues and hard-drinking gullets, tall flat Finns and Norwegians with bony, yellow faces . . . southern Europeans, Montenegrins, Serbs, Bulgarians, Slovaks, Greeks. All these miners had their own societies and clubs and meeting places. And the Finns were always fighting the Irish and the Bohunks. . . . Or they were fighting amongst themselves."[4]

The miners sang their own songs marching home from work. Yet Irish miners learned Finnish words, and Cornish pasty became household food to all the nationalities. A town composed of this explosive stew celebrated a citywide Tolerance Day each year. Dispossessed Indians lived on the edge of town, and they were poorer than the poorest miner. They had their own annual fair, and all the nationalities turned out to watch the Indian horse racing.

The town was a lively contradiction, at once the most destructive of human lives in its uncontrolled and rapacious individuality and also a place kindly and humane from person to person. The miners thought of themselves as an elite work force. They made high wages for a life of dirt, danger, and uncertainty. They endured and hoped decade after decade, believing that each one of them was fortunate in being where he was and in doing what he was doing, sharing somehow in the larger fortunes of his bosses. After-work hours were free and easy and open. Drinking, fighting, and visiting the "girls" of the line were carried on without any sense of shame, and with a western sense of the individual being who he was and what he was, unconnected with past, family, or background. Personal courage counted for much; the fact that one of the "copper kings," F. Augustus Heinze, went unafraid into the danger of the mines over and over added to the miners' admiration of his other qualities.

The work underground was dangerous every day. Drilling year by year went deeper and deeper into heat and gases and unforeseen collapses. A blast from the whistle on a mine superstructure electrified the whole town to an underground disaster, and people ran to help. The place lived by explosives. Once a warehouse loaded with mining explosives blew up and destroyed the entire fire department assembled outside. Only one firehorse, Jim, survived, and in that deeply feeling, sentimental town Jim was revered and honored from that day on. He was given the freedom of a stall without bars and allowed to wander the streets at will, poking into candy stores and grocery stores for handouts.[5]

The town in which the miners and storekeepers and firemen and housewives and prostitutes lived was also the home of the notorious copper kings, notably three, at first the colossal figures and rivals William Andrews Clark and Marcus Daly, then the impudent, ambitious latecomer, F. Augustus Heinze. Clark had arrived first in 1872, on a schoolteacher's savings, from Missouri, and busied himself cleverly in buying and cultivating one property after another. Daly had come in 1876 from mining work in Utah and added to silver mines the first of the copper ones. Heinze had come from New York City in 1889, gone back to the East to raise money, and returned in 1891, to try, spectacularly, to make a fortune from his share of the diggings of the hill. What these three did mattered greatly to themselves. For the people of Butte, the public careers of Clark, Daly, and Heinze added to the color and excitement of the general life of the place, giving a hectic and deceptive sense of imaginative worth to all those diggers whose lives might otherwise have been hard to bear.

Cold, correct Clark was a small, well-dressed man who burned not only for money but also for social position. He amassed and held onto his mines and other interests until he was one of the richest men in the United States. He hungered for the public sphere, and in 1884 and in 1889 he presided at the state constitutional conventions. He wished to be the territorial delegate to Congress, but was balked of this ambition by his rival, Daly. The rivalry becoming notorious, Daly at first prevented Clark from another ambition, a Senate seat from the new state. When Clark at last gained this seat in 1901, it was at the cost of a morass of corruption on the part of both fighters, a virus of buying and selling offices, manipulating news, and poisoning the development of democracy in a new American area.

How Clark and Daly first became rivals has not been untangled, but a difference in manners and temperament was probably enough to ignite the fire. The history of this rivalry makes it an example carried to an extreme of the more ordinary and accepted entrepreneurism and business individualism of the time.

Marcus Daly was a simpler soul than Clark. With a great deal of native ability and also a warm and unpretentious surface manner, he lacked education except in the practical engineering that allowed him to plow ahead with a successful buildup of money and power. He built an efficient smelter town, Anaconda, added coal mines and forests to his domain, built power plants, and established banks. He could hate as well and strongly as Clark. It broke his heart that he lost the fight to make Anaconda the state capitol. Clark won, for Helena.

Daly's hobby of buying, training, and racing thoroughbred horses was something his miners understood and enjoyed, taking pride in "their" winning horses in races back in the East and in California. Daly remained a down-to-earth man usually well liked by his miners, and he was remembered as given to sitting on a sidewalk curb and sharing talk and a sandwich with one of his men come upon by chance in the city.[6] Unlike Daly's common man's love for horses, Clark's love was for paintings and sculptures and a respectably decorated life. That his collection has gained value as that of a rich man would not have added to his miners' sense of his being congenial. He was respected, feared, and admired, but not loved.

The third figure who entered upon the public stage of Butte rivalries was liked and almost loved. This was Frederick Augustus Heinze, "Fritz" to his friends, and he had many, for he was a charmer. The well-educated son of a German-American family, he had studied engineering in Germany and at Columbia University. On his first visit, Heinze kept his eyes open as a surveyor in the mines. He knew what he wanted, went back to the East to raise money, and returned to undertake a campaign of shrewd purchases of mining properties. In 1893 he built a more efficient smelter than those already on the scene. In 1895 he purchased the Rarus Mine, then he acquired others, off the profits of which he became formidable in the affairs of the city. He acquired a public voice in politics, while privately acquiring compliant judges. These judges served him well in the bewildering variety of lawsuits he instituted to protect his questionable use of convenient mining laws to drill into other men's properties.

In 1903 a literal warfare broke out underground between the two forces still fighting cases in the courts. Men from Heinze's mines and from Daly's Amalgamated (another name for Anaconda) "fouled the opposition drifts by burning trash and rubber and pouring slaked lime through vents. They fired back and forth with high-pressure hoses, tossed grenades, even dynamited tunnels and electrified the metal turn-plates on which ore cars moved around corners. Wild fist fights ensued when crews came suddenly upon each other."[7] Two men died. (Yet episodically the men underground made up their own fights for brief reprieves, and they even sat down together to talk and eat.)

During these years, Heinze, ostensibly linked to Clark, had worked for himself. He made himself a hero to the miners by advocating high wages and decent working hours. He seemed a sort of David against the Goliath of the Standard Oil interests that had come into the control of the properties of Daly as he weakened and died in 1900. In a showdown move, Amalgamated shut down its mines and left miners and their families in the face of starvation. Heinze reached the pinnacle of his popularity by addressing a huge downtown crowd: "These people are my enemies, fierce, bitter, implacable, but they are your enemies too."[8]

In the midst of his phantasmagoria of court cases, Heinze appeared indestructible and triumphant at this moment. But this was an illusion. The larger eastern interest, now in control of Daly's properties, gained control of the court system and caused Heinze to lose control of his two complaisant judges, who always decided in his favor in Silver Bow County. Now court cases could be moved out of that county. Heinze lost Clark's money and support. Holding onto his money sources in Butte and else-where, Clark threw over his alliance with Heinze and took on one with Amalgamated and Standard Oil. He wanted his Senate seat, long sought and previously frustrated. He attained that place in 1901 and held it until 1907, becoming an implacable and vocal foe of Theodore Roosevelt's conservation policies.

Heinze was alone against what was becoming known now in Montana as "the Company." Michael P. Malone and Richard B. Roeder, historians of Montana's history of two centuries, wrote judiciously of Heinze's turnabout: "The question must always remain: did Heinze fight Standard Oil on principle, or did he merely shake them down? The answer, perhaps, is—both."[9]

Heinze did what makes him an interest and a puzzle and perhaps a tragic hero; the West had had no room for such a figure up to this time. In the town's public spectacle, the striking personality of Heinze had pleased the people. He was tall, heavily but athletically built, with good manners for the beginnings of Butte's "good society." Parents did not fear their daughters attending his elaborate parties, for these affairs were well-chaperoned. Heinze also pleased the back streets and alleys by his hospitality and camaraderie for barmen, prostitutes, and gamblers. He drank heavily but in these years never appeared drunk. Through these years he glowed with good will and good health.

In his memoir of the time, the uncritical newcomer Berton Braley shows how easily one could be taken in by the legend of Heinze. Braley had come in at the end of the story and did not know all the ins and outs of it, but he incorporated Heinze into his count of the individuals of his youth in Butte: "Take Heinze—a young mining engineer who came out of the East with nothing but his unscrupulous brain. A roisterer, a boozer, a gambler—who with no money, but with sheer intellect, effrontery, imagination and courage, bucked all the Standard Oil millions behind the Amalgamated."

Braley exaggerates. Heinze had behind him a family with money and had efficiently raised money in the East to make his first purchases. Braley ended his praise for Heinze by stating, as a matter to be cheered, that he "departed after ten or fifteen years with twenty-five millions partly taken from Butte's Hill, but mostly taken from Amalgamated stockholders."[10] The cold truth is that in 1906 the champion of the common miner against the wicked company had secretly negotiated with these much abused eastern interests and sold himself to them, not for twenty-five, but probably for ten or twelve, million.

His case is interesting because it is the one that, among the single-souled strivers rising or falling in the city, might be considered as complex enough to be tragic. He bought a Wall Street bank. It failed partly because it was not his kind of business and partly because of a plot against him by his faithful enemies in the Standard Oil Company. This particular bank failure helped initiate the national financial panic of 1907. The brilliant, forceful, charming Heinze found himself very shortly burned out, a great deal of his money gone, his power gone, alien in the older world of the East, and his health finally brought down by drinking. He died in 1914 of liver trouble at the age of forty-five. However, he had briefly returned to Butte for a visit. The miners seemed still to admire him. They would have been Heinze, if they could.

The miners left few personal records. It is difficult to see more than the exterior of the lives of these men, who were needed at this time to dig out the mineral that made wealth for a very few others. When a disaster occurred underground, the whole town knew it, for the whistle blew at the pithead, all the other whistles joined in, and people rushed to the scene.

Braley retold in front-page sensationalism one story of a miner's death and its aftermath. The reporter was cheerfully manipulating his readers. But in the process his story, repeated day after day, gained a certain end, the payment of insurance to the miner's widow, and let a little light into the fearsome depths of the mines. John Lubik, a Polish miner, had been overcome by bad air in a low shaft. Joe Pinazza, an Italian miner, at great danger to himself, had climbed down into the dangerous territory and rescued Lubik, who survived. Pinazza died. Pinazza's widow applied for insurance, but was turned down. She went to court. Braley saw a story here. He paraphrased the policy on the front page and in particular its stipulation that "carried a blanket insurance on the lives of its men, representing year's pay for a miner killed on duty." But in this case the company refused payment because Pinazza had, it stated, "taken an unnecessary risk in entering said stope for the purpose of saving a fellow miner's life. Defendant therefore moves the complaint be dismissed and costs assessed to the plaintiff."[11]

With sarcastic repetition, the reporter headlined the story on the front page day after day. To his delight, the account attracted widespread public attention and indignation. The judge in the case quoted Braley's story in his hearing and granted Mrs. Pinazza her award. The case nearly ruined the insurance company and gave the reporter the biggest single story of his career in Butte.

By the spring of 1909, after his personal hero, Heinze, had gone, Braley also was ready to leave. He wrote ten doggerel songs, *Songs of a Mining Camp,* and sold them to the *Saturday Evening Post.* He set out for the East, where he thought there would be a larger scope for his talents. He had minor successes in this other world but probably never again had the kind of fun he had had in the coppertown.

An adventurer such as Braley came and went. A hero such as Heinze rose and fell, but a memory of him lingered. The lives of thousands who had not his good or bad fortune were forgotten. A more sober memoir of one who was born and remained there reminds history of the variety of human life possible even in places given to extremes of personality. The "Elizabeth Ann (Rose) Morrow Rust Reminiscence," unpublished and held in the archives of the Montana Historical Society, preserves the essence of one unnoticed life of the copper region. [12]

The memories of Rose Morrow Rust were taken down and preserved by her daughter. Elizabeth Ann, called Rose by her family, was born in Butte in 1885, but lived her first ten years in Basin, a settlement thirty miles north of Butte on the road to Helena, the new state capital, the celebration of which her father took her to see. Rose's father and mother had met and married in Butte after migrating from eastern Canada. Her father, William Morrow, was a Presbyterian of stiff rectitude who lived up to the professions of his faith. He managed small gold mines in the Basin community, where his family lived in frontier conditions. Wandering, hungry Indians frightened the settlers. Bears and mountain lions seemed to be occasional menaces. Children fell into rivers and enjoyed wild rides on untrained horses. For Rose, her father's mines were a fascination to peer into, even when trapped miners were being fed from above by food tubes. Her overworked father died when Rose was ten. The event plunged the mother and four children into a hand-to-mouth existence in Butte after a trusted lawyer had taken the mine properties away from the family.

Rose did not stop going to school, but worked before and after school hours. The memories told to her daughter reflect a keen child's mind reacting with gusto to new circumstances in the life of shops and streets in the mining town. She was thrown upon her own resources to find a way to help the family. She worked first in a bakery from 4:30 to 8:45 in the morning, then walked nine blocks to school. Although school began at 9:00, the principal gave Rose a little leeway on her arrival time. After school she worked until 10:00 at night and all day Saturday and six hours on Sunday.

Rose got a better job as a cashier in a café and connived with the wife of the owner to hide the cash from him when he went gambling once a month. At the same time she attended Butte Business College. (Already the city was establishing institutions of various kinds.) She later found better jobs with an insurance company, then a newspaper. She had become a city girl. She bowled on the insurance company's team. She went to dances and became an expert. She won a beauty contest as "the most beautiful girl in Butte." In 1906 she was a delegate to a convention (the narrative does not say what kind) in San Francisco. Almost grown, she took along a younger brother "to see the U.S. Fleet come to the Pacific," as she said, and remembered the effects of the earthquake: "The streets were in terrible shape from the earthquake, deep holes all down the middle." She told her daughter about a day of exploration in a strange city: "We left at four in the morning to be sure to get a seat in the cars, but even at that time we had a hard time to get on the cars. We had to walk a long way from the end of the car line. Different men carried Archie, he was only two. We also went out on one of the boats and had lunch in a fisherman's inn on the beach." That they both woke up the next day with the mumps seems not to have dampened her gusto for a good time. As an older person, Rose apparently retained her Butte gusto for living, a citizen of her time growing from pioneer conditions into the more settled life of the state.

The time of Rose's coming of age was the beginning of the consolidation of the wild mining town into a more solid, controlled, and institutionalized place. Rose probably thought little about this, her attentions directed toward her own life and that of the individuals with whom she interacted in work and play and love. She and others came to their later years in a town more efficient but in some ways harsher than in its earlier days. All power was now consolidated in one company: Amalgamated had again taken the name Anaconda. "The Company" controlled all mining, all power production, much of the forestry, and, in what seemed an inexorable growth of its influence, all politics and all communication—it also owned most of the state's newspapers. Tax laws were written and passed at Helena which exempted this great complex from paying proper taxes to the state while copper was being efficiently taken out of the earth and shipped elsewhere.

Another source about the individual life of this time in Butte is the rescued diary of one month in the life of Beatrice Murphy. The preservation of this artless journal of a night nurse in Murray Hospital during November 1909 reveals something of the new institutionalized respectability that was changing the mining camp. Apparently she paid little attention to state or world affairs, which were affected by the copper under the ground on which she lived. She was sufficiently aware of each night's difficulties and sometime joys, which she encountered in her rounds. The diary survives in the Butte–Silver Bow Archives and was reprinted in *Montana: The Magazine of Western History* (Autumn 1989). In her account, one finds a zest for existence, a youthful confidence, and an intense self-respect by one who enjoyed her duties.

Butte was not an exotic place to Rose Morrow as she grew up. Nor was it that to Beatrice Murphy. It was simply the town in which each one lived and had a hard but interesting job. Murphy took Butte's everyday existence for granted, although a considerable portion of her nursing was taken up with miners hurt underground, a distinctive medical difference from other towns in the number of injuries and casualties that the miners of Butte suffered.

The miners who were often brought into the hospital for summary treatment were lucky to have Murphy as their nurse. She was young, healthy, lively, and cheerful, and also full of humorous self-appreciation. She took a kind of joy in her hard life. Excerpts from the diary illustrate her temperament. "Nov. 1 [1909] Handed in my nightly report to Miss McGregor. She seemed pleased. Tripped down the stairs with a light heart. Worked some more. Everything done nicely. Tired feet, but nothing more. Walked 200 miles all told since 7 P.M. No scraps, no biffs. Very uneventful night."[13]

Murphy never saw the interior of the mines, but almost every day she saw the human debris that they sent her. She patched up these men and liked them, but separated herself from them and their fate. "Tues. night, Nov. 2, 09. Answered door bell. Admitted miner with bruised head, saved his life by performing surgical operation on head, broke one needle (didn't swear), Assisted at operation by Dr. McCrackin first assistant. Miss Donovan second assistant. Floated up to the 5th floor. Ate supper of fried chicken."

She had a strong, tongue-in-cheek sense of herself. "Wed.n. Nov. 3–09. Visited all the patients administering smiles and cheers hand over fist. Admitted three men. One with a rock in the tail of his eye. Another with a dilapidated finger and still another who declared his hand was broken but which proved to be a ruptured vein. Tried to get a little sleep on the table with a roll of cotton under my head." On Saturday night, November 6, she wrote: "Visited my dear patients. One man offered me a bottle of beer. Which I refused with becoming dignity. Elevated my nose among the clouds & tried to look horrified. One of my lady patients started to have fits which lasted one half hour. Four miners decided to get hurt for a change. Fixed them up & sent them on their way rejoicing. . . . Finished work. Ate breakfast. Good Night." These diary notes of a hard-working young woman illustrate a job that was beginning to be a profession.

Butte had seemed a wild and eccentric place to outsiders. It had been without the ballast of traditions. Yet in the last years of the copper kings, and in the first years after their decline, Butte began making its own traditions out of a meager past. Columbia Gardens, endowed by Clark, was a pleasant and innocent place for family picnics and pleasurings. For those who could pay, singers, actors, and lecturers stopped over in this remote place and delivered light to the heathen. These innocents responded eagerly. Plays and talks and musical performances of all kinds were well attended and reported in the local papers. Culture was sought with pathetic insistence.

Butte's camaraderie of democratic manners had a new and superficial respectability. It did not reach very deep, but it was impressive in the extremity of its fine clothes, polished carriages, and well-groomed horses, as well as its well-reported elaboration of private parties among people such as Senator Clark and his circle. This thin layer of propriety was appearing in other places, long enough settled by Montana standards. The Conrad mansion in its walled garden in Kalispell, at the head of the green and prospering Flathead Valley, was proudly furnished with heavy Victorian furniture and darkly curtained by draperies that shut out the light, clear air of the outside. In Helena, some of the goldminers who had struck it rich built fantastic three-story fortresses for their everyday life, creating a residential area of proud and pompous respectability.

Butte seemed unconventional to the rest of the nation. But to a particular girl growing up there, it seemed restrictive to her cabined, confined, and aspiring desires. She had had a conventional high-school education, had written for the school publication, and had been inspired to be a writer by a teacher. Even as a schoolgirl, she had been somewhat solitary, reading a great deal, and taking walks into the austere and stimulating air of the Butte high country. Somehow the new ideas of women's identity and unjust place in society reached her through reading. Among the books she read

was Marie Bashkirtseff's *Journal,* full of an outraged longing for freedom
for all women's so far suppressed desires, ambitions, and capabilities. Mary
MacLane, not yet twenty, leading an outwardly dull and quiet life, in 1901
scribbled about her sense of rebellion and exultation. She sent the diary,
unsolicited, to a publisher in Chicago, Herbert S. Stone and Company. A
reader in that company, Lucy Monroe, a sister of Harriet Monroe, and thus
part of a radical community of new critics and writers, recommended the
book, and, remarkably, the firm almost immediately accepted it for publication. The obscure Butte girl's book, *The Story of Mary MacLane by Herself,*
became "the talk of the nation, from Butte to New York."[14]

What MacLane wrote might seem tame to later generations, but to her
own time it was shocking, even to most of Butte, which was used to rough
living, but not to writing about it in a "literary" style. The book, now
lost to public memory, as is its author, has a quality that makes it likable—a
piquancy of expression, a youthfulness of defiance and aspiration, partly
amusing to the knowledgeable, but also appealing in its sincerity.

The girl who had been lonely, the untried woman in an unused youthful
body, found a voice. It was first one of superior exasperation with what
MacLane thought of as dull, confining surroundings. Out her window she
saw not a daring city of wild acts, but one that was going to put barriers
in her way. "As I look I have a weary disgusted feeling." Life would not
be very rewarding if she did not rebel. "Under each of the roofs live a man
and a woman joined together by that very slender thread, the marriage
ceremony—and their children, the result of the marriage ceremony. How
many of them love each other. . . . And I think, therefore, that I should
prefer some life that is not virtuous."[15]

MacLane's favorite writer was John Keats, who wished to press the grape
of experience to his palate. She was going to resist the drabness of everyday
life and insist on the enjoyment of seeing, touching, feeling. She proclaimed
the pleasure she had in the simple act of sensual taste. A passage from her
book much quoted, and made fun of, was that of her delight in eating a
cold potato: "I stand in the pantry door leaning against the jamb, with a
tiny glass salt-shaker in one hand and the sweet dark pink cold Boiled
Potato in the other. And I sprinkle it with salt and I nibble, nibble, nibble.
And I say aloud. 'Gee, it's good!'" (487–88). Of course, sex was to be
included in her enjoyments. She proudly proclaimed, out of her inexperi-
ence, "I am now bent on reckless sensuality" (485). She was quite consciously mischievous. Proclaiming loyalty to a personal Devil, she asserted

that he "has given me, among other things my admirable young woman's body, which I enjoy thoroughly and of which I am passionately fond" (481).

MacLane's cry of revolt was heard, and her book (published in 1902) was a season's sensation. Hamlin Garland and H. L. Mencken praised her writing. Newspapers all over the country reviewed the book. She received enough money in short order—early royalties of $17,000—to feel rich and precipitately escaped from Butte. She was taken up by journalists and writers, first in Chicago, where Harriet and Lucy Monroe welcomed her, and then in Greenwich Village, where she became a fixture to be pointed out. Her second book was not sensational and fell quite flat. Her third, *I, Mary MacLane,* tried in 1917 to repeat the sensation of the first. In it she wrote, with perhaps a little more experience of the wear and tear of Bohemian life, "I am not Respectable nor Refined nor in Good Taste. . . . And no woman but a dead woman in her coffin is in complete Good Taste. Every live woman has for instance, a working diaphram: and in a diaphram there is, in the final analysis, simply no taste at all" (487).

Butte was shocked by MacLane, or at least some of its newspapers were. She mixed categories of women in a confusing way. Yet there was a good bit of perverse pride in her in Montana. Some newspapers praised her. Despite the local library's ban upon her book, or perhaps because of it, she was widely read in her own state. Outside notice—even in vaudeville acts such as that of Weber and Field's—made the local citizens know that at least Butte was being paid attention to. Beyond the good reception she had had in Chicago by serious critics, and the notoriety and companionship she gained in New York and other eastern cities, she was called upon to make a movie, a not very good one in which she acted and for which she wrote the script. Filmed in Chicago in 1917, it was entitled *Men Who Have Made Love to Me.*

MacLane was becoming the victim of sudden fame, and some of the writing she did briefly for two different newspapers, one in the East and the other in the West, shows that her talents might have matured differently if she had not floated on the reputation of her very youthful work. If she had been allowed more than two small opportunities to do everyday reporter's work, she might have developed in that direction, for she showed on these two occasions that she had a flair for down-to-earth observation of matters outside herself.

Some of this reporter's work has been rediscovered. In 1985, Virginia Terris, in *The Speculator: A Journal of Butte and Southwest Montana History,* resurrected excerpts from MacLane's New York reporting for the *New York World* and for the *Butte Evening News*. The articles for the New York paper appeared in 1902 between August 24 and November 9, when she was in the full flush of notoriety and being given a chance by an editor. She showed a talent then that might have been developed if she had gone on in this vein, a gift for putting down vivid, objective vignettes of street people and street scenes. She had a lively sympathy for the down-and-out of society. But her public wanted more personal sensation from this young westerner.

Some of her writing in New York showed that MacLane was capable of looking outside of herself and seeing other people. In Coney Island she came upon "a stout old lady who was sitting upright while another packed sand around her in a damp heavy bank. These were not wearing bathing suits but were in ordinary clothes. The old lady sat stiff for this process as she would have sat for a shoe polish or a shampoo." In the *New York World* MacLane as reporter and commentator criticized Wall Street as a place of "hell and damnation" and found the rich at Newport to the "human beings grasping, arriving madly after treasure, each for himself . . . utterly cursed . . . / and / know not one moment's peace." [16]

When MacLane returned to Butte in 1910 and wrote for the *Butte Evening News* between March 20 and May 22, she seemed to look more closely and appreciatively at her hometown than she had before. It was fresh to eyes that had been elsewhere:

> little mines in unexpected mid-town blocks with their engines and hoists and scaffolds and green coppery dumps; the big mines on the Hill busily working night and day—the desolate wind-swept cemetery of the Flat . . . the Brophy grocery-window full of attractive grocery-food; the St. Gaudens statue of Marcus Daly; the few sweet green trees on Montana Street by the courthouse; the edge of Walkerville; Ex-Senator Clark's old-fashioned closed house on Granite Street; the surprisingly steep Idaho Street hill; the old Reduction works reminiscent of the bygone Heinze and the bold buccaneering days . . . the Mexican tamale vendors in the early night . . . the brilliant sparkling look of the town from out on the Flat late in the evening.

Neither paper for which MacLane wrote feature stories wanted this kind of material. These were temporary jobs. She was defeated by her own early success. Readers and publishers wanted only sensation from her. She tried to live in the enjoyment of freedoms not acceptable to middle-class people, who read her with a vicarious thrill. But she could not make a living out of it for long. She tired. She died in a hotel room alone in Chicago in 1929, and her body was not discovered for several days.

Whether MacLane died in actual penury has been a question. The sadness of a lonely death made good copy; perhaps, according to a sister-in-law, the story was not so dire. Yet MacLane outlived a kind of success and found no place for herself in society. She spent too much, gambled too much, and failed to find companionship in men or women.

For a time MacLane turned back to the place where she had started, where she had her first joyously rebellious thoughts, to Butte. In a fevered passage, she wrote of her ineradicable love for that strange town: "There is nothing benign, nothing enlightening—no gentleness, no pity in its barren beauty. [But, beyond reason, she felt something for the town] a fascination beyond plaisance or pain—I feel love for this Butte."[17]

Perhaps Fritz Heinze, beaten by his well-earned enemies in New York City, remembered Butte as a place of hope, energy, and triumphant good feeling. His career, as did the careers of the other copper kings of his time, and even the mine heroes of that time, took on the color of legend to a later, drabber Butte. Coppertown people of a later day tended to view the past of their town as legend, and they did not look too closely at the costs endured to make that legend.

Outsiders were able to view the place with a merciless clarity, unlike the natives. Dashiell Hammett did private detective work in the city and used the extremity of civic conditions in Butte as the setting for his first considerable novel, *Red Harvest*. He called the place Personville, pronounced "Poisonville." This was in the 1920s, when the management of the one company had succeeded the boisterous rivalries of the early days, and, as Hammett saw it—perhaps with some unfairness—municipal corruption was complete.

By this time the work of copper mining, still hugely profitable to a succession of management changes, was run in the classic style of the modern corporate organization with national and international connections. Historian Malone described the total domination of "the Company" during the first half of the twentieth century. "In time, the people of the 'Treasure State' came to realize that consolidation was a mixed blessing. . . . No longer facing real competition for master of the hill, the Amalgamated monopoly now bestrode the state like a great, insensate colossus."[18]

The legislature in Helena became noted for passing laws that spared "the Company" its share of state taxes. When an economics professor at the university in Missoula wrote a book that questioned this policy, he was fired. [19] The second great controller of the sources and manufacture of energy in the state, the Montana Power Company, was in league with the Anaconda Company. In the Montana newspapers, only the message of the Anaconda Company appeared. The company owned all but one of the newspapers in the state. Therefore, when the public strayed from the comics and local obituaries to read about politics or business, they learned the views of the one dominant corporation. Political independence came, and in some measure political moderation did not die. There were, as if throwbacks to pioneering individualism, state and federal politicians from Montana whose voices were joyously discordant or smoothly modifying to the view of the company: Thomas J. Walsh, Burton K. Wheeler, Joseph M. Dixon, and Sam C. Ford. In Butte itself, unionism was notoriously militant and aggressive.

The people of the earlier days—the miners who went underground, the copper kings who gained their wealth from this dangerous work, the shopkeepers, the reporters, the women who rode in the carriages of the newly rich, the prostitutes, the wives with their pasties and stews, the new generation of clerks, bookkeepers, nurses, or would-be writers—could not have foreseen the final insult to their place. For after the era of the deep mines, there was developed a method new to Butte—open pit mining. In this process, all the ground containing a metal becoming very thin and scattered was dug up, leaving a gigantic hole where parts of the living city had been, a hole deepening, widening, turning into a pit. This was the gigantic spiral of the Berkeley Pit, with its circle of roadway leading down to the center, where gigantic machines looked like toys. More and more of the ground on which the people of the copper camps had lived and worked and loved disappeared and was carried away for the separation of great quantities of earth from very small amounts of the metal.

The descendants of the original settlers saw a growing, chancrelike wound eating away at the city itself: their houses, their pleasure gardens, themselves. One neighborhood after another, each with its own distinctive talk, kind of food, and way of life, disappeared into the Berkeley Pit. Fewer and fewer of those who would be miners could be. The Company (and after many successive adjustments of management and changes of ownership, it was still "the Company" to Butte people) employed a smaller number of workers. It consolidated its investment in a new technology of mining, the tools of which were digging machines and giant trucks and a negligible number of men skilled at handling the machines.

In the end, Butte was not worth the effort. The rich lodes of copper seemed no longer to exist. During one of the city's usual strikes in the summer of 1980, the Company abruptly came to the decision that it was giving up the game, leaving Butte, Anaconda, East Helena, and Great Falls. After decades of entangling itself with every facet of life in these places and in the whole state, this was a two weeks' notice.

It had taken only one hundred years for the entire process to take place: discovery, frenzied use, methodical and careful use, and, in the end, abandonment. The descendants of the original coppertown people would be called upon to find new and ingenious ways of making a living in this community.

TEN

Mr. Gibson and the Cowboy:
Paris Gibson and Charles M. Russell

The lives of two men who lived at the same time in the same small city exemplify, by a happy coincidence, the opposite ways Americans would have—into the twentieth century—of being westerners. The city was Great Falls, founded in the mid-1880s by one of these men in a curve of the Missouri River still flowing toward Canada before turning to the east. This particular lonely section of Montana in 1920, the year the founder died, was busy transforming itself out of an already mythical frontier into the Main Street of Sinclair Lewis. But at ninety, in the final year of his life, Paris Gibson had the satisfaction of seeing his small place becoming what he had planned. His younger contemporary and friend Charles Marion Russell, by this time the most famous inhabitant of Great Falls, was the painter, sculptor, and storyteller who had captured the transient reality and romance of the older West in his arts.

Great Falls remains an oasis of human habitation in an almost boundless area of rolling high plains, flat-topped buttes, and blue mountain views. The large, rattlingly empty international airport, built upon the westward bluff above the river, proclaims to the incoming traveler by a sign above the entrance from the planes: "This is Charles M. Russell country." But it is not Russell's West that one comes into beyond the airport, but Gibson's. It is the city that the founder planned in 1884 when he came upon the bare sagebrush plain alongside the many waterfalls of the great river of the mountains; it is a city of sober commerce, wide clean streets, and a planned parallelogram both of business and residence, with a greenness of planted trees.

By 1920 Great Falls was a well-established city, although most of its inhabitants had come here from elsewhere and only the children were natives. Even in its first thirty-six years it had undergone changes so complete as to be astonishing even to those who had lived through them. From cattle town to wheat town, from frontier town to comfortable boom town. In the decade after World War I, when an oil boom made for change once again, the city had grown into a kind of stability. The residents of other Montana towns called Great Falls dull; the inhabitants called it a good place to live. But after many changes, it is a city still haunted by the ghosts of Russell and Gibson, whose lives passed each other and hailed each other in a recognition of opposites. Few other small cities have had two such opposite heroes.

In imagination then, in order to understand who and what they were, return to 1920, when Gibson was ninety years old and Russell was fifty-six. This was the year when his city honored Gibson with a celebration. Among those who took part was Russell. He composed a piece of doggerel for the occasion, tossing off the lines effortlessly, for he and Gibson were on home territory together. About Old Senator Gibson (who had been a U.S. senator from Montana from 1901 to 1905), he wrote:

> There are men who claim honor for notches,
> Take nations with powder and lead;
> They never done nothing for live ones,
> But built up great cities of dead.
> But I drink to one with no notches on his gun,
> No knife or gun record to give.
> On windswept ground, you built up a town
> Where humans could come, grow and live. [1]

Although Russell never liked the modern world of which Gibson's city was a well-adapted place, he was fond of the founder and the place itself, where he had been comfortably at home for the years that succeeded his cowboy vagabondage. When the artist, in his later, prosperous years, went away to Chicago, New York, Pasadena, or to London—to sell paintings— he looked back with longing to that one spot in the universe, as he said, lying between Square Butte and Belt Mountain.

If temperament and opportunity had not led them in different directions, Gibson and Russell might have led similar lives. Both came from families of solid position in more settled parts of the country—Maine and Missouri, respectively; both were reared in a self-respecting tradition of modest service to a settled society. But when each one went into the still unshaped Northwest, he found himself answering a particular appeal toward a certain kind of behavior, and their ways were opposite. Today the West holds in uneasy equilibrium these opposites still struggling against each other. In Great Falls one can see the still unresolved qualities of the West embodied in its two local heroes.

Paris Gibson was born on July 1, 1830, in Brownfield, Oxford County, Maine. [2] He attended Bowdoin College. He served in the Maine state legislature, but he was stricken with a westering impulse on a visit to the frontier town of Chicago in 1852 and to Saint Anthony Falls, Minnesota, in 1854. He moved there and was one of those who helped transform that place into Minneapolis. It became his town. He founded a flour mill and a woolen mill. He helped establish the first public library. He served on the board of regents of the state university. He married Valeria Sweat in 1858, but he did not allow her to settle down to a placid life in Minneapolis. After getting that place well started, and suffering some embarrassment from a downturn in his financial fortunes, he became attracted to the possibilities in the improbable wilds of the Montana territory. In 1879, in his forty-ninth year, he decided to start all over again farther west. He set up headquarters in the riverboat town of Fort Benton on the upper Missouri River and established himself as a sheep rancher near today's towns of Belt and Armington.

There was no settlement as yet at the falls of the Missouri upriver and forty miles southwest of Fort Benton. The new Montana man was curious about the famous waterfalls. He made an expedition with his son Theodore to that region in 1880. He had read the journals of Lewis and Clark. What he was to see, striking out across the grassland from his ranch, was little changed from what had met the eyes of the explorers seventy-five years earlier. This was an area that had never been settled and that white people rarely even trespassed upon, after some early efficient killings by the Blackfeet, who had frightened off all tentative attempts to set up a trading post at the falls. The fear was now gone. Chief Joseph had been defeated, and the Sioux were scattered and discouraged despite their striking victory at Little Bighorn. The Blackfeet had been tamed by the infamous Baker massacre.

Benchland and river prairie now lay open to the gaze of a modern man bent upon improving the West. Gibson recalled:

> I can never forget the impression made upon my mind as I looked down for the first time upon these falls and beheld, below them, the deep canyon with its projecting cliffs far above the foaming current. I could readily understand the feelings of Captain Lewis seventy-five years before. [He and his son killed a buck and made camp at midnight] and were aroused from our sleep by an attempted stampede of our horses, probably by a mountain lion or a bear.[3]

This quote and other personal quotes about the first days of Great Falls are from Gibson's account, "The Founding of Great Falls," a brochure printed by the *Great Falls Tribune,* dated January 1, 1914, by the author.

Gibson was fascinated by the place and came again many times to survey what he thought might become a scene of his own future activities. Struck by an inspiration, he was convinced that the falls area could be made a site for a prosperous modern city. It was settled in his own mind that he was to found the city. This is the way he looked back upon his resolution, which had solidified by 1882:

> Although I had traveled much over Northern Montana and the country between the Missouri River and the Yellowstone during my three years residence in Fort Benton, I had never seen a spot as attractive as this and one that at once appealed to me as an ideal site for a city. Before me I saw a plain, unbroken by ravines, gently descending, for two miles, to the broad Missouri with its low grassy banks, while beyond I beheld the Sun River as it runs through the beautiful valley and unites its waters with those of the great Missouri. This scenery, composed of valleys and rivers, flanked by smoothly rounded table lands, formed a picture never to be forgotten. I had looked upon this scene for a few moments only when I said to myself, here I will found a city.

Gibson paced out the boundaries of his imagined city and found no evidence that anyone had ever lived here except a nameless fur trapper who had left behind a "half decayed log cabin in a thick clump of willows at the water's edge." The only settlements nearby were isolated ranches and farms along the Sun River and the army post some miles away at Fort Shaw. From the plains on which he envisioned his city rising, he followed the sweep of the river's current to the beginning of the series of waterfalls, the first of which, Black Eagle, would lie within his planned area. This place and all other named places in the vicinity had been given English nomenclature by the first explorers. On an island in the middle of the quickening current of the first waterfall, Meriwether Lewis had seen a pine with an eagle's nest in it. It was on the north shore beyond this site that the great copper smelter and its stack would rise in time. But, with nothing but the naked hill before him, Gibson saw an appropriate place for power plants, mills, factories, dams—all the resources to give energy to a new community. With the single-mindedness of the late nineteenth-century entrepreneur, he saw no harm in the founder making money out of discovery and development.

From this time on, he devoted his will to making his inspiration come true. He exhibited here the drive and planning that had distinguished his earlier exploits.

> The all important object before me at that time was to acquire title to the lands required for the future city and to secure the lands along the river adjacent to the several important water power sites. As this step involved the expenditure of much more money than could command, I decided, after weighing the situation carefully, to open communication with James J. Hill, whom I had known for many years while living in Minneapolis and who had recently acquired great wealth through the purchase of the bankrupt St. Paul and Pacific Railroad.

The founding of the city, which went ahead under Gibson's push during the 1880s, was tied to private corporate purchase of U.S. government land, to the judicious placing of stock in the hands of President Benjamin Harrison and his cabinet officers, and to the subsequent reselling of lots to settlers. It was the typical thoughtlessly corrupt way in which most corporations grew in the nineteenth century. Yet Gibson was successful; he founded a well-designed city; he attracted eager settlers; the place grew and thrived. The story of Gibson's financing of his city is in James G. Handford's "Paris Gibson, a Montana Yankee."[4]

The success of the settlement, as Gibson shrewdly foretold, depended upon the advance of James J. Hill's western railroad. It was a disappointment to Gibson and the new townspeople that Hill laid his road straight across the map like a ruled line near to the Canadian border and thus bypassed Great Falls. But he was induced to promise to extend a branch line south to Gibson's city. In 1887, three years after the city might be said to exist, the branch line did reach Great Falls. The citizens built a bonfire to celebrate the first train. Two large towered stations were to arise, one for Hill's Great Northern line, the other for the rival Milwaukee line. Today both have been abandoned for passenger use, but they stand as monuments of the railroad era.

Even before the first train arrived, the new settlement had flushed into life under Gibson's prodding. By 1884 two hundred people were living within the tentative outline of the founder's plan. For Gibson was everywhere; he not only conceived the idea and financed the purchase and reselling of land but also laid out a plan for the city's orderly settlement and growth. In 1884 the first child was born and the first election was held. In 1885 the first schoolhouse was built and the *Great Falls Tribune* was established. Inevitably, Gibson was elected the first mayor.

He had made the design for geometrically regular avenues and streets; he had decreed parks and trees; he had initiated waterworks, schools, industries, and a library. By 1890 the town only dreamed of in the previous decade had a population of 3,979, and the first dam on the river, that at Black Eagle, was completed. On the hill above the dam, ground was broken for the Boston and Montana Smelter. This was to become the nucleus of the great Anaconda complex of copper smelting and the refining of lead and other metals. Its stack and deteriorating buildings were razed with some difficulty shortly before the city's celebration of its first hundred years; this destruction made a deep emotional impression upon the city's population.

The tireless Gibson extended his interests to ranching near the city and to promoting the coal deposits at nearby Stockett and Sand Coulee. From Minneapolis he brought the remaining members of his family to the West to settle in a tall stone and brick mansion, which stood for a time in lonely splendor on one of his logically numbered and so far unfilled avenues. His gently reared daughter-in-law could look out her windows, she wrote later, and see in those early years a tall line of native willows, which were the only screen between her and the river as it made, at some distance, a giant curve around the city site.[5] But within a few years, houses, streets, and planted trees totally obscured this large view. Wild starving cattle ate the tender young trees during the terrible winter of the great blizzard, 1886–87, but they were carefully replanted.

The benefits of Gibson's foresight extend into the present. All along the older residential streets there is now an overarching shade from elms and ashes planted in this otherwise open and windswept space.* Dating from Gibson's time, a city ordinance decreed the municipal watering and care of these boulevard trees. The sound of water trucks coming through one's street every other night, cooling the summer grass and soaking the sunken ground around each precious tree, was a sound of childhood. Gibson's design in another respect has helped make Great Falls an attractive city. There is no tangle of wires or line of poles down every street, downtown and residential. Each laid-out block has an alley splitting its innards lengthwise, and along the alley run the telephone and power lines. Downtown, service for the stores, as well as garbage collection, is channeled through the alleys.

Everything about Gibson's career—with the exception of a brief collapse in Minnesota—belongs to the tradition of well-ordered, progressive success, and his life in Montana was a triumphant vindication of this conscious disciplined aim. On the other hand, everything about Russell's career—at least his early one—was haphazard, chancy, and doubtful of a good outcome. It also had a kind of picturesque charm, the story of which affects us today. But one would not in his youth have predicted world fame for him, although a doting father had seen to it that the little childish works the boy did—bas-reliefs and modeled figures—were sent to the Saint Louis annual fair, where they won prizes.

Charles Marion Russell was born on March 19, 1864.[6] Russell was to be a westerner of a generation younger than Gibson's. He also went to the West at a younger age. Both facts would be important. He was impressionable when he first saw Montana. Montana helped make him. Montana and the West were, when he arrived, changing rapidly. Although he was younger than Gibson, he was to outlast the older man by only six years.

The future western artist was the third child of well-to-do, upright parents in Saint Louis, Charles Silas and Mary Mead Russell. His father was the head of Parker, Russell, and Company, a firm that manufactured fire brick. There was always clay handy at the brickworks, where the little boy was taken by his father. At twelve he was already modeling figures and persuading workmen to fire his clay horses and men in the company kilns. It was very natural that the busy, prosperous father wished his son

---

*Unfortunately, at this writing the original elms are dying. Maples are being planted to replace them.

to succeed him in the manufactory. But, in a fatal kind of way, the frontier tradition lived in the family. A great-uncle had been William Bent, the fur trapper and mountain man, the founder of Bent's Fort, a trading post on the Arkansas River near the present town of Pueblo, Colorado.

Charles's imagination was occupied with the fur-trapping relatives of the family past and by the human relics of the fur trade still lingering on the Saint Louis riverfront. He had dogs and ponies and liked to hunt and camp. One time he played hooky and ran away to the nearby woods for a number of days. His father's most energetic attempt to bend his son to his way was to send him to a New Jersey military academy for a year. This did not work. He allowed Charles to attend briefly an art school in Saint Louis, but this ordered instruction was a failure. Charles was already firmly committed to going his own way in painting and modeling. He was also determined to see something of the still half-wild West. Therefore, the good-hearted father, thinking to cure his son of his itch, sent Charles, just before his sixteenth birthday, on a trip to the Montana territory with Wallis W. (Pike) Miller, a family friend.

Miller had a sheep ranch in the Judith Basin south of the Missouri River in the north-central plains and butte area of the territory. In the spring of 1880 (Gibson had reached Montana only the year before), Charles Russell accompanied Pike, by train, stagecoach, and horse and wagon, to the ranch, getting step by step farther into a land occupied so far by Indians, trappers, miners, and a very few ranchers. He found it as difficult, sometimes as scary, and altogether as appealing to his imagination as his sixteen-year-old mind had conceived it to be. Helena, where, less than fifteen years before, gold had been discovered in Last Chance Gulch, was still a town of bull whackers cracking whips over teams laboring in muddy ruts. Here Pike bought a wagon and four horses to take the two of them and their supplies across the Belt Mountains to the Judith Basin. One can deduce from Russell's scattered recollections that the slender, sandy-haired boy, newly outfitted in western clothes, found the experience enthralling.

Open to every new impression—the light, the space, the people— Russell entered into his inheritance. Left alone in Pike's lonely sheepherder's cabin one day, he was broken in upon by aggressive Piegans, who told him, gruffly: "White papoose cook." He cooked everything in sight to pacify them. Very early he was known to Pike's acquaintances as "Kid Russell," a raw but willing boy. Kid Russell found out very soon that he did not like sheep. He left Miller and was fortunate to fall in with Jake Hoover, a benevolent old hunter willing to teach him how to survive. He spent two years hunting and trapping with this experienced mountain man. He learned to live on the land and to be part of it, as well as to be independent but also to depend upon the help of other isolated men. After this initiation, he was taken on by a combined cow outfit and, despite his youth, was put in charge of the four hundred horses for the drive to the railroad. He had a knack with horses. He survived and was respected and had time to dream and sketch and count himself lucky to be where he was. For he took to this life with the whole force of his imagination.

The cattlemen united for this drive thought that the Northern Pacific had by this time reached Miles City in the southeastern part of the territory. Therefore, seventy-five men from several ranches, thousands of cattle, and four hundred horses set off on the long, difficult, aggravating push toward railhead. Russell thrived as a horse wrangler. He had time to learn the ways, the songs, and the tales of these men and to be thoroughly initiated into a rough, adventurous, and free-wheeling life. He found he liked the way time stretched out, the look of the country through which they passed, and the friendliness of men isolated from their kind in a demanding trade. They reached Fort Keough near Miles City and found there was no railroad there. They had to trail the herd farther, 125 miles northeastward to Glendive, to which point the rails had penetrated.

By this time Russell was lost to civilization. For the next twelve years he drifted from one cattle outfit to another, years in which he soon saw that he was involved in the end of a way of life. At the same time, he was becoming assimilated to that life and passionately attached to it. He purchased his own horses. One of the first was Monte, a pinto bought from Indians, which he kept for over twenty years until its death. He always kept horses for their natural lives and was devoted to one after another.

In 1888, a few years after his beginnings as a cowpuncher, Russell went a step farther into the unknown West. With a friend he traveled north into Canada, knew intimately the life of the Bloods, one of the three associated tribes of the Blackfeet, and learned not only their spoken language but also their sign language, which he was to use with grace and ease for the rest of his life. He developed an understanding and liking for the Indians' way of life. The surviving Indians were trying to live their old life in this last

West while settlers crowded in, set up homestead cabins, began to fence the range for farming, and founded towns, destroying the native life so well adapted to this land and the transient life of open-range ranchers.

The two men who had come to this country within a year of each other—Paris Gibson and Charles Russell—loved the land but loved it differently. Gibson saw a future of cities, industries, and a settled agriculture. Russell, even before the old life was gone, saw it going and was homesick for it in its passing. Cowboy life and Indian life had given him a vision. His wandering had not interrupted his habit of modeling in clay or sketching and painting. He impressed friends and trail bosses with his renderings of their homely daily life. He traded pictures for drinks in an innocent, heedless sort of way, but he soon learned that barkeepers would hold a painting and sell it for him. These were his first agents. As the old fenceless kind of ranching began to die out, he decided to try to make his living by his self-taught art. He settled on the city by the falls of the Missouri as the place where he would do it.

Russell was to recall his first sight of Great Falls. It had not yet achieved Gibson's desired state of middle-class respectability. "The street were teeming with activity—saloons, dance halls and gambling joints running full blast." Russell and a friend had ridden their horses 125 miles from Chinook (east of Havre) to try their fortunes for the winter in this new cluster of human beings, very different from the lonely cattle outfits where cowpunchers usually spent the winter, or in little towns such as Chinook, picking up odd jobs. Russell had had an offer from Charlie Green, a bartender in Great Falls, to take a monthly wage and give to this frontier patron all his paintings, presumably for sale across the bar. The amount named was seventy-five dollars. Russell found out immediately that working for a salary did not suit him. He broke off. He and several friends took a shack together and lived out the winter in a happy but haphazard way on the south side of town.

> I put up with a bunch of cowpunchers, a roundup cook an' a prizefighter out of work. . . . We rented a two-by-four shack an' I'll never forget those bachelor quarters of ours that we bunched up in that winter. It was one of those old-fashioned tar-paper wickiups with buttons on it, an' 'twas quite a long walk from Central Avenue.
>
> We didn't have no beds; the dirt floor was our bunk. We had dry goods

boxes for chairs; there was a small stove, a few pans and some kettles. I remember the water turned on outdoors.

Civilization came early and settled in placidly. An early helpful influence in Russell's life was the rancher Albert Trigg, who aided him in finding purchasers for his paintings. The Triggs and their daughter Josephine became lifelong friends. It was the uncalculating friendship of such people that roped the cowboy into a beneficial relationship with the city. He and his paintings had had a hazardous existence in his early roaming years. Cattle owners and horse wranglers liked his work. This circle of friends had particularly admired and talked about his postcard sketch *Waiting for a Chinook,* done during the fierce winter of 1886–87. This quick sketch, which was made in part to convey information, showed a bony, starving calf in a blizzard. It was sent along with the foreman's more conventional report to one of the owners of the ranch, Louie Kaufman. The rancher showed the post-card sketch to his friends. This was Russell's first fame. It had happened before he moved to Great Falls.

In addition to Albert Trigg, the owners of two of the Central Avenue bars, the Silver Dollar and the Mint, sold paintings for Russell. The Mint, owned by Sid Willis, eventually became known in the art world and among tourists for its collection of Russell pictures—some of them simply given to Willis. (The Mint collection went to a millionaire's collection in Texas during the hard times of the Great Depression when the city, the state, and private collectors could not afford to keep them. These paintings are housed today in the Amon Carter Museum of Western Art in Fort Worth, Texas.)

A visitor to Montana brought Russell a new kind of life. Nancy Cooper, a seventeen-year-old from the East, met the artist when she came to what she thought of as the Wild West to stay for a while with the Ben Roberts family in Cascade, southwest of Great Falls toward the mountains. Charles was living with these people, helping out with chores in between times in Great Falls. Nancy Cooper was to be Mrs. Russell. She recalled that she met Charles when he was washing dishes. Romanticizing a bit, she recalled:

> He was a little above the average height and weight. His high-heeled riding boots covered small arched feet, his heavy riding breeches of heavy blue army cloth were snug fitting. They were held up by a wonderful bright colored French half-breed sash that clung just above the hips. The sash was

wound around twice, the ends twisted and turned into a queer flat knot, the long fringe tucked into his hip pocket. He wore a gray flannel shirt unbuttoned at the throat with a necktie hanging loosely. . . .

His face, with its square jaw and chin, large mouth tightly closed firm lips, straight nose, high cheek bones, gray deep-set eyes that seemed to see everything. . . . His hands were good-sized, perfectly shaped and with slender, long fingers. He loved jewelry and always wore three or four rings. . . .

He looked like a blond Indian.[7]

This was in 1895. They were married on September 9, 1896, in the Roberts home and lived first in a one-room shack in Cascade. He was thirty-two; she was eighteen. His prospects were not bright. He received all of twenty dollars for 125 painted postcards for the Park Hotel in Great Falls. But then, as his biographers say, Nancy took over the management of the business side of his life and to an extent made him superficially respectable. She annoyed some of his old friends. However, she was very good at the job. Russell happily relinquished the care for survival to his wife and had time and leisure for his own kind of work. The couple moved into the city and eventually settled on land next-door to the Triggs on Fourth Avenue North and in a house made possible by his generous father, who came from Saint Louis to visit his son and daughter-in-law.

Eastern illustrators visiting the West began to take respectful notice of his work and urged the Russells to visit New York City for the advantage of learning techniques and selling paintings. Russell did so for the first time in 1903. He shared a studio with some other painters and quickly picked up what he wanted that the city could teach him while his wife began to make him known to eastern art dealers. Thereafter, Russell and his wife made regular trips to New York to show his work. He had his first one-man show there in 1911, and the exhibit of twenty-five paintings began to make him famous. But he said: "I'll take Central Avenue, bumps an' all, instead of Broadway." He continued to dress, to talk, and to behave in his idiosyncratic way, his personality attracting as much attention as his art. It was in these early days that he met the youthful Will Rogers, a displaced person like himself belonging to both the West and the Indian tradition, and they became friends.

Russell's hometown changed very rapidly in the early decades of the twentieth century. Automobiles coursed up and down Central Avenue.

There were three busy motion-picture houses showing the silent films of the Pickfords, Charlie Chaplin, Buster Keaton, and Lon Chaney and, with unconscious irony, Westerns. Kiwanis and Lions and Rotary clubs had meetings in the splendid Palm Room of the new Rainbow Hotel. There were City Beautiful campaigns. But Russell did not drive a car and was not a joiner, although with some tolerance he gave talks to these clubs when asked.

Alongside the plain white clapboarded two-story house in which Russell lived, he built a log-cabin studio. Here he spent solitary hours painting and, when ready to relax, met his old and sometimes barely presentable cronies, some of whom were Indians. Behind his house he kept a stable with one or two horses in it, usually one of them aging and no longer ridable. Russell had easy and sociable manners. He often ended his day by walking downtown and visiting on the sidewalk with friends.

Russell's street was paved and grew shady as the years passed, green in summer with the elms and ashes that Gibson had decreed. For Gibson's dream of a small, well-kept, thriving city came true. The waterfalls that Meriwether Lewis had admired provided electric power. The harnessed energy of the river made wheels turn in flour mills, lighted houses along the ordered streets, powered streetcars. Copper mined in Butte and smelted in Anaconda was moved on James J. Hill's branch line to the great plant on Smelter Hill and was there refined. A wire mill was added on, and zinc and lead and silver were profitable by-products. The coal that Gibson had surveyed a few miles south of Great Falls turned the little towns of Stockett and Sand Coulee into busy, ugly centers for new clusters of Finns and Slavs. Here and on Smelter Hill a rich mélange of European languages and customs contrasted to the middle-class habits, stiffening into respectability, of the more staid streets.

Surrounding the oasis of the green city, sheep and cattle ranching changed the structure of the wild grasses of the plains. After the terrible winter of 1886–87 discouraged cattle raising, wheat became a staple crop, and Great Falls was the apex of a triangle of golden grain. Along the Missouri and the Sun rivers, irrigation allowed green crops of hay and alfalfa to grow, and bees from many farmers' beehives pollinated these grains.

The city prided itself on its modernity. In the 1920s its citizens thought no town had better lighting, cleaner streets, less poverty, and less flaunted wealth. Its most famous citizen lived in this place but was not ever entirely of it. In his art and in some of the habits of his daily life, Russell memorialized other loyalties. The earlier transitory life of the plains had become the subject of his painting and sculpture.

Russell was quiet about his work. He called himself an "illustrator." But he knew very well that he was doing something important, and he pleased himself with making the almost extinct life of the Indians and cowboys continue in some sense to live. To his old friend Teddy Blue Abbott, he was frank about his loyalties. In his memoir, *We Pointed Them North,* Abbott recalled a conversation he had with Russell (which was perhaps cribbed from a very similar passage in a letter to him by Russell):

> Coming up Dog Creek, I met Russell. I said, "God, I wish I'd been a Sioux Indian a hundred years ago," and I told him the story [about the good life an Indian bragged of to him, of moving easily from good grass to good grass, from old wife to new wife].
>
> He said, "Ted, there's a pair of us. They've been living in heaven for a thousand years, and we took it away from 'em for forty dollars a month."[8]

Despite such yearnings, Russell managed to live well in Gibson's town. He was comfortable with everyone, including the people on the streets of Great Falls and the wealthy men from elsewhere who bought his paintings. The local citizens knew that they had an authentic famous man among them and were proud. Women's club members arranged visits to his studio to hear him "explain" a painting. But he was sardonic about these people who had come in and transformed his old West. Occasionally he became explicit. Invited one day to make a talk to a men's club, he spat out straight at them: "I have been called a pioneer. In my book a pioneer is a man who comes to a virgin country, traps off all the fur, kills off all the wild meat, cuts down all the trees, grazes off all the grass, plows the roots up, and strings ten million miles of wire. A pioneer destroys things and calls it civilization. I wish to God that this country was just like it was when I first saw it and that none of you folks were here at all."[9] The talk was quoted with approval by John K. Hutchens, a Montanan who went East to make a living and a reputation as a book critic.

Those clubmen who may have squirmed a bit under Russell's frank hostility remained, however, tolerant of their local eccentric great man. They probably shook off his words as foolishness and failed to take his strictures to heart. After all, didn't Russell succeed by their own standards? Did he not receive thousands of dollars for each picture? His paintings seemed accessible to these good business and professional men, as well as to anyone. He had become popular among people who knew nothing about art and often prided themselves on that fact. Yet Russell was every bit as self-conscious an artist and as devoted a craftsman as those who did not seem understandable to the average viewer. His self-deprecating manner hid a strong-headed confidence and commitment, as well as a private search for the various ways to attain his ends. The manner also made it easy for a transient generation of critics to patronize him as a regional artist. Time has righted his reputation. It has persisted. He has come to occupy a secure place in art history, and his native gifts have been recognized. His work has been seen to have preserved and memorialized an epoch.

Russell's death made it possible for his own people to idolize him and to sentimentalize his memory and his work, for in his work they thought they saw themselves as old-time westerners. Russell's time had irremediably passed. But these city westerners, pursuing the aims of Gibson, had wistful moments of wishing they had shared the time before power plants were built to take the power from the falls of the Missouri. Indeed, even city westerners—adding shopping centers to their towns, increasing traffic and smog, competing in commercial and industrial skill—still lived under a western sky and endured the weathers of these Northern Plains, and, outside their urban centers, they went out into a wilderness not different from what Russell had known in his youth or even very different from what Meriwether Lewis had known; so they were not the same as easterners. It was impossible for them to lead the kind of free life Russell had led; yet they had a fellow feeling for such a life. This contradiction in their lives made for their self-defeating, yet ennobling, individualism.

Russell's funeral in 1926 in Great Falls was a poignant celebration of a myth. An old, forgotten, glass-bodied hearse was found in a stable in Cascade. Horses were hitched to it. Russell's casket was placed inside. His horse, Redwing, was led behind with stirrups reversed. All the schoolchildren of the city were let out, and the procession wound through downtown streets lined with quiet people moved to tears by a beautiful dead past. In daily life they lived in a world of streetcars and automobiles and office jobs on Central Avenue, smelter jobs on the hill, or oil-refinery jobs west of town. Yet something in their behavior and emotional set had been strengthened by the influence of Russell's character and art. They had mistreated the land, but they felt a strong love for it. Seeing it fixed in art solidified a vague emotion. Some of the strongest environmental laws have been put into effect in this state where "progress," in Gibson's prescription, has made for the most heartless destruction of water and land and people.

The cemetery where both Russell and Gibson are buried is an island of green on the prairie. To reach it, a visitor leaves the city behind and moves south across a lilt of brown land and sees ahead a crown of trees. The cemetery is situated on a slight uplift of ground. To a traveler from the South, a magpie on the gateway seemed like a bird of fantasy, with its grossly long tail, shining iridescence, and croaking voice. The tall, square-cut marker engraved "Paris Gibson, Founder of Great Falls" stands in the shade inside the gateway. His end was here, although his beginning was in Maine. The grave of Russell, his fellow, opposite, and friend, is on the other side of the cemetery, where the land slants toward the south and where one can still look out beyond low branches and from underneath deep shade to the golden plains and eastward to the blue line of the High-woods. The cowboy's marker is an appropriately rough large boulder, to which has been affixed a copper plate bearing name and dates; a foot marker has on it only *C. M. R.* In midsummer, a few geraniums gloomed against the uneven stone, the color almost disappearing in the shade.

The city has a handsome memorial to Russell outside the museum dedicated to his work and that of other western artists. Bob Scriver's larger-than-life figure of the artist in cowboy garb strides forward on a pedestal near the building. Gibson's statue is in Gibson Park, removed from its original commanding position at the western end of Central Avenue. The Civic Center now blocks the view west, which once led one in imagination toward the mountains.

The Gibson statue is decently marked by a circle of flowers. The figure's stance is determined and authoritative. His right arm is raised in command or blessing, but the drama of his position has been lost. He once had all of the movement of Central Avenue to gaze down upon. It is probable that with the passing years he is less and less known to his townspeople. Art lasts longer than enterprise. Yet the city is, for the most part, living Gibson's dream of the good life, rather than Russell's. However, it is Russell's feckless dream of irresponsible freedom in the great space surrounding this urban center which still has mythical power.

In some sense the good life of Great Falls still lives in a lazy equilibrium between the opposite view of its two heroes, its founder, Paris Gibson, and its cowboy artist, Charles Russell. The citizens of this modest self-contained city are proud of their wide streets, green parks, good library, first-rate newspaper, relatively progressive business community, and decent city government. They also enjoy the easy way one can get out of the city and into the occasionally welcome loneliness of wide spaces. The contemporary airport embodies a potent contradiction. Not so well used as its ambitious builders wished, it has every modern convenience for the traveler—long runways, clean high hallways, an imposing central space where the scattered comers and goers seem half lost, comfortable waiting areas with deeply cushioned seats, escalators, curio shops, a coffee shop open at four in the morning before a commuter plane to Denver or Salt Lake City leaves.

The citizens of Great Falls wish to be both dwellers in the latest minute of today's world and also inhabitants of their own world of the past. They wish for more development, of the kind Gibson preached—more engineering of the present so that they can travel confidently into an assumed good future. (They are only slightly uneasy about the Minuteman missiles still ringed around their city.) And in contradiction to this, they passionately believe that the past, at least here in the West, was better, that Russell and his friends had all the fun, and that when they get out into the wild they are sharing the past. They are torn between making that great alien otherness of mountains and plains serve them; either by law or custom, they are hopeful of leaving it alone so that it can continue to give them an identity separate from that of other Americans.

ELEVEN

Who Was Calamity Jane?
A Speculation

There were probably many unknown thirteen-year-old girls as well as boys riding a horse alongside a hard-pressed family in a makeshift wagon going west in the 1860s, and learning to shoot and hunt and fish along the way, collecting wood or bison chips for a fire, or helping in the bad spots when the men of the train needed a push or a pull. One child who made this journey soon lost her mother, then her father, and then her numerous brothers and sisters, who were deposited with willing families. She was turned loose—or, rather, broke loose—at fifteen, to make her own way in the high prairie and mountain world of the last West. It could not have been predicted that she would become well-known in her own world and later luridly famous in a broader world that came to hear of her as Calamity Jane, in a story that is part truth and part legend.

For who has not heard of Calamity Jane? She could ride a horse like an Indian warrior, she could flick a bullwhip and drive any team, she wore men's clothes, she told tall tales. She could gamble and curse and face up to danger with a gun in her hand. She knew Buffalo Bill Cody. She was a friend or something more of Wild Bill Hickok. She was an inhabitant of Deadwood when it was a wild town and later when it was too tame for her, and she had roamed the settler and railroad towns of the whole Northwest. She was a scandal and a heroine. She shocked the respectable, and she drew, even from them, admiration for generosity and for helping out in a crisis, as when she nursed smallpox victims when no one else would stay with them in a stinking, shut-up cabin in Deadwood. Her grave, which took her body when she was prematurely old and worn in a time that was no longer hers, is next to Hickok's.

Who Was Calamity Jane? A Speculation

American memory has been puzzled by what to do with Calamity Jane. She has been either a movie-star heroine of a West that never quite existed, or she has become lately a drunk and a whore, a disgrace to all the good, hardworking settlers who transformed the dusty and disorderly world of the West into the peaceful settlements of grassed yards and tree-lined streets—an approximation of a new paradise hiding the compromises and corruptions that settlement had entailed.

Two deep-seated impulses have gotten in the way of a clear look. The brief days of the old West are dear to settled Americans today, especially to the well-behaved descendants of the original unruly pioneers. Today's sober citizens wish to belong to a brave, carefree, careless, even violent, and yet overall good community of the past, and they do not want to disturb the legendry of that past. On the other hand, it has been easier to depreciate the reputation of a woman such as Calamity Jane than to denigrate even the palpably exaggerated deeds of the Bill Hickocks, the Buffalo Bills, the Kit Carsons, the George Armstrong Custers.

The verified facts about the life of Martha Jane Cannary Burke are sparse but sufficiently remarkable. What Jane had to say about her very earliest years is probably largely true. Her little pamphlet, *Life and Adventures of Calamity Jane,* which she tried to sell for a small sum or a drink in her later years, tells us that she was born in Princeton, a small community of the frontier edge of north-central Missouri, in 1852. At thirteen, Jane traveled west toward Montana by wagontrain, with her parents and her five younger brothers and sisters. She was orphaned of her mother at fourteen, and of her father at fifteen. The younger children were disposed of in apparently willing Mormon families in Utah, where, among other places, the family lived for a time. After two deaths and the disposal of the siblings, Jane set out to lead an independent life in the frontier world of men and their activities.

Then details become vague. But in the last frontier world of the Rocky Mountain north, Jane emerged fully fledged as a bold young woman, sometimes dressed in man's clothes, doing such things as driving stagecoaches, riding horseback, driving teams in the service of one or another of the lonely military outposts of the Dakotas or Kansas, or doing gang work at the railhead of the frantic forward push of one of the rail lines bringing change to the plains and mountains. When she could not find man's work, she washed dishes, washed clothes, cooked in a home or a restaurant, hosted a saloon, nursed ill people, gambled, and, it was easily assumed, lived a loose life outside the conventions of a society unconventional for men only; women were either nice or bad.

Jane had a rough tongue and a forthright disposition. She caused her peers to accept or reject her on her own terms. Most of those who remembered Jane spoke of her as plain. The photographs bear them out. But in her younger days, with her quick and clever movements, her horse-rider's good figure, and plenty of red hair, she gave to at least a few the impression of good looks. In her later years, the photographs show harsh and forbidding features, a look out at the world as if its owner were saying: try to cross me.

It is possible that Jane went along with the Jenney Geological Expedition looking for confirmation of rumors of gold in the Black Hills. This was before the 1874 army column moved into the Black Hills under the already notorious Colonel Custer to confirm the fact. Several writings confirm that Jane went along as a teamster in General George Crook's crack wagontrain in 1876, moving north into the Rosebud and Tongue River country in what was thought would be a grand pincer movement to round up recalcitrant Indians and place them on reservations. She was a known associate of Wild Bill Hickok in Deadwood in 1876 before his death there, but how close a friend she was then, or had been earlier, would be in dispute.

After the wilder day of this region subsided, Jane was never again at home in the changing West. Her edge of aggressive insistence on being part of a man's world, in which most women were either drudges or whores, did not sit well with an increasingly respectable public. As she grew older, she exaggerated her real and considerable past exploits. She embroidered and encouraged tall tales about herself. She was a good cook and kept an inn for a few years near the Yellowstone River, a few miles from Billings. She volunteered for tough nursing duties.

Her drinking got heavier, and Jane suffered in her health and in the good opinion of respectable folk. She was married at least once, to Charley Burke. She appeared in two Wild West shows, in Buffalo and Minneapolis, but was not a success. She may have appeared for a time in Buffalo Bill's show, relegated to a nonstarring part because of her known drinking habits.

Along the way, single or as Mrs. Burke, Jane picked up stray children as if they had been helpless, mangy dogs or cats and cared for them. Some of the children may have been her own although she never admitted this. She would be remembered warmly for her offhand way of helping when help was needed. Good old Calamity! But no one held open a solid place for her in the new world of the settled West.

Jane was alone and ill and without funds when she died in Terry, South Dakota, on August 1 or 2, 1903. To her friends, it was appropriate for her to die on August 2 because it was the twenty-seventh anniversary of Hickok's death. They may have adjusted the date. These friends claimed her body and carried it back to nearby Deadwood, as she was said to have requested. Then Deadwood, glorying in its own past, remembered her. It was easier to do so with gusto after she was safely dead. The Methodist minister and the whole town gave her a whopping big funeral, and they buried her, as she wanted, next to Hickok's grave.

Many years after her death, when the legend of Jane had taken many fantastic forms, there appeared a document that would become the center of the continuing controversy as to who and what Martha Jane Cannary was. In 1941, a woman who said her name was Jean Hickok McCormick appeared, holding an old bound album that had been used apparently as a diary of unsent letters by Jane to an unknown daughter in England. McCormick said that she was that daughter, that her mother was Calamity Jane (Martha Jane Hickok Burke), and that her father was Wild Bill Hickok (James Butler Hickok). The album diary contained entries dated from 1877 to 1903 and purported to show the interior life of Jane during those years. The controversy as to the identity of Jane—that is, the making out or the filling out of the character—would never be the same again.

The legend of Jane grew before and after the appearance of the album of letters. Movies of the thirties and forties and later found Calamity Jane a handy peg on which to hang a Western. She was an endearing tomboy played by Jean Arthur to Gary Cooper's Hickok. She was impossibly a glamorous, exotic Yvonne de Carlo in *Calamity Jane and Sam Bass*. But after 1941 many writers, both popular and scholarly, attempted to assess a darker side of Jane, and sometimes a more complex aspect, in books that poured forth.

A pamphlet appeared in 1946. Its main purpose seemed to be the reprinting of an early assessment of Hickok, but it included comments on Jane by William E. Connolley from his *Wild Bill and His Era:* "So we can discard that coy charmer, the buckskin clad belle of the plains whom so many writers have fused into Calamity Jane, and yet have a fascinating woman, and a most interesting personality, with whom to deal."[1] This writer concluded that Jane had never had an intimate relationship with Hickok.

In 1948 Stewart Holbrook wrote about Jane in his book *Little Annie Oakley and Other Rugged People:* "There is no shred of evidence to show she ever served, either as man or woman, in any military body of the U.S. Army—that is, not in an official capacity. The Army did not carry camp followers on its muster rolls."[2] This assessment is careless. Jane was hired as a teamster in the wagontrain that General Crook considered an essential part of his army.

Some of the popularizers were determined to make the most of the picturesque dark side of Jane's later days. In *Desperate Women* (1952), James D. Horan wrote, as if he had seen her: "Jane wandered about the West, a grotesque creature, dressed in a ragged black dress, battered flowered hat, worn boots, a drunken grin framing two yellow teeth."[3] However, he recorded that he had talked to a few old hands who said they remembered Jane. Some scoffed at the story of her friendship with Hickok. But another, the rancher Ben Greenough, prosperous after leaner times, said to Horan: "I am convinced they were great pals."* Horan also wrote, trying to be judicious about the album of letters, "of course, without an opinion of a handwriting expert it cannot be flatly labeled spurious."

In 1969, Harry Sinclair Drago, in a book whose title promised a certain kind of treatment, *Notorious Ladies of the Frontier,* wrote about Jane: "By the time she was twenty-four, she was a confirmed alcoholic. She could outcurse, outshout and outdrink most of the men with whom she consorted. She was also fearless."[4] Drago thinks she "would be largely unknown today were it not for what the fictioneers and the romanticists, bent on presenting her as a tragic, misunderstood soap-opera heroine, have done with her— mindless of the facts." He is harsh with gusto: she "was a widely traveled, coarse, slovenly frontier whore!"

Another writer, Joseph G. Rosa, wrote with considerable care about both Hickok and Jane. In two books, *They Called Him Wild Bill* (1964) and *The West of Wild Bill Hickok* (1982), he expressed a thoughtful disbelief in the legend of the romance between the two personifications of the last golden West. He believed that the album of Jane's supposed letters was probably not authentic. He checked out certain details and found them to

---

*Ben Greenough appears in the disputed letters as a boy whom Jane befriended when he was destitute.

be discrepancies easily proven. He was bothered by the fact that there was no example of Jane's handwriting extant except in the album. He claimed to have found out the whereabouts of Hickok at the time of the supposed marriage of the two, but he had not found out, and no one else had, where Jane was at that time—a nagging uncertainty, very aggravating.

In 1958 there appeared a book promising a more considered approach. This was Roberta Beed Sollid's *Calamity Jane: A Study in Historical Criticism.*[5] The book sorts out claims and counterclaims and assesses what was probably true, an extravagance made up by Jane, or a tall tale told by others later. Sollid agrees that Jane was with Crook, that she was probably a bull-whacker, that she appeared in at least two eastern show engagements, in Minneapolis and Buffalo, and that she deteriorated into drunkenness in her older years, for which she served time in jail. She attempts to account for the probability of the story of Jean McCormick being the daughter of a properly married Jane and Hickok, and her presentation of the famous album. Sollid believes that the story is a fraud and that McCormick had an ulterior need to authenticate a parentage. But Sollid is ultimately baffled; she has no way to say whether the makeshift marriage certificate in the album is genuine, and she states that there was no way of knowing when Jane and Hickok met or married. She quibbles about discrepancies in dates, but in the end leaves a reluctant question hanging in the air.

What is remarkable about Sollid's scholarly attempt at finding out the truth about Calamity Jane is its emotional bias. The writer's tone deplores not only the lack of evidence that she has carefully tried to find but also Jane's character. She writes in the "Preface": "Like most prostitutes and drunkards she left little behind in the way of tangible evidence." Moral condemnation plays a part in descriptions: "Martha was compelled to forage for herself and chose the easiest path. In her life of shame she associated with the lowest types of miners, soldiers and railroad workers. . . . She made herself conspicuous by her immorality and also by her kindness to the sick and unfortunate. . . . She accumulated numerous 'husbands,' by whom she may have borne children." Sollid's praise is always tempered; she admits that Jane was a nurse to smallpox victims in Deadwood, but maintains that she was anxious to leave a patient in order to tank up.

The "Note from the Publisher" presents the book to the reader as "a truly scholarly effort to set the record straight concerning Calamity Jane."[6] If this is so in the book's analysis of facts, it is, however, remarkably lacking in emotional objectivity. In one instance, the author, having dug up old newspaper stories about Jane's having been jailed for public drunkenness, is judgmental: "Her very nature indicates that her whole mature life was spent in and out of jails and that the above mentioned incidents are but a few that received extra publicity."

Fictional treatments of Calamity Jane have shown a remarkable sea change over the years. In 1959, Glenn Clairmonte published *Calamity Was the Name for Jane,* a novelized life smoothly put together from the questioned album diary. The author used the source as if it were Gospel truth and buttressed this foundation with rationalizations. The Jane presented here is purified, shorn of earthy contradictions.

By the 1980s and the 1990s, perhaps following the trend in historical revisionism to take a larger and more severe look at the old West, novelists depicted Jane as a part of a flawed development in American culture. In 1986 Pete Dexter in *Deadwood* characterized Jane in 1876 (surely too early) as a dirty slut, who slept without a qualm with the most repulsive villain of the piece and habitually passed out drunk. She is shown as self-deluded in her regard for Wild Bill. Dexter has portrayed Hickok in the last summer of his life as polite and handsome on the outside, but utterly empty inside, syphilitic, and going blind.

Buffalo Girls (1990) by Larry McMurtry shows the older, sadder, if not wiser, Jane as taking part in Wild West shows that are a sort of humiliation. However, he pays a tribute of form to the controversial album diary. The novel is in the form of such letters, as if the older Jane is writing to her daughter, "Dear Janey," in England. McMurtry has at least a kind of admiration for the aesthetic truth of the disputed letters.

It is now in order to try for gleanings of truth from primary sources. Something can be gained from the first-hand impression of a few who wrote about Jane after having known her either casually or as a friend in the early days in the West.

In his older years, a former territorial governor of New Mexico, Miguel Antonio Otero, wrote with great satisfaction about the life he had led as a young boy in the raw town of Hays City, Kansas, where his father was a merchant.[7] In 1868 he had admired Hickok, the marshal chosen to the office by a "Vigilance Committee," and the way in which he had meted out swift justice with his gun. Cool, well-mannered, and handsome, the marshal was a figure for a young man's hero worship. Otero and most of the townspeople justified the deaths that Hickok very efficiently served out. Hickok said that he never killed except in self-defense, but perhaps the self-defense had been provoked. This frighteningly swift and efficient justice later stimulated gunmen to rival or possibly extinguish him. This story of his career would become a legend for dozens of book and movie Westerns to imitate, some with utmost banality, a few with an Oresteian tragic sense.

Otero also remembered that Jane, then only twenty, he thought (she was sixteen), was also in Hays City at this time, "extremely good-looking," as he recalled. Perhaps memory and the blur of what he was to hear about her from others made him think that he at that time admired her for all the traits for which she would become famous. Or perhaps she already possessed these talents: her horsemanship, her ability with a pistol or rifle, her gambling, her careless and generous use of money. He gives no evidence that he ever talked to her or knew her personally, as he said he had known Hickok. But he reports that she "was regarded by the community as a camp follower."

Between 1867 and 1869 Otero was an impressionable boy, the son of a retail storekeeper, keeping his eyes open to the entertainment that the figures of a wild railroad town afforded his imagination. His testimony does not include any kind of alliance between Jane and Bill, but it is important that he shows them inhabiting the same space at the same time, early in their history. He believed she had gone on from Hays City from railroad town to railroad town, in a role (following community judgment) as "camp follower." But he also wrote admiringly: "As she grew older, she developed into a rather bright woman."

The best reported episode of Jane's life was her turning up as a teamster in General George Crook's well-disciplined advance of troops and supply train in the movement he led north from Wyoming into Montana in the spring and summer of 1876, a part of the army movement that was planned to put an end to the wanderings of the Lakotas (Sioux) and place them on a reservation. In this ambitious and, as it turns out, overweening design, General Crook was to move from south to north, Colonel John Gibbon was to move from west to east, and General Alfred H. Terry (with Colonel George Armstrong Custer—"General" only by courtesy, demoted after the Civil War—under his command) from east to west. They were all to come together and trap the hapless Sioux. But this was a land without telegraphs or rails, and communications among the three arms of the pincer movement very early lapsed.

Crook's army was the best equipped, the most carefully organized and ordered by the most experienced of the Indian fighters, and, in the end, the one most sympathetic to Indians. Crook scorned flash and show and preferred dependable mules above high-stepping horses. He himself often rode a mule at the head of the column, his rifle across his arms, ready for a shot at whatever game the troops raised as they moved. That Jane, presenting herself as a man, was accepted into his tightly disciplined wagontrain makes one believe that she was equipped to do the job. Crook had an obsession about supply, and he required the best in his teamsters.

John F. Finerty, a correspondent of the *Chicago Times* who accompanied Crook's campaign, later wrote a book about the experience.[8] (By this time the American newspaper tradition had made it commonplace for correspondents to be part of each of these western campaigns.) Finerty's description of the troops and the wagontrain is colorful, but a little finicky in his distaste for the loud and obscene language of the teamsters. Surely he exaggerated, but Finerty found the officers "models of the early Christian type of mankind," and the teamsters as unattractive as their animals. "Ears polite would be immeasurably shocked by the sounds and observations that accompany the starting of a pack train." However, he admitted that the packtrain made a fine sight as it paraded north from Fort Fetterman into the unknown: "The wagons, 120 in all, with their white awnings and massive wheels, each drawn by six mules, covered the rising ground."

Finerty apparently did not know of Calamity Jane either by name or reputation at this time. Fourteen years later, writing his memoirs, he reported what seems a garbled account of her discovery in Crook's wagontrain. He said that along with the teamsters came a peddler who sold whiskey, and "two abandoned females, disguised as mule drivers, who also came into camp." He stated that the general had the whiskey dealer and "the harlots put under arrest, to be sent back with the first train." In reality there was only one "harlot," and she was Jane. It was very difficult for a man such as Finerty to see any woman who was not a "nice woman" as anything but a "harlot."*

Jane was young at this time, twenty-four, and strong, and proud of her ability to handle horses and mules like a man. She preferred men's dress because it made it easier to do men's things. The only way she could have been a teamster on General Crook's wagontrain was to have been able to

---

*This labeling of Jane would follow her the rest of her life. Although she may have took part in one or another brothel, prostitution did not seem to be a chosen profession. Any woman who felt free of her own will to sleep with whomever she chose was always treated and labeled differently from a man who might do the same thing.

perform as well as the men. This, it seems, was what she was doing until somehow it was discovered that she was a woman.

One of General Crook's officers, Captain ("Colonel" by courtesy of a war rank) Anson Mills, also remembered the incident.[9] For when Jane was discovered and was being hauled off the job unceremoniously, she spoke up familiarly and impertinently to him (having known who he was back at one of the forts). Mills incorporated this memory of a woman who would become famous or infamous, in a talk he made before a group of old soldiers, the Order of Indian Wars, on March 2, 1917. By then brigadier general, retired, he spoke with some relish of being hailed by Jane: "The day she was discovered and placed under guard, unconscious of the fact, I was going through the wagon-master's outfit when she sprang up, calling out 'There is Colonel Mills, he knows me,' when everybody began to laugh, much to my astonishment and chagrin, being married."

The elderly man recalled with humor how he had been embarrassed and yet pleased by the teasing he got: "It was not many hours until every man in the camp knew of the professed familiarity of 'Calamity Jane' (as she was known) with me, and for several days my particular friends pulled me aside, and asked me, 'Who is Calamity Jane?'" Mills kept insisting—all the time enjoying, as a shy, well-behaved man, his sudden notoriety—that he did not know her. His backward look at her was not scornful:

> We carried her along until a force was organized to carry our helpless back, with which she was sent, but she afterwards turned out to be a national character, and was a woman of no mean ability and force even from the standard of men. I learned later that she had been a resident of North Platte, and that she knew many of my soldiers, some of whom had probably betrayed her. Later she had employed herself as a cook for my next-door neighbor, Lieutenant Johnson, and had seen me often in his house, I presume.

Another account of Jane's being in Crook's wagontrain exists in *On the Border with Crook,* the memoir that Crook's aide-de-camp John G. Bourke wrote. His view was neither romantic nor prurient:

> It was whispered that one of our teamsters was a woman, and no other than "Calamity Jane," a character famed in border story; she had donned the raiment of the alleged rougher sex, and was skinning mules with the best of them.

She was eccentric and wayward rather than bad, and had adopted male attire more to aid her in getting a living than for any improper purpose. "Jane" was as rough and burly as any of her messmates, and it is doubtful if her sex would ever had been discovered had not the wagonmaster noted that she didn't cuss her mules with the enthusiasm to be expected from a graduate of Patrick and Saulsbury's Black Hill Stage Line, as she had represented herself to be. [10]

It is known that later in the same summer (1876) Jane turned up in Deadwood, sometimes in the company of Hickok and some others, gadding up and down the street on horseback, cheered or stared at in the saloons, joining the drinkers who stopped stock still to watch Hickok gamble. Hickok was a private person, and a gambler, not a peace officer in Deadwood, as he had been in Hays City and Abilene. But as an onlooker was to tell, Hickok would be called on to aid "law and order" when needed. Some accounts state that Jane came into this new town with Hickok; others said not. In any case, she was in and out of Deadwood after her adventure with General Crook; she watched and admired Hickok; she knew him at least casually, perhaps more intimately. She was apparently not on the scene when, on August 2, Jack McCall shot and killed Hickok at the gambling table. Jane was to claim that she caught the assassin. This turned out to be one of her tall stories; the crowd at the saloon caught him at the door. She was there when McCall was tried and acquitted (to be hanged later in another place). But it is clear that the event crystallized Jane's memory of Hickok and made it a lifelong obsession.

One gets tantalizing glimpses of Jane in the memoirs of Otero, Mills, Finerty, and Bourke; they knew about her and in a sense enlarged on their own experience of the Wild West, by telling that they had brushed past her or spent time with her. But none of these men knew Jane as a friend. But two others, E. C. ("Teddy Blue") Abbott and William Lull, did.

Abbott's story of the great final cattle drives in the unfenced spaces of the West, and the move north from the closing ranges of Texas to the last open ranges in Wyoming and Montana, has become a classic in the version of his life which he uninhibitedly told to Helena Huntington Smith, published as a book entitled *We Pointed Them North*. Abbott ran into Jane from time to time and they became friends. William Lull, whose memories have never been published, recorded his friendship with Jane in papers that his family has kept through several generations and that until now have never been used as source material for information about Jane and about the life of Deadwood.

Abbott wrote that he remembered seeing Jane first in 1878 (although he was shaky about exact dates, as a later memory shows). This was in Deadwood. "I didn't meet her then, but I got a good look at her, when she was at the height of her fame and looks. I remember she was dressed in purple velvet, with diamonds on her and everything. As I recall it, she was some sort of a madam at that time, running a great big gambling hall in Deadwood."[11]

By the 1880s in Miles City, Abbott was good friends with Jane. In 1883 he says that he ran into her in a hotel where he and his fellow cowhands, having concluded a cattle run, were staying; he offered her drinks, then enlisted her in a prank. This was a roughhouse practical joke he wanted to play on a dour, puritanical trail boss whom he and the other men of the outfit despised. They saw the elderly man (Fuller, as he was called in a made-up name by Teddy Blue) sitting in the bar glumly trying to police his cowhands to prevent them from getting a drink. Teddy Blue took Jane apart and said to her:

> "I'll give you two dollars and a half if you'll go and sit on his lap and kiss him." And she was game. She walked up to him with everybody watching her, and sat down on his lap, and throwed both her arms around him so his arms were pinned to his sides and he couldn't help himself—she was strong as a bear. And then she began kissing him and saying: "Why don't you ever come to see me any more, honey? You know I love you." And so forth.

When freed from her grasp, the man, to the delight of his cowpunchers, departed the hotel, and they saw him no more that night.

Abbott's last two memories of Jane concerned money. He had borrowed fifty cents from her one day in the Belly-Ups stagecoach stop on the way from Miles City to Deadwood. He said he had money back at a ranch but needed the sum for a meal. "I thanked her for the fifty cents and said: 'Some day I'll pay you.' And she said: 'I don't give a damn if you never pay me.' She meant it, because she was always the kind that would share her last cent."

Abbott got the date wrong of his last encounter with Jane. He said it occurred in 1907, whereas Jane had died in 1903. However, the incident remained vivid to the older man as he was telling his story in the 1930s:

And I never saw her again until twenty-four years later. It was in 1907, and she was standing on a street corner in Gilt Edge; which was more of a town than it is now, since they took half the buildings away. I walked up to her and said: "Don't you know me?" and gave her the fifty cents. She recognized me then and said: "I told you, Blue, that I didn't give a damn if you never paid me." And we went and drank it up. She had been famous a long time then, traveling with Buffalo Bill's show and so on, and she was getting old.

He jibed at her a little, asking her how she had liked, having been back in the East, to have been civilized. "Her eyes filled with tears. She said: 'Blue, why don't the sons of bitches leave me alone and let me go to hell my own route? All I ask is to be allowed to live out the rest of my life with you boys who speak my language. And I hope they lay me beside Bill Hickok when I die.' "

Abbott was as authentic a westerner as Jane, but generations went by fast, and he was to belong in his later years to the next one after her, that of the cattlemen. He married Granville Stuart's daughter and so also linked himself to the generation before that of Jane, that of the earliest settlers; but Stuart, by the time Abbott became his son-in-law, had traveled on into another era: that of the brief period of the cattle kings of eastern Montana. The generations closely and quickly trod upon each other in the West's changing northern mountains and prairies.

Authentic and poignant memories of Jane in Deadwood have come to light in the private papers of William Lull. [12] He was a fresh-faced boy from the East who had come West to the Black Hills and its environs in August 1875, first to try his luck at gold digging, then at other ways of making a living in the new town of Deadwood. In addition to one job of supervising the grading of the town streets, he took on a position as assistant to the owner of Porter's Hotel, where Jane occasionally stayed. Billie Lull, or Baby-Face Lull, as he was known, was laughed at and also admired by the wild town for not drinking or smoking and somehow keeping the look and reality of youthful innocence. From the evidence of letters he wrote home to his family in New York State,* the young man, enjoying new experiences

---

*These letters were kept by the family and passed on from one generation to another and from several pages of an account that Lull wrote fifty years later and entitled "Calamity Jane, Deadwood City in Pioneer Days," kept with the family letters.

in a world strange to him, was good-humored, tolerant, and observant. It had been a great adventure for him to come here from a staid Methodist family. He recorded for the family and for himself his admiration for Hickok, who was in Deadwood in 1876 and was killed there that year. Lull also recorded his liking for Jane, whom he would know for several years longer than he had known Hickok.

The high point of Lull's connection with Hickok was service with him on a hastily organized posse that was sent out from Deadwood one hundred miles west to rescue some miners who were said to be threatened by Indians. On August 9, 1876, Lull wrote a long lively letter to his family about the expedition. (The proud boast of the family from this time on would be that Lull "rode with Wild Bill Hickock.")[13]

Lull told how Hickok led an "every-man-for-himself-charge" up a hill held by the Indians. Lull's horse fell on him, and a new friend, Charlie, was killed. Burying Charlie, who had told him he was sixteen years old, Lull found that he was burying a girl. (Jane was not the only woman who tried to do things like a man.) Over the last campfire before the posse went home, having buried their dead and left twenty-seven Indians for the wolves, Lull had a talk with Hickok, who stopped to ask how he and Charlie had gotten along, and who stayed to talk more about life in general, and death. Hickok talked, as if obsessed, about his own death. He told Lull he would not be killed by an Indian, but by some unknown white man looking for revenge for the life of a friend or relative whom Hickok had shot. He knew that he had killed too many in earlier days—in his own way of thinking, always for duty or in self-defense—to believe much in his own longevity.

As Lull told his family dramatically, this prophecy had been fulfilled only seven days before he sat down to write this letter. For Hickok, who had brought his troop of Indian fighters home to Deadwood on the past Saturday morning, was killed that night, August 2, sitting at a poker game in a saloon, with Lull himself among the watchers as McCall shot him, approaching him from behind and aiming at close range and at his head a gun suddenly and unexpectedly brought into view. McCall was caught at the door. But he was to be freed in Deadwood on his excuse of killing to revenge a death, and only later to be hanged in another place.

Lull, writing about Jane many years later, with his memories perhaps somewhat colored by the importance of the fact that he had known her on common and everyday terms in that long-off and faraway Deadwood, recalled her as a somewhat taciturn woman who did not talk about herself, who was marvelously skilled in the teamster's abilities of riding, driving, and wielding the long bullwhip, and who was generous and honest.

In 1876, the year of going on the Crook march north toward the Rosebud and the Little Big Horn, and also the year of Hickok's death, Jane was twenty-four, a woman not pretty, but striking, with the fine figure of a good rider of horses, and also the look of having weathered under sun and wind. Lull's report implies in Jane an attitude of having not been put down as yet by fate, but also the wariness of one who knows how ready fate would be to jump.

Against the weight of other opinions, it is worth noting that Lull, who knew both Hickok and Jane, thought that they were friends. Lull wrote that "another, a friend and frequent companion of [Hickock's] in the search for adventure, was Calamity Jane." Lull noted that, "like Bill, she had little to say about anything, but was more prone to act." "Her notoriety sprang rather from her utter fearlessness." Lull said that "Jane was well known in most of the frontier towns. In gold stampedes and new railroad construction camps she was among the first to appear."

Lull had watched her demonstrate her proficiency as a teamster: "She could sit in the saddle of one of the wheel team, and with a jerk line extending to the bit of the lead team guide eighteen or twenty mules over the unbroken trails and through mountain passes, with skill unsurpassed by the most experienced mule skinners, while with a fifty-feet whip lash she picked a horse-fly off the ear of the lead mule."

When Lull took on the job of running the hotel, he deepened his knowledge of the life of the place. Porter's Hotel was where the "girls" stayed, who he said usually had gamblers as "paramours." He remembered that Jane was one of the eight "girls" occupying rooms in the hotel. But he termed Jane "a lone wolf." He wrote that she had "neither partner nor paramour." (Lull knew all about the lives of these other girls, yet treated them with courtesy.) Jane seemed to be a special case. She did not, to his knowledge, take part in the activities of the other girls, but he deduced that "she had never before been treated as a lady," as he treated her. "It was something new, and not to her taste, and her reply was always, with a sneer on her face, 'Go to H——, Baby Face.'"

Writing his narrative about Calamity Jane in the third person, Lull remembered: "For some reason, Billie was more interested in Jane than in any of the other girls. She had a personality of her own, and he felt that the surliness was a cloak to hide something that she was ashamed to let appear on the surface." He tells the story of a crisis in her life when there was no one to take care of her when she fell ill in a room in the hotel. He got her a doctor, who said her illness looked like typhoid. Lull gave her medicine once a day. He bullied the other girls, under threat of being kicked out of the hotel if they did not do what he asked, into taking care of Jane twice a day for "her woman's needs."

Jane's disputed letters confirm the episode. Under the date July 1880, Coulson, appeared this entry (and Jane never had any knowledge of Lull's writing later about her in an article never published): "I met a man here today from Deadwood who knew my best friend there, Mister Will Lull. I was sick with a fever of some sort while rooming at his hotel. The Hotel Baby Face took over from New Orleans man, Porter, and Lull was so good to me. He knows his business. I like him very much, he always treats me with 'Howdy Jane, little girl. Keep a stiff upper lip, remember you're a good girl.' "[14]

Lull remembered that, after getting better from her illness, Jane took a job "serving customers with refreshments" at the Bell Union Saloon. One time she waited on Lull and he asked her to take his poke of gold dust to have it weighed. Bystanders jeered at Lull and told him he would never see his money. But the next day Jane brought the poke to him in the hotel. "Slamming my poke down on the desk she turned and walked away with a half shamed look. At the moment of giving him the money for the gold dust, she exclaimed to him reprovingly: 'There is not another man living who would ever have seen it if he had done such a d——-fool thing.' " Lull concluded that "Jane was not all hard and calloused, as she would have people think."

Lull set down other telling memories. Jane helped Lizzie, one of the girls who had cared for her in the hotel. She stuck a gun in the midsection of a man who had cheated Lizzie with black sand in place of gold in her poke. Jane made him measure out the equivalent amount of gold for Lizzie in the saloon. After Jane had recovered from her typhoid, Jane, with gambling gains, repaid Lull for the doctor, and the girls for their help, during her illness time in the hotel. She had had luck and paid back her debts of four hundred dollars in twenty-dollar gold pieces.

Jane gave Lull a tintype of herself and said: don't show this to your girl back in God's country, for you won't stay out here. "If you show it to some nice young girl, don't tell her it was your sweetheart or she might give you the bounce!" Lull did indeed return to the East and, after saying good-by, never saw Jane again. He read about her at intervals. One time he read that she had given up her wild life and married Clinton Burke, a rancher. Another time Lull saw that Jane had appeared at the Centennial in Buffalo. "Ten more years passed, when Billie saw in the papers that Jane had passed away." He was glad that the report told him that she had been buried alongside Hickok. His belief in their friendship persisted. "Jane and Bill had been friends and partners in many a search. What more fitting than that they shared rest side by side!"

After the glory days of riding with Crook, the camaraderie of life in Deadwood, and the admiring friendship of upright men such as Abbott and Lull, there was not much more of achievement or drama in Jane's life. Her expertness in men's work, her generosity, and her courage had made Jane famous in a limited world. But that world very quickly disappeared. Mining settled down into a corporate affair. After their last desperate battles, the Indians were rounded up and put on reservations. The rugged railroad workers drove their last spikes, and railroading became a workaday matter of conducting and engineering on preset schedules; tourists began riding the trains west to gaze with curiosity out of the windows at the dwindling number of bison. A layer of culture and new kinds of sophisticated corruption buried forever the hell-for-leather, free-and-easy, and awful life of the brief old West. Yet the new culture preserved a wishful nostalgia for that past.

The woman who had been named "Calamity" was left in a drab and long-enduring present. She was guilty of the sin of trying to make an even better story out of her past than it had been. She worked the story to eke out a precarious existence. She did not to have the talents of Buffalo Bill Cody in exploiting his own considerable past for monetary gain in his Wild West shows. She took part in at least two stage engagements in Minneapolis and Buffalo, possibly even with Buffalo Bill, who, if he hired her, hid her by then drunken presence in anonymity among his extra riders. She did not do very well with the curious little telltale pamphlet that she wrote about her life and tried to sell. [15] She did not know how to ingratiate herself with a curious public.

Nevertheless, the legend of Calamity Jane grew. It did not help her materially during her life, but, after her death, the story generated books and films; it put money in the purse of those who dealt with a possible

Jane in fiction, semifiction, and the popular forms of regional western history and biography. There also came, somewhat later, a scholarly search for the real Jane; it uncovered, for the most part, the sad and unsavory details of her later days.

This might have been all there was to say about Martha Jane Cannary, but in June 1941 Jean McCormick, calling herself the daughter of Jane and Hickock, appeared in Billings. She said that her mother had written a part of her life story in the form of letters to a daughter (herself) given away in infancy to the safekeeping and prosperous upbringing of an Anglo-Irish gentleman, James O'Neil. McCormick said that her foster father gave the album of letters to her to read in 1912 to make her aware of her true parentage. Before her death in 1903, Jane had sent the album to England to be kept until O'Neil judged that it was the right time for her daughter to learn the truth about herself. The story excited a great deal of temporary interest, and believers and scoffers continued to argue about it from that time on. McCormick's background was simply the tale that she told of herself, and not much of it was ever verified.

Presumably, after having grown up in England, McCormick had come to the West. At one time she taught in the public schools of Butte. She had been married more than once, and she said that her last marriage had been to an officer in World War I, when she had served as a nurse. He had died of wounds.

Upon proclaiming herself the daughter of the two most notorious figures of the old West of the region, McCormick was given a great deal of public attention. The *Billings Gazette* printed an extensive interview. The well-known radio commentator Gabriel Heatter interviewed her on national radio. In his book *Desperate Women,* Horan quotes a letter written by her, dated in 1947, source not indicated, in which she detailed her birth and upbringing, agreeing with the facts in the letters.[16]

McCormick died in Billings on February 22, 1951, ten years after her disclosures. Many discrepancies in the letters were noted, but the essential claim of the birth and the association between Jane and Hickock remained, if not proven, at least unprovable.

Stella A. Foote of Billings purchased the album containing the letters and the accompanying mementos from McCormick. Foote copyrighted her ownership in 1950, renewed the copyright in 1978, and holds not only the album, locked away in a safe deposit box, but also the unshakable conviction that the letters and McCormick's story are authentic. She and Don C. Foote have published various editions of the letters over the years.[17] Others have published editions without permission.

The personality of Jane as disclosed in the letters has been added onto what was known of her before, or imagined or made up about her. The controversy has not been resolved. Other books will doubtless be written. Stella Foote's own story of Jane is expected.

It is possible to illustrate a life from the letters and to make a tentative judgment. The first letter in the album is dated September 25, 1877, and Jane notes: "You are 4 years old today." Although from this time on the letters are not always appropriate reading for a child, they recount the vivid details of a chancy life. They seem to become a way of pouring out intimate thoughts and feelings for one who almost always presented a crusty, defiant, sometimes self-defeating exterior to the outside world. The continuing motive in the letters written over many years is to convince the unknown daughter, and to emphasize for the writer herself, the legitimate birth of the child and the obsessive memory of a man already dead before any of the letters were written. In addition, the frank and lively entries seem to mirror a whole existence. Caught up by the moral and aesthetic interest of the letters, a reader can only wonder: if somehow they came out of Jane and her life, with all due regard for some errors or misrepresentations in them, then Jane was a more interesting and complete person than the outward circumstances of her life indicate; if the letters are a fraud and the production of another person, then they are a work of remarkable literary achievement.

Jane also wrote in this first letter in the album: "I visited your father's grave this morning at Ingleside. They are talking of moving his coffin to Mt. Moriah Cemetery in Deadwood. A year and a few weeks have passed since he was killed and it seems a century—without either of you the years ahead look like a lonely trail."

In letters that followed, Jane poured into an unhearing ear more details about her meeting Hickock and caring for him after he had been wounded in a fight and about their quick decision to marry, and "then while on the trip to Abilene we met Rev. Sipes & Rev Warren & we were married." Sipes and Warren were real people; they turned up again in Jane's letters and also in the memoirs of Abbott and Lull. The date of the wedding on the makeshift wedding certificate, a page from a Bible pasted into the album of letters, is September 1, 1870. The child of this marriage was born in

1873, according to Jane's word in the letters. Deserted by Hickock at the time of the birth, ill, and without means, she had impulsively given the child into the care of a prosperous British sea captain and his wife. They were traveling in the West at this time and came upon and aided Jane and the baby out of a tight spot. The child was always "Janey" to the mother, but she was aware in correspondence with James O'Neil, with whom she kept in touch through the years, that the little girl was known as Jean in England.

In the following years Jane does not bother to tell someone who cannot respond all the details of the good and the bad in her relationship with Hickock, but she tells a good bit. She says that she was alone when the child was born. Hickok had left her. She says that she gave a divorce to him when he asked for it, although no document substantiates this. She remains scornful of the acknowledged wife, Agnes Lake Thatcher, whom Hickock publicly married on March 5, 1876. She has some sense of triumph that Agnes did not stay, but for some reason left the country.* Jane has no regret or shame that she and Hickock were together again in some sort of friendly accord, and were thus seen riding about together in Deadwood shortly before he was killed in the late summer of 1876.

Joseph G. Rosa, in one of his two books on Hickok, *The West of Wild Bill Hickok* (1982), relates that he found the register of his marriage to Agnes Lake Thatcher and the minister's remarks in the ledger: "I don't think they meant it."[18] The minister is named Warren; is he the same one who married Hickock and Jane?

Whatever the exact truthfulness about these matters, as Jane retold them, asking for future sympathy from an unknown daughter, the sequence of letters, at least in the early years, is also concerned with lively daily matters. The writer shows a kind of hard-earned courage necessary for a defiant and solitary woman living in a harsh world. As an example of her not yet downed spirit in 1877, Jane wrote toward the end of the letter of September 2: "Tomorrow I am going down the Yellowstone Valley just for adventure and excitement."

The letters were written into the album intermittently, sometimes several in a year, sometimes after a break of a year or more. They are full of quite trivial and homely details, which are very revealing of Jane's likes and dislikes. Whenever possible she did work connected with horses. It

*Others would attest to Hickok's at least public appearance of devotion to Agnes.

was easy for her to like animals, perhaps easier than to like people. She had one beloved black horse, Satan, which Hickock had given her. It had been a doglike pet, coming to her when she called and understanding, as she said, what she said to it.

Everyday life became harder. Not as many of the new citizens of the West were willing, as Jane was, to pick up stakes and set off for some Yellowstone Valley of adventure. There was a yearning in these towns for respectability. Jane's reaction was usually a kind of self-defeating defiance. She would show them, she seemed to say, and did one outrageous thing after another, never explained herself, and endured disapproval.

However, when respect was shown her, Jane was almost abjectly grateful. She wrote in a letter dated July 1880 that she had met someone who had known "Mister Will Lull." She remembered warmly that he had helped her when she was ill in his hotel and had always treated her with respect. There would be other references to friends such as Lull and Abbott. Both of these respectful acquaintances recalled Jane in their memoirs, neither of them having had any chance to read her "letters." Lull's unpublished narrative about Jane confirms in detail the incident of her falling ill in his hotel and being attended by him.

Jane's thoughts, in the same letter, tended to go back to Hickok. She said of him, here, wonderingly, that he "never seemed to mind killing, but I do. I've never killed anyone yet, but I would like to knock some of Deadwoods women in the head." She railed at these women in August of the same year: "I hate the women here. The majority of them are no better than I am but they cross the street rather than speak to me or pass me." Jane was rough in tongue and thought. "One smell under their arms would be enough for me were I a man."

She had self-pride. She told of her care (July 1880) for the dictionary and the books O'Neil had sent her and said that she had recovered some of the reading ability her father had given her as a child. Her claim was that her father, as well as being a farmer, was a preacher, and so had the book learning at least of the frontier.

What one sees in the letters—whether true or made up—is a woman thinking about her past, herself and her situation, and life in general. After relating to her album, which was a diary of a sort, how she had met and married Hickok, she admitted to herself in September 1880 "how jealous I was of him." "It drove your father from me."

The letters continued through less good years. In January 1882 she wrote: "I miss my friend Will Lull to stake me. He was always willing to stake me. One night he loaned me a 5 spot & when I saw him the next morning I had $1000 but it goes Janey. Easy come easy goes . . . I sometimes get a little tipsy Janey but I dont harm anyone. I have to do something to forget you & your Father but I am not a Fancy Woman Janey if I were I wouldnt be nursing and scouting & driving stage."

In another letter, undated, possibly a postscript to the above, she wrote: "The poker game is over. I won my $20000 & paid back the $500 I borrowed from Abbott to start with." In a letter dated only May 30, probably in 1882 or shortly afterward, happy with herself, Jane wrote that she was able to give O'Neil $10,000 of her winnings to help pay for her daughter's education.

An undated letter, probably in 1887, shows Jane being scornful of people thinking that she had had numerous children. She says she had indeed adopted or simply taken care of one abandoned child after another, some of them having grown up and done well. "I have them all on pins & needles with my lies about my many children I am supposed to have given birth to. You are the only one I can truly call mine, & now you are 14 yars old in September."

In the same letter, she wrote: "I am going to get a job of some kind. For awhile I worked in Russells Salloon. Abbott got me the job. They want me to drive stage coach again. For when I worked at Russells the good virutous {sic} women of the town planned to run me out of town." She had an exhilarating revenge on the righteous troop who had indeed come into the saloon vowing to shear her hair. In a knock-down drag-out fight, she wiped up the floor with them. "If Abbott & Sipes hadnt showed up just then I would have had them all in their birthday gowns."

The stagecoach-driving job came to pass. In October 1890 she wrote that "Rev. Sipes & Teddy Blue Abbott got me the job . . . they seemed to think it was better than a saloon hostess. You see your mother works for a living. One day I have chicken to eat & the next day the feathers."

She was capable of impulsive and dangerous action while on the job. On September 25, 1891, she wrote about an adventure. From her stagecoach seat, she saw some hungry Indians cutting out the tongues of living range cattle. The animals were bleeding to death. "I got so damned mad I shot one Indian. Not to kill him and then I took them prisoners locked them in the stage coach & took them to Deadwood also took the tongues along to prove it."

She wrote in the same letter: "I did a most crazy thing sometime ago. I married Charley Burke. He got me in a weak moment and we were married. He is a good man, honest and on the square but I dont love him dear. I'm still in love with your father Bill Hickok." The marriage lasted for a few years; then she was on her own again.

By 1893 Jane was forty-one, still strong, her figure and face square and worn. She was, as recorded in a photograph, a straight, stocky person directly looking at the viewer with a stare that said: Do not try anything on me. She had no resources, but gained money from time to time by various jobs, by gambling, or possibly, as gossip said, by prostitution.

On May 10, 1893, she wrote her unknown daughter that she was thinking of homesteading on Canyon Creek, near Billings. She had found a cabin she could live in, and in it she could serve meals to passers-by, or to a group of men living in the vicinity whom others said were outlaws. She told her daughter that she did not worry about the character of those she fed but, she detailed on July 25, 1893, that she "baked them two dozen loaves of bread this week, 8 cakes, 15 mince pies. they paid me fifty cents for a pie, twenty cents a loaf for bread, one dollar a cake." She used up space in the album to write down in detail a number of recipes.

If one believes other letters in the album, she took up Buffalo Bill Cody's invitation to join him in his Wild West show, performed in some eastern cities, and also in England, where she felt the chill of the class system. She was ill at ease and glad, at last, to return to the West, ending again in Deadwood, or on the Clark's Fork, or in Canyon Creek. Perhaps it was true that Buffalo Bill helped her go home with passage money.

Her horse died; it was a connection that by this time meant more than any accessible human relationship. She wrote: "My horse Satan is dead. I had him buried up in the hills near Deadwood. He was so old too" (May 10, 1893). She was a woman alone, poor, and ill. But she laughed at those who tried to worm out of her her life story: "A man named Mulog ask for my life's history & you should have heard the lies I told The old fool. He said he would make some money for me for selling them. I didn't mention being married to your father or knowing him very well. It is better so Janey but I lied & if he wants to print lies to make money out of it its up to him. I pretended I couldn't hardly write. So it is 1 hell of a lifes story" (January 20, 1901).

The worst horror, beyond the stiffness and numbness in her arms and legs, was a growing blindness. "I hate poverty & dirt & here I shall have

to live in such in my last days. Dont pity me Janey. Forgive all my faults
& the wrong I have done you" (April 1902).

Jane died the next year on either August 1 or 2, 1903. The date may
have been juggled by those who were with her when she died, because they
said that her last spasm of consciousness was to note that this day was
the anniversary of Hickock's death, August 2, 1876. She was buried on
August 4, 1903, next to Hickok in the Mount Moriah Cemetery in
Deadwood.

The actual life of Martha Jane Cannary might seem ended. However,
those who told tall tales about her puffed her memory into a legend; those
who dug away at facts in painful scholarship pulled the legend down. A
further complication attended McCormick's public claim in 1941. If one
were to believe the contents of this pathetic album, then Jane had been a
more complex and interesting person than had been known before. Or the
whole presentation of the album and its contents was a fraud.

Those who have been disturbed by the lack of proof in the matter have
been very plain in their statements. In "Calamity Jane White Devil of the
Yellowstone," a chapter of his book, *Desperate Women,* Horan concludes that
"he fails to conjure up" an ill, old Jane, in "a befuddled alcoholic haze,
writing a 'Dear Janey' letter."[19] In her study of Jane in 1958, Roberta Beed
Sollid referred to the document as "a forgery."[20] In 1964, Joseph G. Rosa
wrote that "there are no authenticated specimens of Calamity Jane's handwriting which can be used as a comparison to that in the diary," and so
the diary "cannot be accepted as genuine."[21] In 1969, Harry Sinclair Drago,
in his book, *Notorious Ladies of the Frontier,* thought, categorically, that Jane
was too ignorant to have written the diary. He writes of McCormick's
having given us "a series of alleged documents which she had devised over
the years."[22] In a Montana conference of regional historians, Dan Gallacher,
as reported in the *Great Falls Tribune* of October 29, 1989, noted the lack
of connection between Jane and Hickock: "The only verifiable fact is that
both were in Deadwood, S.D. when Hickok was shot to death in 1876."
In his letter of December 5, 1990, to me, Professor James McLaird, of
Dakota Wesleyan University in Mitchell, South Dakota, engaged in a serious study of Jane, wrote: "I consider the 'Diary & Letters' fraudulent."[23]

However, some of the readers of these letters have wondered: Where
did all this information come from, some of it admittedly garbled or wrong,
and yet some of it true and intimate? After questioning the authenticity
of the letters, Horan noted: "Yet for all its improbability, someone who

knew a great deal about Calamity Jane must have written those letters."[24]
After finding a plausible reason for forgery in the desire of McCormick to
authenticate her parentage, Sollid wrote: "No real denial can be made to
Mrs. McCormick's tale."[25] After citing the lack of handwriting testimony,
Rosa wrote: "But it exists; we cannot deny that. Whoever compiled the
diary originally was cunning, but not very clever."[26]

What does history do with Jane? She lives vividly in two different ways.
From the episodic scraps of fact known and surmised, in the reminiscences
of the few who recorded acquaintanceship, in the bemused remembrance
of those who saw her pass like a comet across their scene, and in the digging of researchers, the presumed objective observer re-creates a lonely,
valiant woman, who achieved a brief, self-glorifying bedazzlement of her
contemporaries, and a late life of bedragglement.

If one reads the disputed letters, putting aside for a time the problem
of authenticity, one finds a woman of strength and complexity hidden behind the bravado and the jeering self-reliance and stoicism. It is tempting
to want to believe in the letters. Yet even for the reader inclined to do so,
there are difficulties that are obvious and pile up one upon the other. The
absence of handwriting in any other place hurts the ready acceptance of the
letters. Could Jane write and read? We do not know. There are factual
discrepancies that seem to multiply with the attention one gives the letters
and that researchers have carefully pointed out: no sea captain of Cunard
lines called James O'Neil has been found. No poster advertisements of
Calamity Jane as a part of a Buffalo Bill show have been found; surely he
would not have missed out on this aid to selling tickets.[27] Little is known
of the western years of the supposed daughter, Jean McCormick. Did Jane
spend them digging up facts about Jean? Did Jane put them in a document
herself? Did she discover in the West someone who had written the document, or who would do so to her order? Is the marriage certificate, torn
from a Bible, and stuck in the album, authentic? Who can tell? Where was
Jane at the time of the supposed wedding? Hickok seems to have been in the
vicinity, but was Jane? No one knows where she was at that time.

The supposedly objective reader has other undeniable qualms. Some
passages in the letters seem designed simply to quiet doubts, as in one early
letter when Jane carefully explains to her absent infant daughter how she
had refreshed her reading and writing skills. Some passages of pleading
self-justification and the pushing of emotion seem too much like a contemporary soap opera. Yet one springs to the defense, wishing to believe: the

expression of true emotion in ill-educated, aspiring folk often takes on what the critical call the bathos of soap opera.

So, with a thick layer of doubt remaining in the back of the mind, yet feeling a liking for the person presented through self-expression in the letters, the reader puzzles himself or, in this case, herself. Is there any resolving of these contradictions?

Arguing with oneself, trying to affirm the affirmative, it is possible to find comfort that many passages in the letters are borne out by the testimony of others, testimony that Jane could never have known about: in, for instance, the recollections of Abbott and Lull. It is possible that McCormick could have known about Abbott's book; it was published in 1939. It is not possible that she could have known about Lull's memoirs; they have never been published, but have been held in the privacy of the files of Lull's family into several generations.

A broadly tolerant view comes from the contemporary team of Barb Fisher and Glenda Bell of Billings, who call themselves simply "Storytellers," and who have made a career of stage re-creations of western characters. Bell has performed her one-woman show *Calamity Jane Tells Her Tale* many times. The team advertises that the performance is "based on original research, interviews with Calamity's descendants and serious inquiry."

In a letter of December 6, 1990, to me, the team, signing both names, wrote in part:

> You raised the question about the "Diary and Letters" and its authenticity. Based on volumes and volumes of research, plus personal interviews of descendants, we are convinced that the little "Diary" was not written by "Calamity." . . . However, what is written there does have a thread or essence of authenticity to it. . . . Having said all of that, let me add another point. There are some things in the "Diary" that only family or someone who was very close to "Calamity" would know. It could be one of her illegitimate children, a relative at the time, one of the many reporters who covered her story early on, etc. Who knows? Almost as intriguing is the question: Who really wrote the diary? We have been pursuing this through our research, but the jury is still out. And, were it not for some of the misleading facts and inaccuracies, she could have dictated it to a reporter who embellished great portions. [28]

Therefore, until new evidence shows up, the consideration must be one of a judicious suspension of final judgment. The sense in which Calamity

Jane's life has become a blend of fact and fiction belongs to an American way of looking at the national past, in this case a self-deluding and yet achingly real mix of what one would like to believe of the last West of the high plains and Northern Rocky Mountains. This is an interesting phenomenon, perhaps reprehensible, yet very revealing of what a nation, guilty of a fallible wishful thinking, wishes to believe of itself. It says something about the knack Americans have of regarding their whole history, not only a brief period of the Wild West, as self-glorification.

The letters are a document to move the reader. They create a character who is believable and haunting. This is not a cheap or cunning fraud, for the letters have the authenticity of art. The license of creativity has given Jane a stronger hold upon the imagination than, without it, the lost, pathetic woman would have had for us today.

The person, Jane, is a creation, perhaps made up by Jane herself, perhaps made up in part by others, but nevertheless a convincing character. If Jane's character as shown in the letters is convincing and endearing, then we want to believe, and we superimpose this more rounded and developed Jane on top of the spare outlines of the human being given us by the glimpses of authenticated fact. We acknowledge ourselves charmed, maybe fooled, but pleased. To the creation of the character—whether the artless reality of a human being babbling out inner thoughts and feelings, or the work of a conscious hand—the reaction of the reader remains: this is an encounter with an interesting human being.

In imagination the person lives. We see the ill older woman looking for a drink in the dusty streets of new western towns; before that time, we see the strong young woman guiding her wagontrain north into the Rosebud country in General Crook's army; we see the woman in her prime riding up and down from one end to the other of lusty Deadwood in a fine man's outfit alongside a companion rider who was the most famous man of the time and place. The girl of thirteen helping out on the family's migration to the West has grown into these women.

Persuaded, allowing a leeway to storytelling, we see a woman who lived with both gusto and regret and who gave away something of herself to a legend. Her story is a resource for a nation always hungry for myth.

▲▲▲

TWELVE

Recollection and Renewal:
An Afterword

On the last day of August 1932, when first snow powdered the tops of the mountains east of Great Falls, Montana, a family of five loaded their tent, bedrolls, camp stove, and other belongings on an already old, square-bodied Studebaker and left, not on a pleasant camping trip, as they had often done before, but to flee eastward and southward from a bankrupt family business and hard times. I was thirteen, the oldest of three children, all girls, crowded in the back seat along with a cat named Trouble, our worried parents looking grimly forward in the front seat.

I have remembered that ten-day trip as a dividing point in my life. We set up our tent in authorized or unauthorized camp places each night that followed: two in Montana, one in North Dakota, one in Minnesota, one in Wisconsin, one in Illinois, two in Indiana (rest stop), one in Kentucky, and one in Tennessee. We arrived in Kirkwood, a part of Atlanta, where my grandparents and an aunt welcomed us. Our father and mother, at forty-two and forty-three, beginning life again in the Depression, doled out a total of seventy-two dollars to make our migration. All that I had known of childhood was severed from all that I was to know afterward.

In July 1979, after deaths had depleted the family, I determined to begin going back to the scenes of my lost childhood and knit together the two parts of my separated life. I was also going to try to write about the landscape I had lost. I was not what I would have been if I had stayed in the house of my childhood. I said to myself: I am now an oddity, a southerner who has had an indelible western beginning. My axis has always leaned sideways because of that slightly crank-sided heritage, that is, from Northwest to Southeast.

I had left the high plains and mountains reluctantly, with adolescent anger and regret. I adapted slowly and unwillingly to the older world of the South, to which my parents returned as to home. It was not home to me, I felt, with that stiff-necked and ignorant pride natural to a teen-ager. Slowly, very slowly, I found myself there: in school, in work, in learning about the depths and heights of this South, the old intractable culture that had been, after all, the land of my ancestors for three hundred years. Once fully possessed of that South—in a love coexisting with the deepest and most cutting kind of criticism—no other region of the country could seem as worthy of loyalty.

In three brief previous visits I had been unable to reconnect myself to my earlier life in the West. So, with the occasion of longer visits possible, I set out to mend the break. I would carry all the life I had lived since that leave-taking, when our road east curved around the Highwood chain of mountains and set out straightly across the wide plains toward the unknown. Living, learning, suffering, and enjoying had intervened. I had acquired certain sets of ideas (I hoped flexible) about politics, books, habits of living.

In addition to a load of personal feeling, I had acquired objective views and curiosities. I would try to exercise them upon the new-old scene. I would travel, I hoped, with a wide-open mind. The fact that I had been there before would make for poignancy of recognition. Yet I would charge myself with uncovering the gritty reality underneath the haze of memory. I would move between two centers of interest, the personal-commemorative and the intellectual-objective. At this time I did not know whether I would write a personal or an objective book. But I did know that it would be a return to a haunting past and that it would open up questions and answers about the past, present, and future of an American region in which I had had the accident of childhood.

The starting and ending point of my explorations, both subjective and objective, would be the Great Falls, on the Missouri River. It had seemed, when I was young, to be the safe center of a child's universe. I see now that the happy little town was also a staid, self-centered, limited sort of place. Yet as I confront memory, I see that this isolated cluster of population (no big city to the east but Minneapolis, no big city to the west but Seattle) represented a celebration and a defense.

Within the regularly laid out blocks of streets and houses, life attempted to be rational and sensible. Flowers in gardens and parks bloomed fiercely all summer long, but the bitter blowing winds of winter blizzards remind us of another world outside the compass of green which its founder, Paris Gibson, and its early settlers had created on a sandy plain bordering the five waterfalls of a great river. These proper people were perversely proud of the nearness of the wild. They said that nothing held the wind back but a barbed wire fence between them and the North Pole.

The city was safety, but the most delicious part of life was beyond, on the river that was wild even within the city limits, or beyond in the space stretching toward the mountain ranges to the east, south, and west. Directly west from Gore Hill, where my plane landed, were the steppelike rolling plains upon which sat giant, flat-topped buttes, and, beyond them, the serrated Front Range. East were the blue scalloped tops of the Highwoods, only thirty miles away; south and southwest were the Little Belts and the Big Belts. North was vast space stretching without any eye barrier. I think that I learned unconsciously what is a part of every true westerner's emotional equipment, that life is divided into two desirable parts, of comfort and liberty, and that we need both.

I think that for the elders of the family, who were all young at this time, as well as for the tribe of cousins who were being born and growing up as the years passed, summer and being outdoors meant more than the sensible, everyday life of winter, of making a living. Making a living was a family business, the pioneer drilling and refining of the oil from the Kevin-Sunburst field of north Montana.

On my father's side, we were a colony of six related families transplanted from the yeoman farming country of hilly north Georgia (where there had never been a slave tradition) by way of Atlanta and a stay in the Panama Canal Zone during the construction days, a progression of movement toward opportunity. I think that my father and his next brother spent as much time in the joys of hunting, fishing, and camping as in the weekday life of business. I know that all of them, leading various kinds of lives in the new town on the Missouri, enjoyed the pleasures of talking and visiting, southern style.

The "Stevenson boys," as they were called familiarly in the town where they made a small, transitory splash, as well as their Anderson brother-in-law, who came out of the same north Georgia culture, had a pride in their recently created family company. The five brothers and the brother-in-law had convenient talents that let each one fall into a particular role in the business: promoter, accountant, manager, field man, advertiser, and engineer. They hired clever geologists who saw where to drill on the dome of a hidden oil reserve and to establish, between Glacier Park and the Sweetgrass Hills along the Canadian border with Alberta, a moderately profitable oil field.

While fly-fishing, my father and his friend, one of the geologists, ran into a party of Blackfeet near the border and went off with them for three days to a sacred place on the Milk River over the border, Writing on Stone. There they were initiated into the tribe and some of its mysteries, and given Indian names. My father had always a self-deprecating and humorous pride in the event. He attributed the attention to the fairness that the company had shown in gaining leases of Blackfeet reservation land on which to drill; perhaps, looking back, I also see a canny manipulation by the Indians, cheated by everyone so often, attempting good relations with a new invasive force.

One time I drove north to the little town of Sunburst, now dead, dry, and dusty, once the center of the family's oil activities. It is, like so many western places, deserted of the energy that once animated it with hope. For a little more than a decade the oil taken from the ground here had given six families a modest prosperity, a shelter for a typical kind of 1920s-1930s sense of well-being before the Depression came to liberate them all, the wives and children as well as the men, into the reality and tragedy of American life. Yet, at the best of times, including a few gushers, the output was not more than five hundred barrels a day. They had drilled the first commercial well in the state; they had designed and built a refinery surrounded by greenery in Great Falls; they had piped natural gas to Great Falls, Helena, and Butte; and they had sold their own refined gasoline—"it's powerized!"—to gas stations throughout the region.

I remember one time being held firmly, frightened, on the shaking platform of a wooden derrick, watching the drill rising up and down in front of my mesmerized eyes out of a hole that I was told went way down into the ground. I was two or three, and I have a hazy memory of eating, with my father and mother, among the jovial loud crew under the canvas tent roof beyond which stretched the empty silent plains. The family members of the firm, leading respectable lives on the edge of the somewhat wild 1920s gaiety of which they disapproved, had been briefly notable citizens of this clean new town on the Missouri. This was the last settled part of the United States, and the founder and the original inhabitants lingered on into this time.

Then, very quickly, after some years of deceptive good luck, in the new hard times of the Depression, the brothers found that they had overex-panded, drilling dry holes in the State of Washington. They discovered that they did not have enough capital to invest in new refining technologies. They suffered what the weak are dealt customarily in the ordinary course of American business. They were overcharged outrageously for the transpor-tation of their commodity in the pipelines controlled by one of the Standard Oils. The company failed, and the six families scattered, some remaining, some going back to Panama, my own returning to Atlanta, from which my parents had come and where they had relatives and friends.

I outline their story because it interests me, but also because it illustrates one more example of an enterprise that came into the Northwest with hope and whose hopes ended in dust. An objective backward glance at these newcomers going about the business of oil drilling and refining, joyously and, in a sense, innocently, tells me that my own family had been part of one of the exploitations of the land, contributing mixed benefits and ills to the landscape in which we all very quickly became native.

Coming back, I wished to understand what happened to them and had brought their world—a small colony of Georgians—to ruin in a new place. I could also see, much later, that it was a part of a pattern of generations of heady achievement and bitter failure occurring over and over to different kinds of people in this same land. I looked back at the small personal picture first. In childhood that hopeful world in a new place had seemed a safe shelter for a good childhood. The best of it was our ingenuous enjoyment of the landscape itself, which seemed indestructible, if a little frightening. My family's summer camping was at this time mostly unstructured. We organized our bedrolls on the living room floor and set off at an hour's notice: to the canyons of the Sun and the Dearborn rivers, to the isolated reaches of Deep Creek or Sullivan Creek, to the Highwoods or to Logging Creek, or to the more civilized campgrounds of Glacier and Yellowstone.

This "extracurricular" life, as instigated by my father, and joined in by all the argumentative, independent, unlike members of this camping fam-ily, made for idyllic summers in which we escaped city life, school life, business life. My father was intoxicated by beauty. He made us kneel down and see the tiny, hidden shooting stars in the early spring prairie grass. He made us see the rolling, shifting color of wheat in the sun. He pointed out strange growths on trees when we walked through the woods. He joined us in rolling down grass banks in childlike ecstasy. He went swimming with us in icy streams.

Family camping, which was his idea, found the five of us in a small, square bell tent gazing up in July at snow on its top or noticing the etched edging of ice on a trout stream in October. Camping was learning how to clean out a natural spring for our water supply, or constructing, well away from camp and hidden, a latrine; we seldom set up our tent, except in Glacier or Yellowstone, at an authorized campground. Education was learning the names of the mountains ringing Two Medicines Lake, the calls of camp robbers and ravens in the higher regions, the harsh talk of redwings above the sloughs and irrigation ditches of the plains.

Education also was my father's light-hearted teaching of road manners: stop when someone else is in trouble; wave when you pass someone; enjoy the unmarked middle of the narrow roads until you meet someone—all this on dirt, or gravel, or, very rarely, oil-bound roads in open spaces where each traveler met was an event. Alongside the roads were the upright sentinels, the little gophers; the rounded backs of the prairie dogs running for their holes; the fluttering, crippled balancing of the mother prairie chicken leading us away from her chicks; and the loping gait of the gray-white coyote.

I was resigned to the fact that summer ended and fall began another kind of education in the classes at Whittier School.* I had a lower degree of enthusiasm for this kind of learning. But a quality of that blessed summer life would stay with me. I had an insight that had been taught me without words. There was something to be considered, something to be in awe of, beyond our everyday living. Daily life was legitimate, but was not everything. That insight might have been learned under other skies, but for me it was a high western sky, rolling plains, and the broken edge of mountains. Therefore, this sense of the worth of the wild would be one of the premises I would carry with me in my rediscovery of a particular West.

The journeys that began in the summer of 1979 have continued every year for more than a decade. In addition to the baggage of the past which I carried about with me in searching out my new West, I had also a lot of interests acquired in a partial lifetime of living elsewhere and in pursuing various interests. I wished to look at a remembered landscape and see it again with a kind of critical questioning. I had assumptions gained from reading diaries, histories, and fiction coming out of the region, and I had

---

* All of the grade schools were named for New England poets. The founding father, Paris Gibson, had been born and raised in Maine.

the perspective of having lived in a very different region created out of a history grossly different from that of the inland Northwest.

I wondered if I would see, in its past and present, a western community forming itself. The inadvertent and uncalculated words left behind by individuals who had lived in the different generations might be, to me, as important as the studied documents of scholars. I believed that I would find individual lives, particularly "unknown" ones, helpful in understanding this last West. My history, if it were to be in some way history, was to be told to me, and retold by me, in the lives of these individuals, whether important or unimportant to their contemporaries.

I also wondered if I would be able to see in this assaulted and beloved land some sharp and minatory teaching for a large crisis of our time: what we as human beings are doing to our land. I continued to believe that the shape and color and climate of a landscape influence the people who live under its rule.

I thought that, implicit in these lives, many aspects of the environmental crisis of our time might show up here smartly. The degradation of cities is not as evident here as elsewhere, although it is beginning; but it is shamefully evident, in a bare way with no disguise, where the abused land exhibits a prodigal misuse: minerals dug up and the dross left toxic and wasteful, streams and rivers running with silted poison, topsoil wasted and blown away, grass grazed away, great forests of protective trees cut down, the fertile life of wild creatures depleted. Yet, under the merciless sun, a landscape remains, surpassingly beautiful, enduring beyond the lives of the generations that have inhabited it.

During a day's visit to Fort Benton, I met a rancher whose cheerful, unguilty self seemed to embody a contradiction central to the western character. He had always loved the land and camped and hunted and fished with a marvelous sense of personal freedom. He had put down his bedroll wherever he pleased, often on an island in the wild Missouri downstream from where we talked at the remnant of the old riverboat landing of the fur traders.

Recently the federal government had officially named that still wild stretch of the upper Missouri a "wild river" and put certain limitations upon visitors. These bureaucratic directives, as he scornfully thought them, were now telling him where to put down his bedroll, where to dig a latrine, whether at a particular time of fire danger he could make a campfire. He hated these restrictions and thought that, for himself, of course, they were unnecessary. He loved the land, and no one was going to tell him what to do with it. He had very little sense that other more predatory and better organized individuals, corporations, or the government itself, might, with no love at all, come in and destroy the wild assets of river and shore and all the land adjoining.

The rancher and his wife, who ran the local art gallery, were hospitable and gave lunch to me and my last Stevenson uncle, the artist, who sold them an etching that day. The couple illustrates the two sides of a coin of the new West: she, fostering native painters and sculptors, who, as she said, were coming out from behind every tree these days to commemorate the unique quality of westernness; he, making a traditional rancher's living off the land and practicing, with scorn of organized defenders of the wild, his own brand of freedom. It was possible to argue lightly with the unapologetic man and also to enjoy him as a pure type. He very clearly represented the difficulty that the West is having in coming to terms with its own qualities.

I sometimes questioned myself. What did I have in me that made it possible for me to judge, or at least criticize, as well as to care, about this region? I had had good schooling, a modest background in American history, and a continuing passion for the subject. I was aware of the force of the great, all-encompassing theories about the American movement to the West, and the American mythologizing of, and sometimes falsifying of, its love of the West as it was and is. I saw a basic fact as underlying all theories: that the dry regions west of the ninety-eighth or one hundredth meridian are different from the wetter and more humid regions of the East and that this difference would largely determine the kind of life that could be lived in this vast space.

Frederick Jackson Turner seemed right, in part, in his frontier theory, but he left out whole sets of circumstances as life had been lived on the shifting and varying frontiers of the West—not all alike. I agreed with Walter Prescott Webb when he showed us the dire limits that geography puts upon any people determined to stay in these dry regions. I revered the earlier, unheeded strictures of John Wesley Powell, who said that dryness would always limit what use could be made of this land in his time and ours. I was aware that much of the trouble of the West was shared between the careless living of its scattered inhabitants and ignorant or selfish policies that governmental or corporate powers imposed upon the region.

One wrong-headed federal policy had been, from the beginning, the allocation of too small allotments to homesteaders; other such policies were the overcutting of forests and the overgrazing of grasslands. Ignorance of the climatic conditions of a land different from that of the East muddled the heads of those reared in a wetter, more humid habitat, or having the usual American viewpoint of the endless beneficence of nature. An intensive usage of this land had resulted in policies that seemed right at the time and turned out to be destructive, such as the erecting of great and magnificent dams on all the principal rivers and the enthusiastic use of artificial fertilizers.

Bernard DeVoto was right decades ago in calling the West "a plundered province." He was also right in his continuing polemical crusade to speak with sorrow of the West, especially the interior Northwest he had come to love, as "the west against itself."[1] After Turner, Webb, and Powell, DeVoto had become my guide in discovery, in both his journalism and his histories. However, once I had set myself to traveling during the summer days and to reading during the winter nights, I found many writers trying, each in a distinctive way, to express truths about the life and landscape of the West. I learned more than surface facts about Indian life from writers such as John C. Ewers. I learned to look at the "Indian" wars with new eyes through writers such as S. L. A. Marshall and Robert M. Utley. Carl K. Kraenzel, Michael P. Malone, Frank Bergon, as well as Zeese Paparikolas, Joseph Kinsey Howard, and K. Ross Toole, gave me a view of the present life of the region growing out of its past and growing perhaps into a future of either self-destruction or creation.

I was willing to follow each author through a particular explanation, and I tucked these views away in the back of my mind for future reference. But coming each year to the brilliant high summer of Montana, Wyoming, and Alberta, I was impatient of everything but the land and individual lives that had been lived upon it. I wanted to sense how things looked and sounded to these lovers and destroyers—the sagebrush wind to the cowboy, the bad air underground to the miner, the bleak look of treeless plains to the dry-land farmer, the terrible cold, and the welcome warming of the chinook.

I had a personal bias. I saw history as biography. It was a limitation, but I had no choice but to make the best of it. I was as interested in the ingrown musings of Meriwether Lewis as I was in his discoveries. I warmed to two different men of the Bitterroot, John Owen and Pierre Jean De Smet, and in the way each one in a sense converted himself to Indian values.

I wanted to steal quietly into the unnoticed and heroic lives of women such as the Crow Pretty-Shield and the West Virginian Nannie Alderson. There was nothing more important to me than the progress of a single life, from birth, through growth and change, through a climb to achievement or a fall to failure, then the inevitable slide to death. I hoped that the story of individual lives, from successive generations of effort, might tell me something about that time, that place. I hoped to catch some hint, from chance words left behind, of what it was like to live then, words in a private journal, a considered autobiography, a tale told to others. I needed words from each one of them to help me get inside a mind and a heart.

Then I determined to go, as I could, to the places where each of these people had lived a fortunate or unfortunate life. Away from the determined contemporary shine of the small, bright, isolated cities of the West, I found that the skeleton of the land had not changed. Its breadths and heights were the same that struck the eyes of these others. It was a continuing task to read what was left of these figures in books and pamphlets and unpublished manuscripts sought out in one museum or library after another. But I had to experience the sunrises and sunsets in the places where these people had looked out at the horizon line.

What would be the boundaries of my geography? I found that the edges of this "last West" were not sharp, that they looped unevenly around several present states and included parts of two or three Canadian provinces. There is more of an easy human and commercial interchange between north Montana and the nearby parts of Alberta than there is between the citizens of Montana and those of the neighboring but far-off states to their east, south, and west. Montana, because of its strong residual western outlook, in part a determination of its geography, is at the center; Wyoming, to the south, is intrinsic; Alberta, to the north, in its southern half, is a mirror province; the eastern edge of British Columbia and the western edge of Saskatchewan also belong; there are felt extensions westward and south to parts of Idaho and Utah and eastward into the Dakotas and Nebraska.

This is a great, confused mass of geography, the northern American ranges of the Rockies, as well as the complementary contrasts of plains, buttes, bench lands, canyons, coulees, winding rivers, and willow-lined creeks—all carrying the weight of a westernness in some sense dying and in some sense being born again. This dry, high, cold, inland Northwest differs radically from the far West of the Pacific coastal states, and from the Middle West, into which its plains merge. It is unlike the true East, the true South, and the unique Southwest.

It is not remarkable that geography and climate affected these people. The seasons were different from those of the East; dryness was a factor of a severity unknown in those wetter, humid places; dangers to human beings, animals, and crops existed that had been unknown before in the march across the more temperate zones. It is not surprising that it took a number of generations of hard living for individuals to begin to express the way one might come to terms with living in a landscape that has remained both magnificent and dangerous. There had been mute endurance, wordless joy, fear, pain, acceptance; but only recently have words been put on paper to express for many what a solitary person might say about the experience of living in the High Plains and among the northern Rocky Mountain ranges.

I recognized and felt companionship in the words of a few writers of verse and fiction, and I only slowly realized that there were beginning to be many writers saying things not said before. Some of them had lived a life here; others had come from elsewhere, been caught by something here and become part of it; there was variety, humor, anger, sadness in enough profusion to begin to seem like a kind of western renaissance, perhaps sparer than the lush southern renaissance with which I had grown up. I knew that the South had found itself, had come to terms with itself, in fiction of honesty and power. Perhaps now the last West might do so, too.

As Hemingway said: we all came out of *Huckleberry Finn*. All of us, wanting to understand the aspects and experiences of the West which had seeped into our bones and had nourished our loves and our resentments, assented to A. B. Guthrie's *The Big Sky*. It was a phrase that we murmured, as if it were ours, too, when we left the comfort of paved streets and made our way across the spaces that are the same ones that Lewis surveyed or Osborne Russell traversed. The book as novel or as history is not perfect, and I found it overlong when I reread it recently, but it has the distinction of a great, overarching idea that has satisfied a need. It is a story that has made us understand our condition, that of a people living under an immense horizon and forever reminded of this physical and psychical fact, of a people extravagantly in love with possibility here, yet a people, like Boone Caudill, doing brave and cruel things and, in the end, failing and destroying what it had loved.

One laughs at the crass, clever advertising world that has picked up

Guthrie's phrase "the Big Sky" and affixed it not only to bumpers but also on products, as one laughs at Lewis and Clark Beer. The rueful grin does not kill the fact that one is grateful to Guthrie, when one drives out of Great Falls westward past Square Butte and Crown Butte and sees the extent of land and sky; he found words for us to use to make us understand what we were seeing and feeling under the big sky.

As I loaded up my rented car with suitcase, maps, extra water, a first-aid kit, and high expectations, I included books. They made me realize what I was seeing. Going north from Great Falls to Chinook, seeing in the main street of that town the east-west road, the Hi-Line, decorated with a notable grain elevator, I saw better both the nearby land—across the line—that Wallace Stegner wrote about in *The Big Rock Candy Mountain* and *Wolf Willow,* and also the land that James Welch wrote of in verse in *Riding the Earthboy 40* and in early novels such as *Winter in the Blood* and *The Death of Jim Loney.*

Driving west from the mountain valley of Lincoln, where I had had childhood vacations, though the irregular canyon of the Blackfoot River, I found it much more interesting because I was reading *A River Runs through It.* This was not only the small river of my own past, the river of my father, who had fished it, but also, significantly, the river that became a symbol of a drama of life and death in the short novel by Norman Maclean. Read again and again, the story of the tragedy of a father and two sons who fished for rainbows on the Blackfoot seems to me the one surpassing piece of writing of our time. Maclean has shown his people as integral to a scene, a river that in its swiftness, unpredictability, complex depths, treacherousness, and beauty is the quality of the story told.

Artists and photographers such as William Henry Jackson, and once-forgotten painters such as George Catlin, Karl Bodmer, and Alfred Jacob Miller helped me see the West in line and color. Outsiders such as Remington aided in creating the mythical West, whereas in Great Falls two men of my parents' generation, Charles Marion Russell and Olaf Seltzer, painted closer to the real bone of the disappearing old West. My uncle Branson Stevenson also contributed images of engraved lines, fixing on copper plates moments of truth of what he had learned about the place to which he had come at nineteen to join his brothers in a rash enterprise.

I went again and again to the Russell collections in Great Falls and Helena. Museums were regular stopping places, as were libraries, where I asked that forgotten or unpublished works be pulled out for me. I was grateful that I had fallen into a time when many writers were trying to say, for themselves and for others, how it had been and what it had meant to live in this remote, difficult, and beautiful land. In doing so, they were forming a cultural sense of self for the whole region: for those of us who had grown up here, or for those who had come here from the outside and felt the pang of suddenly and in some sense belonging.

A number of these writers have felt compelled to look back at their own growing up and to tell their stories, either without disguise or in story form. Those of the last generation, of our own one, or of a younger one have touched a nerve. They are of us and near us. The compelling need to come to terms with themselves and their land speaks in the writing of those mentioned above, and in that of Ivan Doig, Ann Marie Lowe, William Kittredge, Mary Clearman Blew, and Rick Bass. Earlier there had been the sardonic but tender view of Indian-white relations in a novel by Dan Cushman, in the tough, unsentimental cowboy or Indian stories of Dorothy Johnson, and in the down-to-earth life of farm families in Mildred Walker's novel.

In the present there is a continuing rush of verse, short stories, and novels attempting to discover some kind of truth in the lives of this extreme tilt of plains and mountains. There is variety here in D'Arcy McNickle, Thomas Savage, Thomas McGuane, James Polk, Ralph Beer, Richard Ford, Michael Dorris, Louise Erdrich, W. P. Kinsella, James Crumley, David Quammen, Deirdre McNamer, and many others. In the crystallization of images and idea into verse, and in his influence, Richard Hugo stands alone.

These are names thrown out as examples. The impression persists that these writers whom I have chanced upon are part of a stream that shows no sign of being dammed. The West seems happy to be hearing about itself. I came upon a librarian in a tiny library in Lincoln who told me knowledgeably about the latest writers. I came upon a bookstore in Bigfork where a collection of regional writing was displayed with proprietary pride.

In books or in movements of travel, the contrasts between what had been and what was now continued to be startling and amusing, as well as sometimes tragic or forbidding. I stood one day on a point of the lawn of the country club in Great Falls where the Sun and the Missouri rivers merge and realized that this place, or one near here, was where Meriwether Lewis, alone, ran out into the water to escape a grizzly bear, its great mouth open, that was charging him.

On another day it was disturbing of my sense of time to be part of an everyday crowd of sightseers on a small launch floating the dam-raised level of the Missouri through the canyon that Lewis had named the "gates of the mountains." I had come easily on the road from Great Falls to this small wilderness area just off the interstate, a place only seventeen miles from the state capital where a band of mountain goats live and where, even today, you can come only by boat or on foot. Lewis and his expedition of army men, now seasoned by a year on the way into an informal, cohesive, voting group, were delighted to be at last in the mountains, although the poling and pulling of the small boats grew very difficult when the canyon walls came straight down to the water. I counted it as a lucky coincidence that I happened on July 19, 1979, to take the boat ride on the very day of the month—Friday, July 19, 1805—when the expedition's leader first saw these canyon walls seem to close ahead, then reopen to let him through, as they did for us, the captain of the launch pointing out the phenomenon and telling us that this was the day Lewis noticed the same effect.

At the great falls of the Missouri, where Lewis indulged in a romantic exhilaration, an ugly dam regulates the flow of the water. Yet the river is still wild in the canyon beneath the falls. A landscaped picnic island in the river below the falls is a contrast to the stark walls bounding the green flow. In these upper reaches, the Missouri is still a good trout stream, and I saw pelicans floating calmly in midstream near the Giant Springs, upriver from the falls.

Here, or near here, Clark was amazed at the spectacle. Here, after a thunderstorm, as customary doctor to the expedition, he looked after the men's cuts and bruises, as well as the temporary indisposition of Janey, as he called Sacajawea, and her baby. This has been a picnic place and a state park. As a child, with a few others, I had pretended to dangers that were not here, and walked back the five miles to the city by way of the narrow path under the river bluffs, rather than on the road. The route is now being made an official paved pathway.

It is not too hard to imagine away the town, with its regular avenues and streets in Paris Gibson's firm design, and its generous trees planted and replanted over one hundred years ago. The cactus prairie, through which the men of the small company dragged their boats on hastily made cottonwood wheels, cannot be very different. Upstream, beyond the curve of the river that now holds the city, is an island that may be the White Bear Island, to which the expedition portaged in a long hard month. It was on this island that I was one of a group of picnicking children who were brought here by boat and left for the day on the delicious pretense of being marooned.

In successive summer travels I set out again and again from Great Falls to trace the pathways of many different individuals who had passed through the canyons, over the mountains, and across the plains to all kinds of fates. I followed Lewis and Clark's little company west from the area of the waterfalls to where they first penetrated the mountains (where only in my last years in Great Falls a paved highway was pushed through). Beyond Missoula, I followed them up and across the rough, tree-cluttered Lolo Pass. On the other side, I saw how difficult the passage must have been until they could put new canoes in water. In the wilds of Idaho I stopped for a few minutes at the cedar grove where a plaque told me that one of the Northwest's first conservationists, Bernard DeVoto, had asked that his ashes be scattered.

Beyond the twin towns of Lewiston and Clarkston, facing each other across the Snake River on the border of Idaho and Washington, I stopped to rest, then went on across wild bare mountains to the Wallowa Valley in northeastern Oregon, Chief Joseph's home country. Returning over the Lolo Pass to Montana, in my imagination I followed Joseph and his whole tribe—men, women, children, dogs, and horses—on a long valiant march toward what they hoped might be safety, pursued by the U.S. Army, which failed again and again in skirmishes and pitched battles. Earlier I had spent a lonely night at Chinook, then drove the few miles south to the Bearpaw Battlefield, where in the end Joseph and his people were defeated and he was said to have spoken the noble, brave, dignified words "I will fight no more forever."

In another quarter of the state during another summer, I stood where Custer and his dubious Crow scouts had stood, looking downhill at a great gathering of Sioux and Cheyenne beyond the little stream called the Little Bighorn. It struck me that, except for a few irrigated green fields beyond the river, this scene looked very much as it had looked then. Turning to read the names of the long-dead white soldiers inscribed on a monument topping the slope, I felt pity for them and for the Indians who had thought this "a good day to die." The natives of this land had won the battle but lost the war. They scattered and disappeared into the hinterland to keep out of the way of subsequent sorties of troops trying to round them up for reservation life.

South of Billings, I saw both the past and the future. The past was the site called the "Indian caves," where a prehistoric people, probably five thousand years ago, had lived in caves on a cliff side. This was only five miles south of the city, but seemed as remote as the moon. A falcon flew ahead of me up a hill, pausing at each steep turn in a narrow road to perch on a fencepost and wait for my car to come close, then to fly ahead.

I climbed a path up the side of the bluff, then looked into a large overhung space and tried to imagine what life was like here. All was still except a rustle in the ravine below, and I looked down to glimpse what I thought might be a fox moving from brush to brush. Ethnologists had carefully dug down and categorized this lost life in the big cave, so it was empty. But those dwellers had looked out across the same space that stretched out for me.

The promise and menace of the future took me farther south from Billings to Colstrip, not far from where the northern Cheyenne tribe, in flight from where they had been placed on a reservation in midcountry, at last found refuge. At this time one great double installation of a coal-powered electrical generating plant was running, the other half yet to be built. This development had come to pass despite the strange and united opposition of Indians, ranchers, and environmentalists. The wires from here were humming with power, and the land lying all around was under attack from the unimaginably large mantislike machines that were stripping the land's surface to find the coal lying just below. Bitter to the protesters was the success of the enterprise, and the truth, that the land was being destroyed, and its power being sent away from this area to light cities such as Seattle and the bright gambling strip of Las Vegas. A brave little gimcrack town surrounded the power plant.

Out of Billings I returned to Yellowstone National Park, where as children we had seen with awe the great gathering of grizzlies at the feeding ground behind the Old Faithful Inn, a very bad practice since abandoned. However, the sight of thirty-three grizzlies at one time was something to remember, and I recalled that it was through this wild uninhabited country that Joseph had led his people on the way to the Bearpaw Mountains. Catching up with the homeward journey of the Lewis and Clark expedition, east from Billings I saw Pompey's Pillar, which the redheaded chief William Clark had named for Sacajawea's little boy, fondly nicknamed "Pompey" for his pompous walk. I climbed the steps up the strange mountain shaped like a round cheese and saw Clark's name and date carved into the soft stone of its side. Already deteriorated, the inscription is somewhat protected by a glass covering. It is the only remaining physical evidence in the Northwest of the expedition.

North from Yellowstone I had seen the remnants of two other passing cultures of this West: Virginia City and Butte. Virginia City, the second capital of the territory, still a county seat, preserves the dead life of the fierce gold city. I sat on the upstairs porch of the Fairweather Inn and watched people come and go along the slanted sidewalk below.

I had sprained my ankle on the way out of Yellowstone, incautiously jumping out of the stopped car to take a photograph of two swans and their cygnet floating on the Madison River. But with an Ace bandage stiffening my hurt ankle, I walked the wooden sidewalk cautiously and imagined scenes that had taken place there: excited citizens moving to east or west on the street, separating themselves into yes or no votes for the latest alleged criminal caught by the vigilantes, while the editor of the *Montana Post,* Thomas Dimsdale, in the shadow of one of these primitive buildings, watched the whole spectacle before retreating to his office down the street to write about another death.

Reaching Butte, northwest of Virginia City, I tried to imagine what it was like for my parents, living here for the first year of their residence in the West, hearing the whistles blowing in the night for an underground disaster, and seeing the great spectacle of a miner's funeral, a walking procession of like-worshipping people from Italy or Ireland or Croatia. The city was drenched in its past, but seemed strangely quiescent in the present.

I revisited Lincoln, the town and the valley cupped high in the mountains, where my family had rented a cabin when I was ten, against the edge of the Bob Marshall Wilderness area. Lincoln is haunted by a dead past of inefficient gold mining. Its diggers of a hundred years ago were buried in a cemetery site half grown over by forest. But it is now a disturbed place, the scene of a new gold-mining project, a plan to take the top off a small mountain and pour poisonous acid through the ground to leach out the remains of the gold, possibly ruining the nearby free-flowing trout stream, that of Maclean's *A River Runs through It.*

Another small expedition another summer took me down (or rather up) the Bitterroot Valley below Missoula. The sharp outline of the mountains with the distinctive peak, Trapper, marked the boundary of Idaho; these mountains seemed typical of Montana mountains—sharp, unrelenting, frightening—yet the valley below was blessed with green fields and spacious sites for ranches, no one knocking elbows with anyone else. Ahead of me was Hamilton, the site of a distinguished biology laboratory, in which scientists discovered the cause and cure for Rocky Mountain spotted fever.

I turned off the highway at Stevensville to visit Father Pierre Jean De Smet's first mission church, Saint Mary's. Nearby, I walked inside the enclosure of Major John Owen's trading post. I found it easy to think, as if of friends, about the two men. I saw the compassionate, intelligent priest sitting companionably on the ground with the Salish, sharing a bison feast. In Owen's compound I thought of his trading amicably with Indians as well as white men, writing fondly of his "old Indian wife" in his diary, and worrying about the latest batch of fruit trees, or his newly planted grain, or his vegetable patch—all things strange and growing in this valley for the first time. I could lift my eyes from De Smet's little church or from the remnant of the rooms in which Owen had operated and see the same mountain peaks that these two men had seen and that they missed when they spent their last days far from the Bitterroots. And that the Salish also must have missed, after they were forcibly removed from their own place.

Beyond Hamilton I climbed higher, past Lost Trail Pass (the one that the Lewis and Clark expedition missed) and through the Joseph Pass and down the slope into the broad ranching valley of the Big Hole. I paused at the battlefield, the most signal victory of well-matched Indians against well-matched white men in our history.

More frequently than going to the southeastern or the southwestern parts of Montana, in the summers I have driven my car north from Great Falls toward the Canadian border where two national parks, Glacier and Waterton, meet, and where I find the ideal kind of northwestern mountain scenery, mountains and lakes shaped as if by an artist. On the way, I had always on my left the overthrust of the Northern Rockies, a jagged escarpment, pushed out over the plains toward the east by a movement of the earth itself. On my right and ahead of me was the most dramatic confrontation of high plains and high mountains on the continent, an extreme and abrupt contrast.

Time stretches forward and back here in my mind. Somewhere in the shadow of those leaning peaks are said to be the ruts indented by the feet of many people passing up and down the Old North Trail, perhaps the first having been the prehistoric Asian settlers of the continent ten thousand or more years ago. The land is still not closely settled. Going north on a two-lane federal highway, I saw few cars. It was intensely quiet, except for the wind in the grass. Bison were here in great numbers not long ago. It was easy to imagine a prime spring season with tens of thousands of the great humped beasts romping and charging in their rut, yet wheeling all in one like a great organ. On the flanks would have been the plentiful, shaggy wolves trailing strayed young and tired old, and in the distance, the white rumps of the antelopes winking in the sunlight. Over to the east, I saw the peaks of the Sweetgrass Hills, not hills, but seven-thousand-foot-high mountains rising like an island out of the plains, the place where my father and uncles had temporarily established a prosperous oil and gas field.

A cowboy in full panoply gallops alongside the road, herding several cattle before him. He waves at me and I wave back. He shows off, rising in his stirrups, delighting in the day and himself. He may be a Blackfeet, and I think of his people's story. They came out of the more fertile areas of what is now the midwest of Canada and, pushed from behind by settlement, for a time had a great freedom here. They adapted very quickly and cleverly to a ranging life on the open plains, becoming bison hunters and migrants with the herds. Today, I see small farms off in the shelter of coulees and evidence of a hard life for each family. In Browning, despite brave efforts at tribal self-reliance, and the splendor of the Museum of the Plains Indians, I see sadness in its dusty streets.

I cross the Marias River (Lewis's Maria) and think about the end of the Blackfeet's overt resistance here, on January 23, 1870, when an ambitious colonel newly appointed to the West, Eugene M. Baker, massacred an almost helpless encampment. Actions of this sort had been for years tacitly encouraged by the attitudes of the generals in charge of Indian affairs, Sherman in Washington, Sheridan in the field.

I told the story to myself again. The women, children, and older men had been left in camp while the young men had gone hunting for winter meat. At dawn the soldiers attacked without warning in a massed formation, firing into the canvas and skin shelters without announcing a reason for being there. The chief, Heavy Runner, who came out toward them with a white paper held high, which said he was a friend of the whites, was among the first shot down.

Count of the dead varied greatly. After self-serving claims had been dismissed, it seemed that one white soldier had been killed and another wounded, whereas, of the Blackfeet in the innocent village who were killed, fifteen were men, ninety were women, and fifty were children. The soldiers burned the lodges and placed, on top of the bonfires, all the food and robes saved up for the winter. Then the remainder of the Indians were turned loose in the cold and abandoned. Luckily for them, the survivors rescued some of their frightened horses. Returning from the hunt, their young men found them and took them to a nearby Blackfeet encampment.

In an account written over a hundred years later, *Death, Too, for the Heavy Runner,* Ben Bennett, having dug up army documents as well as oral accounts, wrote: "General Philip Sheridan issued General Order #1 officially commending Baker and his men for the 'complete success' of their mission."[2] "The Lieutenant General cannot commend too highly the spirit and conduct of the troops and their commander. [The order continues] and . . . congratulates the citizens of Montana upon the reasonable prospect of future security for their property and lives.[3]

The eastern press nosed out some of the truth, and there was a passing scandal. In ultimate command, Sherman asked for a more proper accounting of the incident. Sheridan justified what had happened in a private letter to his commander: "If a village is attacked, and women and children killed, the responsibility is not with the soldier, but with the people whose crimes necessitate the attack. . . . Did we cease to throw shells into Vicksburg or Atlanta because women or children were there?"

When I came back from this western trip, I reviewed the Baker case and was shaken. Who can say that this seemingly empty land has not had its history, a rich mix of good intentions and bad results, of bad intentions and some good results, the mix of which all cultures are made?

It is not difficult to envision in these spaces not only relatively recent tragedies but also, beneath and beyond the deeds of human beings, a life that preceded us. For this was once the land of many varieties of dinosaurs, some of which have only recently been discovered in an area only ten miles west of Choteau on the highway I was traveling.

Beginning in 1978 and 1979, a young paleontologist, Jack Horner, first suspected, then found, with the help of others, the remains of baby dinosaurs, the young of a kind of dinosaur which had not been named before.[4] In a rock shop in what had once been a church at a stop on the highway dignified with a name, Bynum, he saw a small, inconspicuous bone, probably that of a dinosaur. This began the hunt for dinosaurs on the nearby plains.

Dinosaurs were so plentiful that anyone knowing how to look may still find bones on the surface of the land before digging below it. Horner had a hunch that this was important, and it turned out that it was an important find: the location of the territory of a middle-sized dinosaur of eighty million years ago who had built nests, laid eggs in the nests, and cared for their young for a period of time, somewhat like the birds that were to be its remote descendants. With a smile, Horner named his dinosaur Good-Mother Lizard, *Maiasaura peeblesorum,* the Peebles being the ranch owners on whose land the find was made. With the help of eager volunteers season after season, he uncovered not only bones but also a distinct way of life among this kind of prehistoric creature, a way of life not ever substantiated before. Other scientific diggers have independently pursued the work.[5] *Digging Dinosaurs* is Horner's personal perspective on this important discovery.

Traveling across this open country, it is not difficult to imagine first the dinosaurs running about on ungainly legs, then the bison, in their compact herds, and Indians moving their household goods first on travois pulled by dogs, then by horses. The dinosaurs are gone, most of the bison are gone, and the Indians have been segregated from the freedom of their broad range. But one ancient creature is still here. This is perhaps the only place in the United States where people can look out kitchen windows and see grizzly bears in their yards. For this is the eastern extension of the great bears' mountain range, and, when berries are scarce, the bears come down into the outskirts of Choteau, Bynum, and Dupuyer. They are the threatened remnant—as are the elk and antelope—of the abundance of animal life that the explorers and fur trappers knew.

To the east a great inland sea once stretched all the way from what would become the Gulf of Mexico, but then the gulf was the whole inner part of a divided continent. The dinosaurs were on a windy upland not so different from these plains today, but not so far away from wetter lands near a primal sea. Here, with the skeleton of the land always visible, and the extremes of weather threatening one, it is impossible to ignore the nonhuman, the earth itself. I have found it salutary and sometimes exhilarating.

It is sometimes the shock of the nonhuman, the grandly indifferent, which makes me know that I am at home, away from comfortable places. Nothing has ever hit me as hard as when, driving farther north along the Front, nearing the Canadian border, I round a corner and behold Chief Mountain—a square monolith, rugged, stony, solitary—looming at me. Holding the wheel as I circle its base, I glance at it as often as I dare and see it as an exclamation of triumphant stony endurance. For a westerner this is the kind of experience always lying in wait beyond our small attempts at humanizing the scenery. Chief Mountain, like the line of the Lewis Overthrust behind it, makes us all visitors. Although a smattering of geology tells me that Chief also will crumble—"the Rockies will crumble," as the song says—it does not seem to be doing so. We will go first.*

If the oil is mostly gone, as well as the gold, the original prairie grass, the bison, the free-roaming Blackfeet, and portions of several generations of white invaders, the land remains. If this is acknowledged, it makes for a salutary relationship between humankind and the land. It helps to make us humble in the face of the not always manageable. There is always the greatness, the wildness, the untamability of the spaces that surround the bright, complete, small towns. It has induced a contradictory set of reactions. Sometimes the reaction that we give this land is one of a wildness, a lawlessness, an expansion of individual rights and desires contemptuous of governing restraints. On the other hand, it usually becomes clear that each person here counts for far more than the solitary individual elsewhere. There is an instinctive reaching out from one to another in initial trust and reliance, in hunger for company in the great loneliness, and in willingness to help in need.

The perspective of the eternal is not a bad background for the comic and tragic antics of the scattered human beings who have made a short, intense history on this landscape.

---

*In early July 1992, part of the north face of Chief Mountain slipped away, causing an avalanche, the silting of streams, and the closing of campgrounds.

NOTES

Full citations of sources are in the Bibliography.

ONE. THE SOLILOQUIES OF MERIWETHER LEWIS

1. Meriwether Lewis and William Clark, *Journals,* ed. John Bakeless, Sept. 17, 1804, 62–63.

2. William Clark, *The Field Notes of Capt. William Clark, 1803–5,* ed. Ernest Staples. Jan. 6, 1804; Mar. 30, 1804; June 30, 1804; and July 18, 1804.

3. Ibid., July 19, 1804; and July 4, 1804.

4. Lewis, preparing to continue westward, in Lewis and Clark, *Journals,* Apr. 7, 1805, 127.

5. Archibald Hanna, "Introduction," in Thomas Jefferson, *The Lewis and Clark Expedition,* xxvii–xxviii.

6. Lewis and Clark, *Journals,* May 31, 1805, 157.

7. Lewis's notes about the Great Falls in ibid., June 13, 1805, 176–80.

8. Wonders (wolverine, grizzly bear, prickly pears) in ibid., June 14, 1805, 181–86; and June 13, 1805, 180.

9. Lewis and Clark, *Journals,* Aug. 18, 1805, 246.

10. Interchange between Lewis and Cameahwait in ibid., Aug. 25, 1805, 253; and Aug. 26, 1805, 255.

11. Lewis and Clark, *Journals,* Jan. 1, 1806, 287.

12. Ibid., June 27, 1806, 335.

13. Ibid., July 3, 1806, 338.

14. Ibid., Sept. 20, 1806, 382.

TWO. FUR TRAPPER: OSBORNE RUSSELL

1. Osborne Russell, *Journal of a Fur Trapper, 1834–1843,* ed. Aubry L. Haines, 34. Subsequent citations appear within parentheses in the text.

2. Bernard DeVoto, *Across the Wide Missouri,* 159.

3. Russell, *Journal,* 96.

4. Biographical information and editor's "Introduction," in ibid.

THREE. NATURALIST: JOHN KIRK TOWNSEND

1. John Kirk Townsend, *Narrative of a Journey across the Rocky Mountains, to the Columbia River* . . . 364. Subsequent citations appear within parentheses in the text.

FOUR. TRADER AND PRIEST: JOHN OWEN AND PIERRE JEAN DE SMET

1. Pierre Jean De Smet, *Father De Smet's Life and Travels among the North American Indians*, ed. Hiram M. Chittenden and Alfred T. Richardson. Citations are from vol. 1.

2. John Owen, *Journals and Letters of Major John Owen, Pioneer of the Northwest, 1850–71*, ed. Seymour Dunbar, with notes by Paul C. Phillips. Citations are from vol. 1.

3. Paraphrased by John Upton Terrell, *Black Robe: The Life of Pierre-Jean De Smet, Missionary, Explorer, and Pioneer*, 182. From Chittenden and Richardson, *Father De Smet's Life and Travels*, 1.

4. Terrell, *Black Robe*, 106. Quoting *Father De Smet's Life and Travels*, 1.

5. Terrell, *Black Robe*, 241. From *Father De Smet's Life and Travels*, 1.

6. Terrell, *Black Robe*, 302.

7. Ibid., 304. From *Father De Smet's Life and Travels*, 1.

8. Terrell, *Black Robe*, 339. From *Father De Smet's Life and Travels*, 1.

9. Owen, *Journals*, Sept. 24, 1855, 1:111.

10. Ibid., June 17, 1856, 1:132–33.

11. Ibid.

12. Ibid., May 11, 1856, 1:126.

13. Ibid., July 4, 1856, 1:135.

14. Ibid., May 8, 1856, 1:124.

15. Ibid., May 10, 1856, 1:125.

16. Ibid., Aug. 1, 1856, 1:138.

17. Ibid., Aug. 18, 1856, 1:139.

18. Ibid., the account of the fall journey to Fort Benton and back is contained in entries for Sept. 7-Nov. 18, 1856, 1:140–51.

FIVE. SETTLERS: JAMES AND GRANVILLE STUART

1. Granville Stuart, *Prospecting for Gold: From Dogtown to Virginia City, 1852–1864*, ed. Paul C. Phillips. In *Forty Years on the Frontier, Pioneering in Montana, 1864–87*, 2 vols., 1:192–93. Subsequent citations appear within parentheses in the text.

2. Successive quotes about the book search are in ibid., 159–61.

3. Some of the information about Granville Stuart's life is in Paul C. Phillips, "Introduction," in Stuart, *Prospecting for Gold*, 13–18.

SIX. EDITOR AND OUTLAW: THOMAS DIMSDALE AND HENRY PLUMMER

1. Thomas J. Dimsdale, *The Vigilantes of Montana*. This was the first book published in Montana (1866). Quotations that follow are from a University of Oklahoma Press edition (1953).

2. As told by Annie Moran Durnen, at seventy-four years of age, remembering her teacher, in a newspaper article by Mrs. M. E. Plassmann, "First Virginia City School Was Taught by Dimsdale," *Forsyth Independent*, May 9, 1929.

3. Granville Stuart, *Forty Years on the Frontier, Pioneering in Montana, 1864–87*, 2 vols., 2:30.

4. Thomas Dimsdale, unsigned editorial, *Montana Post*, Oct. 6, 1864. *Montana Post* was the first newspaper published in Montana and issued from a storefront on the main street of Virginia City.

5. Thomas Dimsdale, unsigned editorial, *Montana Post*, Nov. 10, 1864.

6. Ibid., Nov. 26, 1864.

7. Quoted in Robert J. Goligoski, "Thomas J. Dimsdale: Montana's First Newspaper Editor," 80.

8. Granville Stuart, *Prospecting for Gold: From Dogtown to Virginia City, 1852–1864*, ed. Paul C. Phillips. In *Forty Years on the Frontier, Pioneering in Montana, 1864–87*, 1:232, 237.

9. *X Beidler, Vigilante*, ed. Helen Fitzgerald Sanders in collaboration with William H. Bertsche, Jr., 27–29. The original was dictated in 1880.

10. Ibid., 92.

11. Dan Cushman, *Montana: The Gold Frontier*, 119.

12. Full use is made of information and speculation about Henry Plummer in R. E. Mather and F. E. Boswell, *Hanging the Sheriff: A Biography of Henry Plummer*, balancing this theory against the tradition.

13. Two quotes about the death of Cleveland are in Dimsdale, *The Vigilantes of Montana*, 29. Subsequent citations appear within parentheses in the text.

14. Two quotes about the killing of the Mexican, Pizanthia, and the author's subsequent comment, are in ibid., 153–54.

SEVEN. SOLDIERS: GEORGE CROOK
AND JOHN GREGORY BOURKE

1. John Gregory Bourke, diary, Aug. 12, 1875, in J. W. Vaughn, *The Reynolds Campaign on Powder River*, 14.

2. Words of the 1868 Treaty are quoted in S. L. A. Marshall, *Crimsoned Prairie: The Indian Wars*, 82–83.

3. Reputed words of Chivington are in Marshall, *Crimsoned Prairie*, 37.

4. Robert M. Utley and Wilcomb E. Washburn, *Indian Wars*, 207.

5. Ibid., 210.

6. From Bourke's diary, quoted in Vaughn, *The Reynolds Campaign on Powder River*, 51.

7. John Gregory Bourke, *On the Border with Crook*, 247. Subsequent citations appear within parentheses in the text.

8. They thought it was Crazy Horse's village, but it was not. His lay intact beyond their march and was to receive the survivors of their attack.

9. Quoted in George Crook, *General George Crook: His Autobiography*, ed. Martin F. Schmitt (who found the unfinished manuscript in the library of the Army War College in Washington, D.C., in 1942), 269–70.

10. Crook, *General George Crook*, 271.

11. Ibid., 273.

12. Bourke's diary, quoted in Joseph C. Porter, *Paper Medicine Man: John Gregory Bourke and His American West*, 299.

13. Cited in Porter, *Paper Medicine Man*, 274.

14. Quoted in ibid., 187.

15. Two quotes on Bourke's death are in ibid., 306.

EIGHT. SURVIVORS: PRETTY-SHIELD AND NANNIE ALDERSON

1. Frank B. Linderman, *Pretty-Shield, Medicine Woman of the Crows*, 235–37.

2. Two quotes are in Nannie T. Alderson and Helena Huntington Smith, *A Bride Goes West*, 192.

3. Linderman, *Pretty-Shield*, 243.

4. Alderson and Smith, *A Bride Goes West*, 4.

5. Ibid.; Helena Huntington Smith, "Preface," in ibid., vi.

6. Two quotes about childhood remembrances are in Alderson and Smith, *A Bride Goes West*, 6.

7. On freedom in Kansas, see Alderson and Smith, *A Bride Goes West*, 8.

8. Three quotes about change for the Indians are in Linderman, *Pretty-Shield*, 20, 23, 24. Subsequent citations appear within parentheses in the text.

9. On the lost baby episode, see Linderman, *Pretty-Shield*, 65–70.

10. Alderson and Smith, *A Bride Goes West*, 25. Subsequent citations appear within parentheses in the text.

NINE. COPPERTOWN PEOPLE

1. Berton Braley, *Pegasus Pulls a Hack: Memoirs of a Modern Minstrel*, 49, 50.

2. Mary MacLane, *The Story of Mary MacLane, by Herself*, in *The Last Best Place: A Montana Anthology*, ed. William Kittredge and Annick Smith, 482.

3. Myron Brinig, *Singermann*, 33, 35.

4. Braley, *Pegasus Pulls a Hack*, 4.

5. The story of Jim the firehorse is in Federal Writers Project, *Copper Camp*, 90.

6. The story of Daly on the sidewalk is in Carl Burgess Glasscock, *The War of the Copper Kings: Builders of Butte and Wolves of Wall Street*, 104.

7. Michael P. Malone, *The Battle for Butte*, 180.

8. Ibid., 174.

9. Ibid., 175.

10. Two quotes on Heinze are in Braley, *Pegasus Pulls a Hack*, 57.

11. Braley, *Pegasus Pulls a Hack*, 87.

12. Elizabeth Ann (Rose) Morrow Rust, "Reminiscence." Biographical details and quotations from these memoirs as compiled by her daughter, Harriette Dommes, Montana Historical Society Archives.

13. Beatrice Murphy, "Diary of a Night Nurse, Butte, Montana, 1909," *Montana: The Magazine of Western History*, 64–65.

14. Leslie A. Wheeler, "Mary MacLane, Montana's Shocking 'Lit'ry Lady,'" *Mon-*

tana: The Magazine of Western History, July 1977. Biographical details are in Wheeler; Virginia Terres, "Mary MacLane, Realist," *Speculator: A Journal of Butte and Southwest Montana History*; and Carolyn J. Mattern, "Mary MacLane: A Feminist Opinion," *Montana: The Magazine of Western History*.

15. MacLane, *The Story of Mary MacLane, by Herself*, in *The Last Best Place: A Montana Anthology*, 483. Subsequent citations appear within parentheses in the text.

16. Mary MacLane, New York City and Butte journalism, quotes in Terres, "Mary MacLane, Realist."

17. Mary MacLane, *I, Mary MacLane: A Dairy of Human Days*, quoted by Wheeler, "Mary MacLane, Montana's Shocking 'Lit'ry Lady,'" 30.

18. Malone, *The Battle for Butte*, 190.

19. Louis Levine, *The Taxation of Mines in Montana*.

TEN. MR. GIBSON AND THE COWBOY: PARIS GIBSON AND CHARLES M. RUSSELL

1. *A Genealogy of Paris Gibson*, compiled by the Great Falls Genealogical Society.

2. Dates and facts of Paris Gibson's life are in James G. Handford, "Paris Gibson— a Montana Yankee."

3. Brochure printed by the *Great Falls Tribune*, Jan. 1, 1914.

4. On file with other early Great Falls material in the Montana Room of the Great Falls Public Library.

5. Mary Douglas Gibson, *Reminiscences*.

6. The dates, facts, and quotations about Russell are, except where noted, in Ramon F. Adams and Homer E. Britzman, *Charles M. Russell, the Cowboy Artist: A Biography*.

7. Nancy C. Russell, quoted in Adams and Britzman, *Charles M. Russell*, 132–33. See also a slightly different version in a biographical note by Nancy C. Wilson in *Good Medicine: The Illustrated Letters of Charles M. Russell*.

8. E. C. Abbott and Helena Huntington Smith, *We Pointed Them North*, 145.

9. Quoted in John K. Hutchens, *One Man's Montana: An Informal Portrait of a State*, 207–8.

ELEVEN. WHO WAS CALAMITY JANE? A SPECULATION

1. William E. Connolley, "Wild Bill and His Era," in James W. Buel, *The True Story of "Wild Bill" Hickok*, ed. J. Brussel, 85.

2. Stewart H. Holbrook, *Little Annie Oakley and Other Rugged People*, 32.

3. This quote and two others are in James Horan, "Calamity Jane, White Devil of the Yellowstone," in *Desperate Women*, 192, 199.

4. This quote and one other are in Harry Sinclair Drago, "Calamity Jane in Fact and Fiction," in *Notorious Ladies of the Frontier*, 208, 212.

5. Three quotes are in Roberta Beed Sollid, *Calamity Jane: A Study in Historical Criticism*, xi, 1, 91.

6. "Note from the Publisher," in Sollid, *Calamity Jane*, v.

7. Three quotes are in Miguel Antonio Otero, *My Life on the Frontier, 1864–1882*, 21, 22.

8. Several quotes are in John F. Finerty, *War-Path and Bivouac*, 63, 80, 200.

9. Three quotes are in Colonel Anson G. Mills, *My Story*, 401.

10. John G. Bourke, *On the Border with Crook*, 299–300.

11. This quote and four others are in E. C. Abbott and Helena Huntington Smith, *We Pointed Them North*, 74, 75, 76. Drago says that Abbott was mistaken about Jane in 1878, and must have seen some other woman, but Abbott got to know Jane much better after this; one doubts that he clung to a mistaken memory.

12. William Lull Papers, quotations to follow from letters Lull wrote to his family, 1875–77, and from his unpublished narrative, "Calamity Jane, Deadwood City in Pioneer Days," by permission of David Lull, Atlanta. David Lull is William Lull's great-nephew.

13. Karen Lull (Mrs. David Lull), letter to the author, Jan. 4, 1991.

14. The quotation is from Calamity Jane, in William Lull Papers, verified as a passage in Martha Jane Cannary Burke, *Calamity Jane's Diary and Letters*, ed. Stella Foote, Billings, Montana, copyright and physical owner of the said *Diary and Letters*. The full information on the *Diary and Letters* to be cited later where appropriate.

15. Martha Jane Cannary Burke, *Life and Adventures of Calamity Jane*, reprint ed.

16. Horan, *Desperate Women*, 198–99.

17. Burke, *Diary and Letters*, 6th ed. and others. The album diary was purchased by Stella A. Foote of Billings, Montana, from Jean Hickok McCormick in 1941. All quotations from whatever edition have been verified as coming from the original source, and are used with the permission of Stella A. Foote.

18. Joseph G. Rosa, *The West of Wild Bill Hickok*, 182.

19. Horan, *Desperate Women*, 200.

20. Sollid, *Calamity Jane*, 44.

21. Joseph G. Rosa, *They Called Him Wild Bill*, 163.

22. Drago, *Notorious Ladies of the Frontier*, 222.

23. James McLaird, letter to the author, Dec. 5, 1990, showing the continuing interest among contemporary scholars in the identity and character of Jane.

24. Horan, *Desperate Women*, 200.

25. Sollid, *Calamity Jane*, 45.

26. Rosa, *They Called Him Wild Bill*, 163.

27. Horan, *Desperate Women*, 198.

28. Barb Fisher and Glenda Bell of Fisher-Bell, Storytellers, letter to the author, Dec. 6, 1990.

TWELVE. RECOLLECTION AND RENEWAL: AN AFTERWORD

1. Bernard DeVoto, two articles from, among many, "The West: A Plundered Province?" and "The West against Itself."

2. The general account and quotes about the story of the Baker massacre are in Ben Bennett, *Death, Too, for the Heavy Runner*, 129–46.

3. William T. Sheridan and Philip H. Sherman, *Reports of Inspection Made in the Summer of 1877*, 143–46.

4. John R. Horner and James Gorman, *Digging Dinosaurs*.

5. Bone discoveries, analyses, and lectures in paleontology at Old Trail Museum, Choteau, Montana.

BIBLIOGRAPHY

The listings under "Background" are those materials that have most helped me for the whole book. Listings under the chapter titles indicate those books, articles, newspaper stories, and unpublished materials that have been most helpful in understanding each separate stage of the growth of the life and culture of the Northern Rockies.

BACKGROUND

Armitage, Sue. Introduction to "Nineteenth-Century Women on the Frontier." *Montana: The Magazine of Western History*, special ed., Summer 1982.

The Arts in Montana. Edited by H. G. Merriam. Missoula, Mont.: Mountain Press Publishing Co., 1977.

Bergon, Frank, and Zeese Paparikolas. *Looking Far West: The Search for the American West in History, Myth, and Literature*. New York: Mentor (NAL), 1978.

Burlingame, Merrill G., and K. Ross Toole. "History of Oil and Gas in Montana." In *A History of Montana*. 2 vols., vol. 2. New York: Lewis Historical Publishing Co., 1957.

Ewers, John C. *The Blackfeet: Raiders of the Northwestern Plains*. Norman: University of Oklahoma Press, 1958.

———. *Indian Life on the Upper Missouri*. Norman: University of Oklahoma Press, 1968.

Federal Writers Project. *Montana*. American Guide Series. New York: Viking, 1939.

Fiedler, Leslie A. "Montana, or the End of Jean-Jacques Rousseau." In *Collected Essays*. 2 vols., vol. 1. New York: Stein and Day, 1971.

Garreau, Joel. "The Empty Quarter." In *The Nine Nations of North America*. Boston: Houghton Mifflin, 1981.

Great Falls Tribune. Great Falls, Mont., 1979–92.

Gressley, Gene M. "Regionalism and the Twentieth-Century West." In *The American West: New Perspectives, New Dimensions*. Edited by Jerome O. Steffen. Norman: University of Oklahoma Press, 1979.

Hoebel, E. Adamson. *The Cheyennes, Indians of the Great Plains*. 2d ed. New York: Holt, Rinehart & Winston, 1978 (c. 1960).

Howard, Joseph Kinsey. *Montana: High, Wide, and Handsome*. New Haven: Yale University Press, 1959 (c. 1943).

Josephy, Alvin M., Jr. "Agony of the Northern Great Plains." *Audubon Magazine*, July 1973.

Bibliography

————. *The Indian Heritage of America*. New York: Bantam, 1969 (c. 1968).

Kraenzel, Carl F. *The Great Plains in Transition*. Norman: University of Oklahoma Press, 1955.

Malone, Michael P., and Dianna G. Dougherty. "Montana's Political Culture: A Century of Evolution." *Montana: The Magazine of Western History*, Jan. 1981.

Malone, Michael P., and Richard B. Roeder. *Montana: A History of Two Centuries*. Seattle: University of Washington Press, 1976.

Martin, Albro. *James J. Hill and the Opening of the Northwest*. New York: Oxford University Press, 1976.

Miller, Robert E. "Life in the Gold Camps of Montana." *Montana Magazine*, July-August 1980.

Montana Magazine. Helena, Mont.: American and World Geographical Publishing Co., 1979–92.

Montana: The Magazine of Western History. Helena: Montana Historical Society, 1979–92.

Powell, Peter J., and Michael P. Malone. *Montana, Past and Present*. Papers read at a Clark Library Seminar. April 5, 1975. William Andrews Clark Memorial Library, University of California, Los Angeles, 1976.

Reid, T. R. "New Western Historians Firing away at Turner's 'Frontier Thesis.'" *Atlanta Constitution*, Oct. 14, 1989.

Reisner, Marc. *Cadillac Desert: The American West and Its Disappearing Water*. New York: Penguin Books, 1987 (c. 1986).

Reps, John W. *Cities of the American West: A History of Frontier Urban Planning*. Princeton: Princeton University Press, 1979.

Sharp, Paul F. *Whoop-Up Country: The Canadian-American West, 1865–1885*. Drawings by C. M. Russell. Helena: Historical Society of Montana, 1960 (c. 1955).

Spence, Clark C. *Montana: A Bicentennial History*. States and Nation Series. New York: Norton, 1978.

Stegner, Wallace. *The American West as Living Space*. From three William W. Cook Lectures at the Law School of the University of Michigan, Oct. 28, 29, 30, 1986. Ann Arbor: University of Michigan Press, 1987.

Thomas, Lewis G. *Ranchers' Legacy: Alberta Essays*. Edited by Patrick A. Dunae. Western Canada Reprint Ser. Edmonton: University of Alberta Press, 1986.

Toole, Kenneth Ross. *Montana: An Uncommon Land*. Norman: University of Oklahoma Press, 1959.

————. *The Rape of the Great Plains*. Boston: Little, Brown, 1976.

————. *Twentieth Century Montana: A State of Extremes*. Norman: University of Oklahoma Press, 1972.

Trenholm, Virginia C., and Maurine Carley. *The Shoshonis: Sentinels of the Rockies*. Norman: University of Oklahoma Press, 1964.

Turner, Frederick Jackson. "The Significance of the Frontier in American History." In *Annual Report of the American Historical Association for the Year 1893*. Washington, D.C.: U.S. Government Printing Office, 1894.

Udall, Stuart. *Beyond the Mythic West*. Salt Lake City: Peregrine Smith Books, 1991.

Webb, Walter Prescott. *The Great Plains*. Boston: Ginn, 1931.

Bibliography

Note: Free and helpful use was made of the *Americana Encyclopedia* and the *Dictionary of American Biography*.

ONE. THE SOLILOQUIES OF MERIWETHER LEWIS

Allen, John L. *Passage through the Garden: Lewis and Clark and the Image of the American Northwest*. Urbana: University of Illinois Press, 1975.

Anderson, Irving W. "Profiles of the American West: A Charbonneau Family Portrait." *American West*, March-April 1980.

Bakeless, John E. *Lewis and Clark, Partners in Discovery*. New York: William Morrow, 1947.

Clark, William. *The Field Notes of Capt. William Clark, 1803–5*. Edited by Ernest Staples. New Haven: Yale University Press, 1964.

Clarke, Charles G. *The Men of the Lewis and Clark Expedition: A Biographical Roster of the Fifty-one Members and a Composite Diary of Their Activities from All Known Sources*. Glendale, Calif.: A. H. Clark Co., 1970.

DeVoto, Bernard. "Introduction." In *Journals of Lewis and Clark*. Boston: Houghton Mifflin, 1953.

Dillon, Richard. *Meriwether Lewis: A Biography*. New York: Coward-McCann, 1965.

Fisher, Vardis. *Suicide or Murder? The Strange Death of Governor Meriwether Lewis*. Denver: Alan Swallow, 1962.

Jefferson, Thomas. "Capt. Meriwether Lewis." In *The Lewis and Clark Expedition*. 3 vols., vol. 1. The 1814 ed. Philadelphia: J. B. Lippincott, 1961.

La Vérendrye, Pierre Gaultier de. *Journals*. Edited by Lawrence J. Burpee. New York: Greenwood Press, 1968; reprint of 1927 ed.

Lawrence, Paul. *Journey of Discovery*. Jackson, Wyo.: Unita Pioneer Press, 1978.

Lewis, Meriwether. *History of the Expedition of Captains Lewis and Clark, 1804–6*. Reprinted from the 1814 ed. Edited by James K. Hosmer. 2 vols. Chicago: A. C. McClurg & Co., 1902.

Lewis, Meriwether, and John Ordway. *The Journals of Capt. Meriwether Lewis and Sergeant John Ordway*. Edited by Milo M. Quaife. Madison: State Historical Society of Wisconsin, 1916.

Lewis, Meriwether, and William Clark. *American Odyssey: The Journey of Lewis and Clark*. Compiled by Ingvard Henry Eide (photographs and text). Chicago: Rand McNally, 1969.

———. *Journals*. Edited by John Bakeless. New York: Mentor (NAL), 1964.

Moulton, Gary E. "The Missing Journals of Meriwether Lewis." *Montana: The Magazine of Western History*, Summer 1985.

Nichols, William. "Lewis and Clark Probe the Heart of Darkness." *American Scholar*, Winter 1979–80.

Parker, Ed. "On the Lewis and Clark Trail across the Bitterroots." In *1967 Yearbook of Agriculture* (Yearbook Separate No. 3463). Washington, D.C.: U.S. Government Printing Office, 1968.

Steffen, Jerome O. *William Clark, Jeffersonian Man on the Frontier*. Norman: University of Oklahoma Press, 1977.

Bibliography

TWO. FUR TRAPPER: OSBORNE RUSSELL

Chittenden, Hiram Martin. *The American Fur Trade of the Far West*. 2 vols. New York: Press of the Pioneers, 1935 (1902).

DeVoto, Bernard. *Across the Wide Missouri*. Boston: Houghton Mifflin, 1975 (1945).

Hafen, Le Roy R., ed. *The Mountain Men of the Fur Trade: Biographical Sketches of the Participants*. 10 vols. Glendale, Calif.: A. H. Clark, 1965–72.

Jackson, Donald. *Voyages of the Steamboat Yellowstone*. New York: Ticknor & Fields, 1985.

Miller, Alfred Jacob. *The West of Alfred Jacob Miller*. Norman: University of Oklahoma Press, 1951.

Russell, Osborne. *Journal of a Fur Trapper, 1834–1843*. Edited by Aubry L. Haines. Lincoln: University of Nebraska Press, 1965 (1955, from 1914 and 1921 eds.).

Vestal, Stanley. *Jim Bridger, Mountain Man: A Biography*. Lincoln: University of Nebraska Press, 1976 (1946).

THREE. NATURALIST: JOHN KIRK TOWNSEND

Audubon, John James. *Audubon Reader*. Edited by Scott Russell Sanders. Bloomington: Indiana University Press, 1986 (in part: introduction, chronology, last journal: "Up the Missouri . . . 1843").

———. *Ornithological Biographies*. 5 vols. Edinburgh, 1831–39 (vol. 5 only—search for credits to Townsend).

Catlin, George. *Letters and Notes on the Manners, Customs, and Conditions of the North American Indians. Written during Eight Years' Travel (1832–1839) amongst the Wildest Tribes of Indians in North America*. 2 vols. (vol. 1 only). Introduction by Marjorie Halpin. New York: Dover Publishers, 1973 (London, 1844).

Goetzmann, William H., Introduction, and Orr, William J., Biography. *Karl Bodmer's America*. Joslyn Art Museum & University of Nebraska Press, 1984 (pictures only).

Herrick, Francis Hobart. *Audubon the Naturalist*. 2 vols. New York: Appleton, 1917 (vol. 2 in part).

Maximilian, Prince of Wied. *Maximilian's Travels in North America, 1832–1834*. 2 vols. In Reuben Gold Thwaites, *Early Western Travels, 1748–1846*. Cleveland: Arthur H. Clark Co., 1906.

Parkman, Francis. *Journals*. Edited by Mason Wade. 2 vols. New York: Harper, 1947.

———. *Letters*. Edited by Wilbur R. Jacobs. 2 vols. Norman: University of Oklahoma Press, 1960.

Townsend, John Kirk. *Narrative*. Lincoln: University of Nebraska Press, 1979. (*Narrative of a Journey across the Rocky Mountains, to the Columbia River . . .*). Philadelphia: Henry Perkins, 1839. In Reuben Gold Thwaites, *Early Western Travels, 1748–1846*. 32 vols., vol. 21. Cleveland: Arthur H. Clark, 1905.

FOUR. TRADER AND PRIEST: JOHN OWEN AND PIERRE JEAN DE SMET

Burk, Dale A. "The Bitterroot Valley." *Montana Magazine*, May-June 1981.

De Smet, Pierre Jean. *Father De Smet's Life and Travels among the North American Indians*.

Bibliography

Edited by Hiram M. Chittenden and Alfred T. Richardson. 4 vols., vol. 1. New York: Francis P. Harper, 1905 (1904).

Florian, Rev. Martin. *The Story of St. Mary's Mission.* Stevensville, Mont.: Saint Mary's Mission Historical Foundation, 1959.

Hungry Wolf, Adolf. *Charlo's People, the Flathead Tribe of Montana.* Invermere, B.C.: Good Medicine Books, 1974.

Miller, Robert E. "Fort Owen: Montana's First Department Store." *Montana Magazine,* Sept.-Oct. 1979.

Owen, John. *Journals and Letters of Major John Owen, Pioneer of the Northwest, 1850–71.* Transcribed and edited from the original manuscript in the Montana Historical Society by Seymour Dunbar, with Notes by Paul C. Phillips. 2 vols., vol. 1, 1850–65. New York: Edward Eberstadt, 1927.

Ronan, Peter. *History of the Flathead Indians.* Minneapolis: Ross & Haines, 1965 (1890).

Terrell, John Upton. *Black Robe: The Life of Pierre-Jean De Smet, Missionary, Explorer and Pioneer.* New York: Doubleday, 1964.

FIVE. SETTLERS: JAMES AND GRANVILLE STUART

Clark, Rob. "The Real Brother: The James Stuart Diaries of 1863." *Montana Post.* Helena: Montana Historical Society, Spring 1988.

Stuart, Granville. *Pioneering in Montana: The Making of a State, 1864–1887.* Edited by Paul C. Phillips. Lincoln: University of Nebraska Press, 1977; originally published under the title *Forty Years on the Frontier . . .* 2 vols., vol. 2. Cleveland: Arthur C. Clark Co., 1925.

———. *Prospecting for Gold: From Dogtown to Virginia City, 1852–1864.* Edited by Paul C. Phillips. Lincoln: University of Nebraska Press, 1977; originally published under the title *Forty Years on the Frontier as Seen in the Journals and Reminiscences of Granville Stuart, Gold Miner, Trader, Merchant, Rancher and Politician.* 2 vols., vol. 1. Cleveland: Arthur H. Clark Co., 1925.

SIX. EDITOR AND OUTLAW: THOMAS DIMSDALE AND HENRY PLUMMER

Anonymous (possible author: John Lyle Campbell, reporter, *Chicago Tribune*). *The Banditti of the Rocky Mountains—Vigilance Committee in Idaho, An Authentic Record of Startling Adventures in the Gold Mines of Idaho.* Notes and Bibliography by Jerome Peltier. Minneapolis: Ross & Haines, 1964.

X. *Beidler, Vigilante.* Edited by Helen Fitzgerald Sanders in collaboration with William H. Bertsche, Jr. Foreword by A. B. Guthrie. Norman: University of Oklahoma Press, 1957. Dictated in 1880.

Callaway, Lew L. *Montana's Righteous Hangmen: The Vigilantes in Action.* Norman: University of Oklahoma Press, 1982 (1973).

Cushman, Dan. *Montana: The Gold Frontier.* Great Falls, Mont.: Stay Away Joe, Publisher, 1973.

Dimsdale, Thomas. Unsigned editorials, *Montana Post,* September 1864 through August 1866. Helena: Library of the Montana Historical Society.

————. *The Vigilantes of Montana.* Virginia City, Mont.: D. W. Tilton & Co., 1866; reprint, Norman: University of Oklahoma Press, 1953 (Western Frontier Library).

T.B.E. "Thomas Josiah Dimsdale." *Anaconda Standard,* July 9, 1893. Copy from the Montana Historical Society.

Edgerton, Mary W. *A Governor's Wife on the Mining Frontier: Letters, 1863–1865.* Salt Lake City: Tanner Trust Fund, University of Utah Library, 1976.

Goligoski, Bob. "Dimsdale Kept Pro-Dixie Readers Hopping Mad." *Great Falls Tribune,* June 20, 1965. Copy from the Montana Historical Society.

Goligoski, Robert J. "Thomas J. Dimsdale: Montana's First Newspaper Editor." Master's Thesis, Montana State University, May 17, 1965. Mansfield Library, Missoula: University of Montana.

Langford, Nathaniel Pitt. *Vigilante Days and Ways; the Pioneers of the Rockies; the Makers and Making of Montana, Idaho, Oregon, Washington, and Wyoming.* 2 vols. Saint Paul: D. D. Merrill Co., 1893 (1890).

Mather, R. E., and F. E. Boswell. *Hanging the Sheriff: A Biography of Henry Plummer.* Salt Lake City: University of Utah Press, 1987.

Mullan, John. *Miners' and Travelers' Guide.* New York: Arno Press, 1973 (1865).

Plassmann, Mrs. M. E. "First Virginia City School Was Taught by Dimsdale." *Forsyth Independent,* May 9, 1929. From files of Montana Historical Society.

————. "Thos. Dimsdale, Montana's First Historian." *Rocky Mountain Husbandman,* Aug. 5, 1927. From files of Montana Historical Society.

Wolle, Muriel Sibell. *Montana Pay Dirt: Guide to the Mining Camps of the Treasure State.* Sage/Swallow Press Books. Athens: Ohio University Press, 1893 (1963).

SEVEN. SOLDIERS: GEORGE CROOK AND JOHN GREGORY BOURKE

Bourke, John Gregory. *On the Border with Crook.* Bison Books. Lincoln: University of Nebraska, 1971 (1891).

Connell, Evan S. *Son of Morning Star.* Berkeley: North Point Press, 1984.

Crook, George. *General George Crook: His Autobiography.* Edited by Martin F. Schmitt; foreword, Joseph C. Porter. Norman: University of Oklahoma Press, 1960 (1946).

Finerty, John Frederick. *War-Path and Bivouac.* Chicago: R. R. Donnelley, 1955 (1890).

Grouard, Frank. *Life and Adventures of Frank Grouard.* Retold by Joe De Barthe; edited by Edgar I. Stewart. Norman: University of Oklahoma Press, 1958 (oral history of De Barthe, 1891).

Hedren, Paul L. *With Crook in the Black Hills: Stanley J. Morrow's 1876 Photographic Legacy.* Boulder, Colo.: Pruett Publishing Co., 1985.

Hoig, Stan. *The Battle of the Washita: The Sheridan-Custer Indian Campaign of 1867–1869.* New York: Doubleday, 1976.

Jordan, Robert Paul. "Ghosts of the Little Bighorn." *National Geographic,* December 1986.

Kadlecek, Edward, and Mabel Kadlecek. *To Kill an Eagle: Indian Views on the Last Days of Crazy Horse.* Boulder, Colo.: Johnson Books, 1983 (1981).

Bibliography

Lang, William L. "Where Did the Nez Perces Go in Yellowstone in 1877?" *Montana: The Magazine of Western History,* Winter 1990.

Marshall, S. L. A. *Crimsoned Prairie: The Indian Wars.* New York: Da Capo, 1984 (1972).

Merington, Marguerite. *The Custer Story: The Life and Intimate Letters of General George A. Custer and His Wife Elizabeth.* New York: Devin-Adair Co., 1950.

Miller, David Humphreys. *Custer's Fall: The Indian Side of the Story.* Lincoln: University of Nebraska Press, 1985 (1957).

Neihardt, John G., as told through. *Black Elk Speaks: Being the Life Story of a Holy Man of the Oglalla Sioux.* New York: Pocket Books, 1972 (1932, 1959).

Neihardt, John G. *The Song of the Indian Wars.* New York: Macmillan, 1925.

Place, Marion T. *Retreat to the Bear Paw: The Story of the Nez Perce.* New York: Four Winds Press, 1969.

Porter, Joseph C. *Paper Medicine Man: John Gregory Bourke and His American West.* Norman: University of Oklahoma Press, 1986.

Rister, Carl Coke. *Border Command: General Phil Sheridan in the West.* Norman: University of Oklahoma Press, 1944.

Robbins, Jim. "Unearthing Little Bighorn's Secrets." *National Parks,* Nov.-Dec. 1986.

Tillett, Leslie. *Wind on the Buffalo Grass: The Indians' Own Account of the Battle at the Little Bighorn.* New York: Thomas Y. Crowell Co., 1976.

Utley, Robert M. *Frontier Regulars: The U.S. Army and the Indian, 1866–1891.* New York: Macmillan, 1973.

Utley, Robert M., and Wilcomb E. Washburn. *Indian Wars.* American Heritage; distributed by Houghton Mifflin, 1985 (1977).

Vaughn, J. W. *The Reynolds Campaign on Powder River.* Norman: University of Oklahoma Press, 1961.

———. *With Crook at the Rosebud.* Harrisburg, Pa.: Stackpole Co., 1956.

Vestal, Stanley. *Sitting Bull: Champion of the Sioux.* Norman: University of Oklahoma Press, 1967.

EIGHT. SURVIVORS: PRETTY-SHIELD AND NANNIE ALDERSON

Alderson, Nannie T., and Smith, Helena Huntington. *A Bride Goes West.* Lincoln: University of Nebraska Press, 1969 (1942).

Call, Hughie. *Golden Fleece.* Lincoln: University of Nebraska Press, 1981 (1942).

Linderman, Frank B. *Pretty-Shield, Medicine Woman of the Crows.* Lincoln: University of Nebraska Press, 1972 (1932).

Low, Ann Marie. *Dust Bowl Diary.* Lincoln: University of Nebraska Press, 1984.

Luchetti, Cathy, in collaboration with Carol Olwell, editors. *Women of the West.* Saint George, Utah: Antelope Island Press, 1982.

"Nineteenth-Century Women on the Frontier." *Montana: The Magazine of Western History,* Summer 1982.

Petrik, Paula. *No Step Backward: Women and Family on the Rocky Mountain Mining Frontier, 1965–1900.* Helena, Mont.: Historical Society Press, 1987.

Stewart, Elinor Pruitt. *Letters of a Woman Homesteader.* Boston: Houghton Mifflin, 1982 (1914).

Bibliography

NINE. COPPERTOWN PEOPLE

Baucus, Max, U.S. Senator. "Taxation of Natural Resources." In *Vital Speeches,* March 15, 1980 (delivered before the Conference on Alternative State and Local Policies, Billings, Mont., Feb. 8, 1980).

Braley, Berton. *Pegasus Pulls a Hack: Memoirs of a Modern Minstrel.* New York: Minton, Balch & Co., 1934.

Brinig, Myron. *Singermann.* New York: Arno Press, 1975 (1929).

Federal Writers Project. Writers Program, Montana. *Copper Camp.* New York: Hastings House, 1945 (1943).

Glasscock, Carl Burgess. *The War of the Copper Kings: Builders of Butte and Wolves of Wall Street.* Indianapolis: Bobbs-Merrill, 1935.

Hammett, Dashiell. *Red Harvest.* New York: Vintage, 1972 (1929, 1956).

Hurlbut, David. "The Day the Company Said Goodbye." *Rocky Mountain Magazine,* March-April 1981.

La Grande, Daniel J. "Voice of a Copper King: A Study of the Butte 'Reveille,' 1903–1906." Master's Thesis, University of Montana, 1971.

Levine, Louis. *The Taxation of Mines in Montana.* New York: B. W. Huebsch, 1919.

MacLane, Mary. *I, Mary MacLane: A Diary of Human Days.* New York: Frederick A. Stokes, 1917. And excerpts in *The Last Best Place: A Montana Anthology.* Edited by William Kittredge and Annick Smith. Helena: Montana Historical Society Press, 1988.

———. *The Story of Mary MacLane, by Herself.* Chicago: Herbert S. Stone, 1902. And: Excerpts in *The Last Best Place: A Montana Anthology.* Edited by William Kittredge and Annick Smith. Helena: Montana Historical Society, 1988.

McNelis, Sarah. *Copper Kings at War.* Missoula: University of Montana Press, 1968.

Malone, Michael P. *The Battle for Butte.* Seattle: University of Washington Press, 1981.

Marcosson, Isaac F. *Anaconda.* New York: Dodd, 1957.

Mattern, Carolyn J. "Mary MacLane: A Feminist Opinion." *Montana: The Magazine of Western History,* Oct. 1977.

Murphy, Beatrice. "Diary of a Night Nurse, Butte, Montana, 1909." *Montana: The Magazine of Western History,* Autumn 1989.

Place, Marian T. *The Copper Kings of Montana.* New York: Random House, 1961.

Rust, Elizabeth Ann (Rose) Morrow. "Reminiscence." Document in the files of the Montana Historical Society, Helena.

Terris, Virginia. "Macy MacLane—Realist." *Spectator: A Journal of Butte and Southwest Montana History,* Winter 1985.

Wheeler, Leslie A. "Mary MacLane: Montana's Shocking 'Litr'y Lady.'" *Montana: The Magazine of Western History,* July 1977.

TEN. MR. GIBSON AND THE COWBOY: PARIS GIBSON AND CHARLES M. RUSSELL

Abbott, E. C., and Helena Huntington Smith. *We Pointed Them North.* Norman: University of Oklahoma Press, 1955 (1939).

Adams, Ramon F., and Homer E. Britzman. *Charles M. Russell, the Cowboy Artist: A Biography.* Pasadena, Calif.: Trail's End Publishing Co., 1948.

Bibliography

Dobie, J. Frank. "The Conservatism of Charles M. Russell." In *Prefaces*. Boston: Little, Brown, 1975.

A Genealogy of Paris Gibson. Compiled by the Great Falls Genealogical Society, 1977.

Gibson, Mary Douglas. *Reminiscences*. N.p., n.d. On file in the Great Falls Public Library.

Gibson, Paris. *The Founding of Great Falls, and Some of Its Early Records*. Great Falls, brochure printed by the *Great Falls Tribune*, Jan. 1, 1914.

Handford, James G. "Paris Gibson—a Montana Yankee." Master's Thesis, Montana State University, 1952.

Hutchens, John K. *One Man's Montana: An Informal Portrait of a State*. Philadelphia: J. B. Lippincott, 1964.

Ladner, Mildred D. *O. C. Seltzer, Painter of the Old West*. Norman: University of Oklahoma Press, 1979.

Linderman, Frank Bird. *Recollections of Charley Russell*. Norman: University of Oklahoma Press, 1980 (1963).

Renner, Frederic G. *Charles M. Russell: Paintings, Drawings, and Sculpture in the Amon Carter Museum*. New York: NAL/Abrams, 1976 (1966, 1974).

Robbins, Jim. "Are Cowboys Killing the West?" *USA Weekend*, April 19–21, 1991.

Russell, Charles M. *Good Medicine: The Illustrated Letters of Charles M. Russell*. New York: Doubleday, 1929.

———. *Trails Plowed Under*. New York: Doubleday, 1927.

———. *The Western Art of Charles M. Russell*. Edited by Lanning Aldrich. New York: Ballantine Books, 1975.

Vaughn, Robert. *Then and Now; or Thirty-Six Years in the Rockies: Personal Reminiscences, 1864–1900*. Minneapolis: Tribune Printing Co., 1900.

ELEVEN. WHO WAS CALAMITY JANE? A SPECULATION

Abbott, E. C., and Helena Huntington Smith. *We Pointed Them North*. Norman: University of Oklahoma Press, 1954, 1986 (1939).

Aikman, Duncan. "Calamity Jane." In *Calamity Jane and the Lady Wildcats*. New York: Holt, 1927.

Bourke, John G. *On the Border with Crook*. Lincoln: University of Nebraska Press, 1971 (1891).

Buel, James W. *The True Story of "Wild Bill" Hickok*. Edited by J. Brussel. New York: Atomic Books, 1946 (pamphlet).

Burke, Martha Jane Cannary. *Calamity Jane's Diary and Letters*. 6th ed., 1951, and other eds. By permission of owner of document, Stella A. Foote, copyright 1950 and 1978.

———. *Life and Adventures of Calamity Jane*. Fairfield, Wash.: Ye Galleon Press, 1961 (pamphlet 1896?).

Clairmonte, Glenn. *Calamity Was the Name for Jane*. Beverly Hills, Calif.: Sage Books, 1959.

Connolley, William E. *Wild Bill and His Era*. New York: Cooper Square, 1972 (1933).

Dexter, Peter. *Deadwood*. New York: Random House, 1986.

Drago, Harry Sinclair. "Calamity Jane in Fact and Fiction." In *Notorious Ladies of the Frontier*. New York: Dodd, Mead & Co., 1969.

Finerty, John F. *War-Path and Bivouac*. Chicago: R. R. Donnelley, 1955 (1890).

Fisher, Barb, and Glenda Bell. Letter to the author, Dec. 6, 1990.

Gallacher, Dan. Talk at Annual Montana History Conference at Missoula, Mont. Report in *Great Falls Tribune*, Oct. 29, 1989.

Holbrook, Stewart H. *Little Annie Oakley and Other Rugged People*. New York: Macmillan, 1948.

Horan, James. *Desperate Women*. New York: Putnam, 1952.

Jennewein, J. Leonard. *Calamity Jane of the Western Trails*. Huron, S.C., 1953 (pamphlet).

Lull, William. Lull Papers. "Calamity Jane: Deadwood City in Pioneer Days," and William Lull letters to his family, 1875–77. Unpublished papers in possession of David Lull, Atlanta, used by his permission.

McMurtry, Larry. *Buffalo Girls*. New York: Simon & Schuster, 1990.

Mills, Colonel Anson G. *My Story*. Edited by C. H. Claudy. Washington, D.C.: the Author, 1918.

Otero, Miguel Antonio. *My Life on the Frontier, 1864–1882*. In *Otero: An Autobiographical Trilogy*. Albuquerque: University of New Mexico Press, 1940.

Rosa, Joseph G. *They Called Him Wild Bill*. Norman: University of Oklahoma Press, 1964.

———. *The West of Wild Bill Hickok*. Norman: University of Oklahoma Press, 1982.

Sollid, Roberta Beed. *Calamity Jane: A Study in Historical Criticism*. Correlated and edited by V. A. Palladin. Montana Historical Society. Helena: Western Press, 1958.

Wilstach, Frank J. *Wild Bill Hickok*. Garden City, N.J.: Garden City Publishing Co., 1926.

TWELVE. RECOLLECTION AND RENEWAL: AN AFTERWORD

Bennett, Ben. *Death, Too, for the Heavy Runner*. Missoula, Mont: Mountain Press Publishing Co., 1981.

Cushman, Dan. *The Great North Trail: America's Route of the Ages*. New York: McGraw-Hill Book Co., 1966.

DeVoto, Bernard. "The West against Itself." *Harper's Magazine*, January 1947.

———. "The West: A Plundered Province?" *Harper's Magazine*, August 1934.

Guthrie, A. B. *The Big Sky*. Boston: Houghton Mifflin, 1947.

Horner, John R., and James Gorman. *Digging Dinosaurs*. New York: Workman, 1988.

Josephy, Alvin M., Jr. "Plundered West: Coal Is the Prize." *Washington Post*, August 26, 1973.

Maclean, Norman. *A River Runs through It and Other Stories*. Chicago: University of Chicago Press, 1976.

Old Trail Museum, Choteau, Mont. Resource for discoveries, analyses, and lectures on the dinosaur digs nearby.

Packard, Vance. "Life on the Nuclear Frontier." In *A Nation of Strangers*. New York: Pocket Books, 1974 (1972).

Parfit, Michael. "A Gathering Storm over Synfuels on the Big Sky Range." *Smithsonian Magazine*, March 1980.

———. *Last Stand at Rosebud Creek*. New York: Dutton, 1980.

Bibliography

Sherman, William T., and Philip H. Sheridan, *Reports of the Inspection Made in the Summer of 1877*. Fairfield, Wash.: Ye Galleon, 1985.

Stegner, Wallace. *The Big Rock Candy Mountain*. New York: Doubleday, 1938.

———. *Wolf Willow: A History, A Story, and a Memory of the Last Plains Frontier*. Lincoln: University of Nebraska Press, 1980 (1955, 1962).

Welch, James. *The Death of Jim Loney*. New York: Harper & Row, 1979.

———. *Riding the Earthboy 40*. New York: Harper & Row, 1971, 1976.

———. *Winter in the Blood*. New York: Harper & Row, 1974.

ACKNOWLEDGMENTS

My thanks are due to Stella A. Foote of Billings, Montana, for her generous permission to use quotations from *Calamity Jane's Diary and Letters,* copyright by Stella A. Foote, 1951 and 1978, from the original document in her possession; to David J. Lull of Atlanta, for his kind permission to use quotations and facts from the William Lull Papers, unpublished family papers in his possession, and for the generosity and encouragement of David and Karen Lull in this matter; to Barb Fisher and Glenda Bell, of Fisher-Bell Storytellers of Billings, for permission to quote from a letter to me, sharing their opinions from their own researches about Calamity Jane; and to the Montana Historical Society, Archives Division, for the unrestricted use of quotations and factual matter from the typescript in possession of the society and declared open to unrestricted use: Elizabeth Ann (Rose) Morrow Rust's "Reminiscence" (1888–1909), compiled by Rust's daughter, Harriette Dommes.

I also give thanks to Dave Walter, Reference Librarian, and Bill Summers, Archivist, of the Montana Historical Society, Helena, for help in finding and suggesting various source materials concerning my figures; to Librarians Kay Courtnage and Kathryn Kujawara and others on the staff of the Great Falls Public Library for access to information about materials of local and state history; to the Mansfield Library of the University of Montana, Missoula, for pulling out two master's theses for the enrichment of my research; Robert J. Goligoski on Thomas Dimsdale and James G. Handford on Paris Gibson; to the Billings Public Library for material on the history of Billings; to the staff and resources of the Robert Woodruff Library, Emory University, Atlanta, for office space, interlibrary loan service, and its collection of nineteenth- and twentieth-century books about the American West; and to the Emory University Faculty Research Committee for a grant for study of the life and culture of the Rocky Mountain Northwest.

Acknowledgments

I am thankful for, and grateful to, many individuals: to Branson and Violet Stevenson of Great Falls, who, through the years of my journeys enlarged my knowledge of family history, including business history, and who, in hospitality and friendship, again opened to me the life of the region; to Candler Professor Emeritus of History J. Harvey Young of Emory University, for encouragement, specific suggestions, and sharing his general knowledge of where to look and what to look for in researching an area of American life and culture; to George Remington, publisher of the *Billings Gazette,* who, during a July 9, 1980, interview, shared his opinions with me on a variety of Montana topics, including Colstrip, Wild River designations, forest controversies, the economic viability of Billings; to Dick Thoroughman of Fort Shaw, Montana, for sharing his expert knowledge on the history of the U.S. Army base Fort Shaw; to Patricia G. Tavenner, proprietor of the Electric Avenue Bookstore of Bigfork, Montana, for help in identifying new books by northwestern authors; to Sherrie Wood, at one time of Lincoln, Montana, for her defense of the environment against gold-mining interests and for her friendship; to Glenda Bradshaw of Helena, for photocopying material that was out of my reach, Rust's "Reminiscence"; to June M. Mann of Emory University, for her intelligent ordering and word-processing of my untidy typescript.

I am grateful for the friends of Fifth Avenue North, who, after many years of separation, came together again: Barbara Kaufman de Chambeau, Iva Brown Carrico, Alvira Klies Smith, and Eleanor Moore Gollehon; for the reawakened memories of a shared family childhood, which Bernice, John, Joan, and Martha gave me; for the skies of Montana, which roofed important years in my life.

My special thanks to George F. Thompson, of the Center for American Places, for many years of support, encouragement, and intelligent editing.

INDEX

Index

Library of Congress Cataloging-in-Publication Data

Stevenson, Elizabeth, 1919–
Figures in a western landscape : men and women of the northern
Rockies / Elizabeth Stevenson.
p.   cm. — (Creating the North American landscape)
Includes bibliographical references and index.
ISBN 0-8018-4676-5 (alk. paper)
1. West (U.S.)—Biography.   2. Landscape—West (U.S.)
3. Montana—Biography.   4. Landscape—Montana.   I. Title.
II. Series.
F591.S827   1994
920.078—dc20
[B]   93-22973